INTERVENTION

IN

PSYCHIATRIC NURSING

INTERVENTION IN PSYCHIATRIC NURSING: PROCESS IN THE ONE-TO-ONE RELATIONSHIP

JOYCE TRAVELBEE, B.S.N.Ed., M.S.N., R.N.

Director of Graduate Education
School of Nursing, Louisiana State University Medical Center
New Orleans, Louisiana
Formerly Professor, University of Mississippi School of Nursing
Jackson, Mississippi

 F. A. DAVIS COMPANY, Philadelphia

Second Printing, September 1970
Third Printing, January 1972

66273

Manufactured in the United States of America

Library of Congress Catalog Card Number 79-79907
ISBN-O-8036-8610-2

PREFACE

The purpose of this text is to assist both students and professional nurse practitioners to establish effective one-to-one relationships with mentally ill individuals. Focus of the text is on the clinical specialty of psychiatric nursing and it is primarily designed to be used by students of psychiatric nursing in collegiate programs.

It is believed that establishing, maintaining and terminating one-to-one relationships with mentally ill individuals are activities which fall within the province of nursing practice. A major assumption is that only qualified psychiatric nurses are prepared to supervise nurses in the practice of psychiatric nursing, and that the nurse who begins interacting with a mentally ill individual for the purpose of establishing a nurse-patient relationship has at her disposal a qualified psychiatric nurse supervisor. Another major assumption is that the knowledge, understanding and skills needed to plan, give and evaluate care during the one-to-one relationship are necessary prerequisites for developing competency in group work.

In Chapters I through IV the nature and purpose of psychiatric nursing, the functions of the psychiatric nurse, and beliefs about the nature of mental health and illness are discussed. The process of psychiatric nursing is explored as are the effects of myths and directives on the behavior of nurses. Goals of the nurse in the one-to-one relationship are discussed.

In Chapters V through VII the concept of communication is defined and the rationale underlying the purposeful use of the communication process is explored. Selection of patients for the one-to-one relationship and the purpose and use of process recording are discussed.

In Chapters VIII and IX phases leading to the establishment, maintenance and termination of the relationship are discussed. Problems frequently encountered by nurses in the one-to-one relationship are explored and ways to solve these problems are suggested.

In Chapter X the supervisory process is discussed and the roles and responsibilities of both supervisor and supervisee are explored.

Appendix I is a Selected Bibliography with suggested reading references for each chapter. References used throughout this work are in the footnotes and are not repeated in the Appendix. Appendix II includes a list of general reference sources in psychiatric nursing and related fields. Emphasis is placed on assisting practitioners to use abstracts, indexes and bibliographies.

The ideas discussed in this book elaborate on concepts developed in each chapter. It is important that learners achieve depth of understanding of these concepts as they proceed into the text.

It is assumed that learners who use this text possess a basic understanding of the major concepts from the natural, physical, biological, medical and nursing sciences. It is also assumed that students will have completed the beginning courses in the behavioral sciences and in the humanities.

ACKNOWLEDGMENTS

I wish to thank the many individuals who have assisted and encouraged me in writing this book.

I acknowledge an incalculable debt to Mrs. Marie A. Combel, my mother, whose life and great courage have been inspiring to me.

It is with deep gratitude that I thank Lt. Ruth A. Johnston R.N. (A.N.C., retired) whose deep understanding of the human condition has taught me much. I am indebted to her for her valuable suggestions and for her encouragement.

I am grateful to Miss Christine Oglevee, Dean of the School of Nursing of the University of Mississippi, for her support and encouragement. I wish to thank the faculty members of the University of Mississippi School of Nursing, especially Mrs. Elizabeth Graves, R.N., and Miss Dianne Denham, R.N.

I also wish to thank my colleagues Mrs. Cora Balmat, R.N., University of Southern Mississippi, and Miss Catherine Treusch, R.N., Chief Nurse, Veterans Administration Hospital, Gulfport, Mississippi, for many stimulating hours of discussion and for sharing with me their views on the one-to-one relationship.

I am particularly indebted to J. M. J. and T. J. M. who helped make this work truly a labor of love.

J. T.

CONTENTS

PAGE

INTRODUCTION

The learner in psychiatric nursing is frequently overwhelmed by the multiplicity of schools of thought which theoretically attempt to describe the behavior of the mentally ill person. Intervention in psychiatric nursing is often based on concepts derived from a particular behavioristic viewpoint; for example, certain psychoanalytic concepts are often used as a basis for the one-to-one relationship in psychiatric nursing which, although offering some benefits, too often must be "bent" to fit the nursing situation or given a specious type of application. In this work the author has used an eclectic approach rather than a particular theoretical framework.

Only a few comments are included on some of the content aspects usually found in most psychiatric nursing textbooks. In this text emphasis is placed on assisting the learner to make wide use of current literature relating to psychiatric nursing and allied disciplines, in order to develop depth of understanding of the various concepts operating in nursing situations. Knowledge of source materials and ability to utilize research findings are essential if the learner is to intervene effectively and to act as a change agent in improving the quality of care given the mentally ill.

Particular attention is given to assisting the learner in the development of critical thinking abilities. Knowledge is not static; "facts," concepts and principles will continue to change as new research evolves. The most effective safeguard against intellectual arrest or stagnation is the development of the ability to think, combined with the ability to adapt or change as the need arises.

A major assumption, with which I agree, is the defining of nursing as a constant, regardless of the clinical specialty area in which the nurse is engaged. Nursing is "an interpersonal process whereby the professional nurse practitioner assists an individual or family to prevent, or cope with, the experience of illness and suffering and, if necessary, assists the individual or family to find meaning in these experiences."[1]

Various ways and means of nursing intervention in the one-to-one relationship are discussed, based on the author's experience in direct patient care and in teaching and supervising learners working with mentally ill individuals, and on research findings in the literature.

---

[1] Travelbee, Joyce: Interpersonal Aspects of Nursing. F. A. Davis Company, Philadelphia, 1966.

Chapter 1

THE NATURE OF PSYCHIATRIC NURSING

In order to develop a conceptual framework for the one-to-one relationship, it is necessary to explore the nature of psychiatric nursing. Counseling, or the one-to-one relationship, is but one aspect of clinical nursing practice, one method of helping ill individuals and their families. How, when, where and why the nurse assists ill individuals are determined by many factors as, for example, the nurse's experiential background and her ability to use it, and her beliefs about the nature of man, the nature of nursing, and the roles and functions in the clinical specialty area.

PART I—A DISCUSSION OF DEFINITIONS OR BELIEFS ABOUT PSYCHIATRIC NURSING

A review of fifteen commonly used basic psychiatric nursing textbooks reveals that in only two texts do the authors attempt to define the nature and scope of psychiatric nursing. A similar review of numerous periodical articles regarding psychiatric nursing again reveals an almost complete lack of definition of psychiatric nursing. Most basic textbooks on psychiatric nursing, however, do focus on the function and role of nurses while evading a definition of the nature of psychiatric nursing. The concepts regarding psychiatric nursing appearing in the literature may be divided into the following general categories: definitions of psychiatric nursing "by setting," beliefs regarding psychiatric nursing as a part of all nursing, and definitions of psychiatric nursing as a process and as a clinical area specialty in, and of, itself.

DEFINITION BY SETTING

The term *psychiatric nursing* has been defined in many different ways. A now obsolete method is to conceive of it strictly as a type of nursing practiced in a particular setting, i.e., in a mental hospital. An analogy of this type of definition, in another clinical area, is the use of the term *operating room nursing*—the definition again being focused primarily on setting.

Defining psychiatric nursing by setting would necessarily eliminate any consideration of the nurse's role and function in the prevention of mental illness and the promotion of mental health. Mental hospitals as we know them today were not established for the purpose of preventing mental illness or for promoting mental health—unless one conceives of the curative functions performed in these settings as being contained within the general category of health promotion.

Actually, the psychiatric nurse of today is no longer bound by a particular geographic setting; there is no one "proper" setting for the practice of psychiatric nursing since it has finally begun to emerge from the hospital into the community. The psychiatric nurse is beginning to practice in a *number* of settings, such as comprehensive mental health clinics, day treatment centers, halfway houses, child guidance clinics, suicide prevention centers, and others.

PSYCHIATRIC NURSING AS "A PART OF ALL NURSING"

Others conceive of psychiatric nursing not as being a distinct specialty area but as an integral and almost indivisible aspect of all of nursing. This particular belief seems fairly prevalent, as exemplified by the fact that psychiatric nursing instructors are often requested, by faculty, to teach psychiatric nursing very early in the program of study so that (hopefully) the student will be able to apply to other areas of clinical practice the understanding and skills gained in working with the mentally ill. It cannot be denied that students will encounter ill individuals suffering from behavioral problems in medical-surgical and other settings. However, the theoretical basis of psychiatric nursing, the knowledge underlying the skills of psychiatric nursing, and the major concepts which must be learned and applied in practice are highly abstract; because of these factors it is recommended that psychiatric nursing in collegiate programs be taught preferably as the last clinical nursing course in the curriculum. The student's experiential background, age, and maturity level do seem to have significant correlation with her ability to understand, apply and test theory in caring for the mentally ill.

PSYCHIATRIC NURSING AS PROCESS

Tudor states:

> From our point of view, psychiatric nursing can be conceived of as these overlapping and definable components: observation, evaluation of the observations, determination of the various alternatives possible within the situation, intervention, evaluation of the intervention with reference to the reasons for success or failure, and further intervention on the basis of the new data obtained.[1]

It would seem that this definition is also a description of the process of nursing applicable to any clinical area specialty.

CLINICAL SPECIALTY AREA

Some nurses use the term psychiatric nursing to refer to a specific specialty within the broad framework of nursing practice. In reference to this belief the American Nurses Association Statement on Psychiatric Nursing Practice, in regard to psychiatric nursing as part of all nursing, reads:

> Psychiatric nursing is described as a specialized area of practice in the science and art of nursing. The scientific aspect of psychiatric nursing is the application of new and complex theories of human behavior based on the sciences that are utilized in all of nursing. The art of psychiatric nursing is derived from the purposeful use of self in the practice of nursing. Psychiatric nursing thus utilizes a broad spectrum of general and specialized nursing knowledge and skill in a variety of settings with different psychiatric approaches to patient care. Through systematic studies of the clinical phenomena, new theories of psychiatric nursing are formulated and new practices are evolved.

> Psychiatric nursing is a service to people affected by pathological thought processes or other personality disorders manifested in such a way as to interfere with healthy or normal living. Psychiatric nursing has functions and practices that are intended to prevent or to have corrective impact upon mental illness, and is concerned with the promotion of optimal mental health for all individuals and families in the community.[2]

The ANA Statement on Psychiatric Nursing Practice does not differentiate between mental health nursing and psychiatric nursing

---

[1] By permission. Tudor, Gwen E.: A sociopsychiatric nursing approach to intervention in a problem of mutual withdrawal on a mental hospital ward. Psychiatry 15:194, 1952.

[2] By permission. Statement on Psychiatric Nursing Practice. Division on Psychiatric-Mental Health Nursing, American Nurses Association. 1967.

because "there is little doubt today that the theory which underlies the practice of mental health and psychiatric nursing is essentially the same. The dichotomy which developed historically has a diminishing meaning for current programs of education and service."[3]

The ANA's definition of psychiatric nursing, while not an operational one, is nevertheless comprehensive; i.e., it is of value as a general guideline to psychiatric nursing practice, as well as large enough in scope to anticipate the varied, emerging (and now almost undefined or unanticipated) roles of the psychiatric nurse in a changing society.

RECAPITULATION

Psychiatric nursing in the preceding discussion has been defined as a setting, as a clinical specialty area and as a part of all of nursing. As has been stated in the introduction to this chapter, beliefs about the definition, role and purpose of psychiatric nursing are necessarily related to, and emerge from, one's concept of the nature of nursing and—especially in the field of psychiatric nursing—are determined by one's beliefs about the nature of mental illness. In Part II the relationship between psychiatric nursing and nursing in general is discussed.

PART II—DEFINITION OF PSYCHIATRIC NURSING

A major assumption of this work is that the definition of nursing remains constant despite the clinical specialty area in which nursing is practiced. For example, definitions of nursing used re "medical-surgical," "maternal-child" or any other clinical specialty area would not become invalid when applied to psychiatric nursing. Some modification may be necessary in terms of explanation or application but, although varied in function, the purpose of nursing remains constant.

In this text psychiatric nursing is defined as an interpersonal process whereby the professional nurse practitioner assists an individual, family or community to promote mental health, to prevent or

----

3 Ibid.

cope with the experience of mental illness and suffering and, if necessary, to find meaning in these experiences.[4]

INTERPERSONAL PROCESS . . .

Psychiatric nursing is an interpersonal process because it is always concerned with people. These persons may be individual patients, families, or groups in need of the assistance the professional nurse can offer, or people associated with the other health disciplines.

PROFESSIONAL NURSE PRACTITIONER . . .

In this work the term professional nurse practitioner refers to a graduate of a baccalaureate school of nursing. A graduate of such a program should possess a disciplined intellectual approach to problems (i.e., she should not only know how to think but possess the facts, principles and concepts with which to think) combined with the ability to use self therapeutically in assisting other individuals, families and the community to solve health problems.

ASSISTS AN INDIVIDUAL, FAMILY OR COMMUNITY . . .

The nurse assists individuals and groups directly or indirectly by the functions performed. The nurse as a knowledgeable individual is an "enabler," interested in assisting others to help themselves (as in prevention of illness and promotion of health), and in assisting those who are incapable, or unable, to help themselves (as in helping the disabled to cope with the stress of illness and suffering).

Most nurses readily comprehend the nurse's role in working with individuals and family members to prevent illness, promote health or help individuals and families to cope with the stress of illness. Now, how does a nurse assist a community?

---

[4] Adapted from "The Definition of Nursing Re-Stated As a Purpose" *in* Travelbee, Joyce: Interpersonal Aspects of Nursing. F. A. Davis Company, Philadelphia, 1966.

N.B. In order to avoid repetition of material published in the above-mentioned book the author will focus only on those aspects included in the purpose of psychiatric nursing which have direct implication for the clinical practice of psychiatric nursing. The reader is referred to the above-mentioned work for further discussion of terms.

Community Assistance

Individuals or groups of persons living within a particular geographical area can be assisted by the nurse's making known to them the resources, facilities and services available. The psychiatric nurse may also assist a community, if given the opportunity, by acting as health teacher or resource person to community groups such as parent-teacher associations. Nurses may assist a community by being represented on, and contributing to, local, state and national programs concerned with health and welfare. It is probably in this area that professional nursing has been most lax. Nursing is not represented on many local, state or national programs because nurses have not requested such representation. In some instances nurses are not invited to participate because it does not occur to health workers or legislators that nursing has anything to contribute. It is not so much that nursing representation is not wanted (this is easier to cope with)—the problem is that nurses are not even thought about or considered to have anything of significance to contribute. It is this latter attitude which must be changed. Nurses can effect no change in a community until they are willing to become involved and to give of their time, effort and energy.

TO PROMOTE MENTAL HEALTH . . .

The promotion of mental health, or indeed health in general, depends on one's definition of mental health. Is mental health synonymous with "average" normality or with the mythical "well-adjusted" person? How does a health worker promote mental health? Is it realistic to conceive of health as compartmentalized and segmented, to focus on mental health as being opposed to physical health or spiritual health? The term *mental health* has not been operationally defined in the literature. The concept of health has been defined by the World Health Organization as: "Health is a state of complete physical, mental and social well being and not merely the absence of disease or infirmity"[5] but the meaning of the phrase "physical, mental or social well being" was not discussed. The problem in defining mental health and health in general derives from the fact that neither is a scientific term. The concept *health* is probably a value judgment and more amenable to philosophical analysis than to rigid scientific definition.

---

[5] Constitution of the World Health Organization *in* Chronicle of the World Health Organization. World Health Organization Interim Commission, New York, 1:12, 1947.

Fundamentally one's concept of the nature of mental health rests on one's concept of the nature of man.

Value judgments regarding mental health are often determined by cultural norms, rules or standards of "appropriate" behavior within a given society at a particular point in time. Hence value judgments are in one sense relativistic and not static; they are caused by a repeated and ever-changing pattern, an unfinished and incomplete mosaic which represents the current views of man, his nature and the nature of the society in which he lives.

Although the term mental health has not been operationally defined, numerous "definitions" or discourses on the nature of mental health abound in the literature. No attempt will be made to discuss the seemingly endless variety of viewpoints regarding the nature of this concept. A perusal of the literature soon reveals that the definitions are, for the most part, theoretical and nonoperational. The reader is referred to Jahoda's excellent book, Current Concepts of Positive Mental Health, for a survey of varying viewpoints on mental health. (See references appearing in the bibliography for a selected survey of the literature regarding the nature of mental health.)

Beliefs About the Nature of Mental Health

Although there is no functional definition of mental health, there are broad standards of reference, or criteria, upon which a judgment can tentatively be made. These criteria are useful in the sense of providing a guideline to health workers who are committed to "promoting mental health."

Obviously one cannot consider mental health without taking into account the fact that man is a biological creature with certain basic human needs, as well as physiological needs, which must be met if man is to survive—much less achieve the elusive state known as mental health. Maslow has written an excellent perspective on basic needs (see bibliography for selected reference readings). Yet an individual may have all of his physiological needs met and still not be mentally healthy. A basic assumption is that mental health is not only "something one possesses" but "something one is," as demonstrated by certain behaviors or abilities. Three such abilities or criteria are discussed below.

Criteria

The first and most important of these abilities is the ability to love oneself and the concomitant ability to transcend self and love others. The term *love* is used in its broadest sense—namely, as the opposite of indifference. Unfortunately the term love has almost become meaningless in our times. Too often it is equated with genital sexuality which may or may not represent an act of love, because genital sexuality is not in and of itself love. Love wills only that which is good to the love object; it is actively concerned and involved. Love is actualized in deeds and not in words and pronouncements. Love is basically an act of the will, not of the emotions (although the emotions are certainly involved) ; the brotherhood of man, a love of humanity, must be willed, but we have substituted a yearly donation to the United Fund for love.

The ability to love self is a precursor to loving others. This does not mean egotism—what it does imply is acceptance of one's self, self-respect, knowledge of, and confidence in, one's capacities and abilities, and an insight into one's human limitations. To love self requires great courage. It is easier to focus on the abilities and limitations of others than honestly to confront one's own. The escape from self is exemplified by over-involvement in activities and by an inability to be alone. Sensory input is sought—whether the source be people, radios, television or some other form. Escape from self is also exemplified by the rising rates of alcoholism and drug addiction and, especially in our times, by the growing use of consciousness-expanding (psychedelic) agents. No one can give to another that which he does not possess. If an individual does not love or respect himself, how can he love or respect others?

The ability to transcend self is basically the ability to get beyond self in order to focus on other human beings; it is the capacity to be unselfishly concerned about others—simply because one is a human being who can empathize and sympathize with fellow creatures. Gratitude is not extracted as a price for one's concern for another person. The ability to transcend self is also the ability to perceive others as unique individuals and not replications of one's self or of individuals known in the past. The ability to love others should not be confused with liking others. It is possible to transcend self and love others without liking others. One may love another without necessarily "liking" all of his personality traits (or quirks) or approving of all of his activities. There is always some degree of ambivalence in every human relationship. Love of another person is not a "constant"; it changes, fluctuates, develops at various stages or levels, or may cease entirely. Love does not "just happen"—it is developed, nurtured and permitted to grow.

We have spoken thus far of love of one person for another. What of love for mankind or for people in general? At the risk of repeating an old cliche it must be reemphasized that it is quite possible to love mankind and dislike (or even hate) people. One needs to ask: "Who (or what) is mankind?" Mankind is one's neighbor, relatives, friends, acquaintances, all of the individuals with whom one interacts—co-workers, students, members of other health disciplines, as well as the ill person(s) one cares for in the practice of nursing. Mankind is the stranger we do not know—he who is different or separated from us by physical distance or by the psychological distance of skin color, religion, race, creed, or a different way of life. Mankind is the derelict, the prostitute, the thief, the murderer, the skid row vagrant, the drug addict, the alcoholic, the mentally and physically ill individual. Mankind is those we know and like, those we know and dislike, those we do not know and those we do not choose to know. Mankind is each and every one of us individually, in our uniqueness and difference. Mankind is each of us collectively. Mankind is the answer to the perennial question "Who is my neighbor?" Each of us, at one time or another, must answer this question and live with the consequences of our answer and our choice.

Love of mankind is exemplified best in action; those who transcend self and love others display this behavior to others. "By their fruits you shall know them" is as valid psychologically as it is spiritually. The human being is truly known by deeds and behavior—not by "kind thoughts" which may never be translated into helpful activities.

In our impersonal age it is often assumed that an individual who gives large donations to charity, or is an active member of some benevolent organization, is an individual who can transcend self and love others. This is not necessarily true. Such persons may be motivated by status needs or the desire to claim income tax deductions rather than by a sincere wish to help others. The individual is not personally involved with the recipients of his bounty, and in this lies the crux of the matter. Perhaps a truer criterion is the answer to the question: To what extent will an individual inconvenience himself to assist a person whom he does not particularly like?

Mankind, as has been seen, can be an abstraction. It is easier to profess belief in an abstraction than to confront and help the individual (or group) with whom we are in daily contact. It is easier to contribute to a charity caring for the starving people of India than to assist individuals living within one's own community; one need not be personally involved in the suffering of those in India.

It is not necessary to search far to find examples or results of the inability to love self, much less others. A woman is attacked and screams repeatedly for help but those who hear her screams do not "interfere" or call the police, because "they do not want to become involved." Indifference, as was stated earlier, is as opposite to love as is hatred—and in some instances more so, since to hate one must at least have some feeling, albeit negative, towards one's hate object; this is not true in the case of indifference.

One could cite innumerable acts of human injustice, cruelty, hatred of others of different skin color, race or creed (best exemplified in the genocide of the Jewish people during World War II). Our own times are beset by wars, civil disorders, riots in the street, bombings of churches and synagogues, a rising crime rate, etc. The evidence is clear—too clear perhaps—with an abundance that is overwhelming in sheer magnitude of human suffering and misery.

However, there is also evidence of ability to love others, of concern of individual for individual. There are no statistics on the number of acts of kindness performed every day, since such acts are not newspaper copy, but increased commitment and concern for mankind are seen, for example, in the increased enrollments of the Peace Corps, VISTA and other organizations.

The Ability to Face Reality

The ability to face reality as it is, not as we may wish it to be, requires the individual to possess a sense of identity as a separate unique human being—as a person able to direct and control personal behavior. It includes the ability to recognize one's participation in an experience, to gain correct, valid, cognitive perception of a situation without the need to distort the experience in order to present self or others "in a favorable light." It implies the capacity to recognize one's feelings, to cope with them or, if one is unable to do so, to seek professional assistance. The strength to cope with conflict is the core of the human condition. The ability to face reality also includes the ability to appreciate the humorous, to be able to laugh at one's self and at one's behavior.

The ability to confront reality as indicated above involves a further step, i.e., problems encountered are resolved or dealt with one way or another. A decision is made. In some situations it is healthier to withdraw mentally from a person or situation; in other situations confrontation would be a wiser course. The individual is flexible in that behavior is not constantly repetitive regardless of the situation faced. Decisions are made on a conscious level, with a knowledge of the consequences of the decision. Then the individual must live with the decision without blaming others for it.

The ability to face reality includes the ability to recognize one's obligation to act, i.e., to intervene when principle is at stake. To fail to speak or take a stand against human injustices which degrade, persecute or make "non-persons" out of human beings is to become like those who perpetrate such deeds. To know the need to speak out when principle is at stake, and fail to do so, is to begin a process of character corrosion which ends in an elusive search for peace of mind. It is no easy matter to act on principle when the consequences of one's actions may be persecution, or the less dramatic (but no less real) loss of promotion or of job, or the cause of misunderstandings with loved ones, friends and relatives. It is far worse, however, to fail to act because of human considerations. The loss to the individual is almost irreparable; he loses self-respect and the knowledge that he could have prevented or protested human wrongs yet failed to do so. To live with such a burden for all of his life is a far greater tragedy than is the loss of job or of friends and relatives. This point is stressed not because many individuals in our society are threatened by imprisonment or job loss for failure to speak out against all that depersonalizes and dehumanizes the human being, but because many individuals at one time or another in life have the opportunity to speak, to be heard and to take a stand even though in a seemingly small way. This does not imply revolt for the sake of contentiousness or anarchy. It does mean that one knows and understands the basic principles which guide life and has a profound respect and reverence for life.

The ability to face reality also includes accepting the capacities and limitations of one's human condition; it is to experience one's finiteness—yet to appreciate life as a great gift. To face reality is to appreciate that an individual cannot be an authentic human being by living life through another. It includes the ability to appreciate the transitory nature of life and of all human creatures, the ability to appreciate the *now* and to live immersed in the now—fully and completely—because the now is, really, all that one has.

To face reality includes—in addition to accepting one's capacities and limitations—the ability to refuse to exempt self from this human condition. It is to realize that as human beings we are subject to joy, love, happiness, to illness, loneliness, guilt, depression and to all of the conflicting emotions (especially the tormenting ambivalence of love and hate) which beset mankind. To face reality requires great courage. As terrible or as depressing as reality may be at times, however, unreality is even more unbearable. It is only by confronting the crisis situations of our human condition that we are afforded the opportunity to grow and develop as authentic human beings.

The ability to face reality includes knowledge of, and orientation to, the world in which one lives. It is more than successful adaptation to stress or simple adjustment to the cultural milieu, more than being "average," "well balanced" (whatever that means) or adjusted. To be "adjusted" to a sick society is no virtue—as for example the millions of men, women and children well adjusted to life in Nazi Germany. To submit to totalitarian regimes or institutions because one wishes to be average, adaptable, well liked and accepted is not health; it is sickness of mind and spirit.

The ability to face reality implies the ability to work productively with others—to collaborate, to compromise and to compete. In our culture perhaps more emphasis is placed on competition than on collaboration. Compromise implies the ability to give and take in human relationships; it does not imply "giving in" or abandoning one's basic principles for the sake of expediency or to be popular or liked. The ability to face reality also includes the capacity for wonder, enjoyment—the ability to experience pleasure and to give or create pleasure for others. The third and last of the abilities required by the mentally healthy person is the ability to find a purpose or meaning in life.

The Ability to Find a Purpose or Meaning in Life

Achieving a sense of one's identity as a person, as a unique human being, precedes the developmental task of finding a meaning or purpose to life. Most individuals, especially during adolescence, ask the questions: Who am I? Why am I here? Where am I going? Sooner or later these questions must be answered, not evaded or answered glibly and superficially as in the case of the perennial adolescent adult. Human beings need a sense of direction and a purpose for living—not merely existing. It is believed that the need for meaning in life is as basic a human need as are the physiological needs for food and water. Perhaps a way to appreciate what is meant by purpose and meaning in life is to ask oneself: If everything and everyone you need and love were taken away from you, what would you have left to sustain you? What would give meaning and purpose to your life? Some individuals construe the meaning in life as the answer to the question: What are you willing to die for? More appropriate is the answer to the question: What are you willing to live for?

A philosophy of life should include the finding of meaning and purpose in living; it must be an operational philosophy, not an abstract belief system. And it is in times of great stress, suffering, pain, illness and loneliness that one's purpose or meaning is most tested. It is in these times that the individual realizes whether or not his philosophy of life is operational. The meaning or purpose one ascribes to, it would seem, must support the person in times of stress, suffering and illness. If not then one can only assume that the individual arrived at a fallacious, meaningless, and unrealistic concept of the meaning of human existence.

Recapitulation

The promotion of mental health is viewed as a function of the psychiatric nurse. To promote mental health one must first know what is being promoted. A basic assumption in this text is that mental health is characterized by three major abilities. The first and most important of these is the ability to love self and others. If one accepts this then the role of the nurse in promoting mental health is clear, nursing functions being to foster, nurture, teach and help individuals to love themselves as a precursor to loving others.

The second ability is the ability to face reality. The functions of the nurse here would be to assist individuals to identify problems, to face problems realistically, to recognize their participation in experiences and to find (if possible) workable solutions to life's problems. The nurse helps others to understand that as human beings they are vulnerable to all of the capacities and limitations of their human condition.

The third and last ability is the ability to find a purpose and meaning in life. The functions of the nurse in relation to this ability is to assist others in developing a philosophy of life which has meaning and purpose, and which will support them in times of stress and suffering.

TO PREVENT OR COPE WITH THE EXPERIENCE OF MENTAL ILLNESS AND SUFFERING . . .

The ability to assist individuals, families, or the community to prevent or cope with the experience of mental illness and suffering depends on one's definition of the nature of mental illness.

Mental illness is no easier to define than is mental health. Mental illness per se cannot be observed any more than mental health can be seen—both are categories. What *can* be observed are various behavioral manifestations which may or may not be labeled as deviant.

Mental disorders are generally divided into two major groups. The first includes disorders believed to be primarily determined by organic factors (for example, acute and chronic brain syndromes associated with infection, trauma, etc.). The second group includes functional disorders such as the affective disorders, the schizophrenias, the psychoneuroses. The specific kind of mental illness an individual is believed to have is a diagnostic label—schizophrenia, acute psychotic depression, chronic brain syndrome, etc. A diagnostic label or an etiology, however, does not sufficiently explore the problem of what comprises mental illness. Especially in the case of the functional mental disorders, mental illness may be viewed primarily as a value judgment—made by an individual who is specially educated or prepared by virtue of his knowledge and skill to give a clinical opinion as to the "sanity" of another human being.

An individual is not mentally ill just because he has been diagnosed as being so. Does it matter who diagnoses or makes the judgment, or, more importantly, what criterion is used as a basis of the judgment—especially in the case of the functional illnesses? Is it sufficient to assume that any individual seeing a psychiatrist or hospitalized in a psychiatric setting is mentally ill?

Why is this point belabored? If a diagnosis made on an individual is that of "schizophrenia," then he is a schizophrenic and that ends the matter. However, this is not entirely true and raises a number of interesting, and for the most part unanswered and still debatable, questions. As stated, the diagnosis of functional mental illness may be viewed as a value judgment on the part of the individual making the diagnosis—i.e., the psychiatrist, psychologist or other health worker. A student of human behavior might well ponder the answers to the following questions: What is mental illness? Is unhappiness a sign of mental illness or is it an intrinsic aspect of the human condition? Are all criminal acts the result of mental illness? If so, should an individual who engages in antisocial or asocial behavior be treated in a mental hospital for his behavior problem or imprisoned in a penitentiary for his crime? Are all individuals who habitually steal kleptomaniacs? What of individuals who attempt or commit suicide? Are all drug addicts, alcoholics, prostitutes and homosexuals mentally ill or should they be classified legally, as in some instances they are, as criminals? How much freedom and responsibility does a mentally healthy person possess? Is there really such a thing as choice in human affairs? Is choice an illusion? Is every choice made by a human being already determined by his heredity, environment, culture and life experiences—or does he possess a modicum of free will even though some of his behavior is partially determined by the factors listed above?

Should "hippies," "yippies," "flower children," "beatniks," "professional" protestors, civil rights or peace demonstrators and others of that ilk be jailed for disturbing the peace or should they be treated and "healed" of their deviancy? Does one accept as a criterion of mental illness the theory of the cultural norm or "average person's" behavior—then subsequently label all deviations from this norm as indicative of mental illness?

Is it possible for a society or entire community to be sick, as has been suggested by some critics of American society? If so, then a community which was considered to be a healthy one emerges as the deviant by accusation. If a community consists of one hundred persons and ninety per cent of the inhabitants suffer from pulmonary tuberculosis—the remaining ten per cent being unaffected—then it can be assumed the "average person" in this community is ill. The healthy ten per cent of the population are deviants in the sense that they do not conform to the norm. It must again be emphasized that *mental illness is a value judgment*. Such value judgments are relativistic and are constantly evolving and changing. What is considered "normal" or abnormal behavior may vary greatly from one culture to another, and from one historic era to another. Perhaps one may consider as abnormal behavior which society does not endorse, condone or approve, and as normal that which is approved, condoned and encouraged by the society in which one lives.

It may be simplistic to assume that mental illness can be viewed as the opposite of mental health. Yet, in a sense, it is generally true that a mentally ill individual is, to some extent, unable to demonstrate the behaviors exhibited by the mentally healthy person, namely, the ability to love oneself, transcend self and love others; to face reality; and to find a meaning or purpose in life.

In summary, mental illness has been considered as a classification, a label, a category, and as a value judgment made on the basis of some criteria. Especially in the case of the functional illnesses these criteria are usually determined by cultural norms, rules, or standards of appropriate behavior in a given society. Mental illness has also been viewed as being on a continuum, with mental health as one extreme and mental illness as the other.

Mental Illness As An Experience

Mental illness is an experience undergone by a human being—not merely a label or a category. The fact that he is mentally ill may be accepted, denied, or ignored by the ill person. Nevertheless it is the individual human being who experiences the symptoms of his malady and must live with the loneliness (and in some instances incommunicability) of his condition, for how can pain, whether it be of mental or physical origin, truly be communicated in such a way that another person comprehends what is being communicated? Mental illness is something one *is* as opposed to a disease one *has*. It affects every aspect of being and is reflected in thoughts, feelings and actions. Above all, it is a malady that is *experienced* by the human being afflicted with the disorder.

Other Views

Mental illness may be viewed as an expression of a life style— a way of life—or as a way of coping with or adapting to stress. It may be viewed (culturally) as a sick way of relating with others. Mental illness is purposeful in one sense: it may provide some elements of security and comfort. Perhaps mental illness is embraced as a way of life because there are no other possible alternatives—no other avenues of expression or escape. Mental illness may also be viewed as a last resort, a last adaptive stand or survival technique. Mental illness (culturally) may be viewed as an irrational solution to an unsolvable life situation.

Are there secondary gains in mental illness, as may be the case in some instances of physical illness? Probably, although the "rewards" of mental illness may be more difficult to comprehend. Secondary gains may include being relieved of all responsibility for one's life or decisions. Other secondary gains, if the individual is hospitalized, may include being fed, clothed, given shelter and care, as, for example, in the event of a physical illness. Perhaps being too sheltered becomes the fate of many of the mentally ill. "Hospitalitis" and "institutional syndrome" are phenomena well known to health workers in psychiatric situations.

Recapitulation

To assist individuals and families to prevent, or cope with, the experience of mental illness and suffering is viewed as a function of psychiatric nurses. In order to accomplish this function the psychiatric nurse must understand what she is preventing or assisting the individual to cope with, namely, mental illness. She must realize that psychiatric nurses *do* need to understand the varied theories of the nature of mental illness as defined and explored by authorities in the field.

It is also necessary to focus on the meaning of mental illness to the individual experiencing the malady. Specific ways of assisting individuals to prevent and cope with the experience of mental illness and suffering will be discussed in this text.

TO FIND MEANING IN THE EXPERIENCE OF MENTAL ILLNESS AND SUFFERING

As in the case of physical illness, one is confronted with the question: "Why did this happen to me?" or to a relative or friend. The etiology of mental illness (or in many instances a "blame object") is sought. Questions are asked regarding the situation or series of experiences, the physiological insults or stresses that predisposed an individual to illness, or the factor(s) which precipitated the illness. The "blame object" may, in the case of the behaviorally ill, be the parents—more especially, it is the mother who is often cast in the role of "etiological agent." There seems also to be an implicit assumption, especially in the case of the so-called functional illnesses, that the mentally ill person is a "helpless" victim of malign outside forces (which may or may not be entirely true) and that somehow he cannot in any way be held responsible for his behavior. This latter point is debatable and has grave implications for nursing intervention.

Meaning

How does anyone find meaning in the suffering of a profound depression or in an uncontrollable behavior so frenzied and hyperactive that no self-control is possible? How does anyone find meaning when immersed and encompassed by an evermounting anxiety that does not lessen, but paralyzingly grows until there is nothing left of the person who was; there is only what is *now* anxiety become incarnate?

What meaning can be found in the immobility, the mute facade of an uninhabited being, frozen in muteness and in the inaccessibility of aloneness, or in the grotesque choreography and posturing of inappropriate grimacing and giggling? What of the "automaton" obeying commands of unseen forces and voices heard by self alone? How does one find meaning in the depths of a suspicion that trusts no one, or in flight from persecutors—the seen and unseen "enemies" who plot and pursue—or in a reality so distorted that the familiar becomes unfamiliar and misinterpreted and may be replaced by imagined and hallucinated voices, visions, smells, tastes and touches? How does one find meaning in a behavior which is so compulsive and impulsive that free will no longer exists and which causes actions which cannot be understood, much less controlled? What meaning is inherent in unreality? How does one find meaning in a shattered self that has lost identity and a sense of "I-ness" or "me-ness"?

"Why did this happen to me?" (or to a relative or friend) is not just a rhetorical academic musing—it is a human cry for help which no one can definitively answer. Difficult as it may be to help the physically ill to bear, cope with, and find some meaning in "physical illness," it is, in most instances, even more difficult to assist the behaviorally ill individual and his family to find some meaning in the suffering and despair that *is* mental illness.

Summary

In Part I of this work, various definitions or beliefs about the nature of psychiatric nursing have been discussed, with special emphasis being placed on the recently published American Nurses Association Statement on Psychiatric Nursing Practice. A definition of psychiatric nursing was stated.

In Part II the definition of psychiatric nursing used in this text was stated as a purpose, a major assumption being that the purpose of nursing remains constant despite the clinical specialty area or setting in which the nurse practices. Terms used in the statement of the purpose of nursing were discussed and clarified. Beliefs about the nature of mental health were considered and three abilities of the mentally healthy person were discussed.

PART III—THE FUNCTIONS OF THE PSYCHIATRIC NURSE

In this text, the term *psychiatric nurse* is used synonymously with that of professional nurse practitioner who has completed study in a baccalaureate school of nursing. What functions does a psychiatric nurse perform in order to achieve the purpose of psychiatric nursing? These functions are varied and numerous, and clearly emerge from the purpose of psychiatric nursing. They are:

A. To promote mental health

B. To prevent mental illness

C. To help the afflicted to cope with the stress of mental illness and assist them (if possible) toward health

D. To assist the ill person, his family and the community to find meaning in mental illness

A psychiatric nurse accomplishes her functions by an understanding and application of the skills of observation, by valid interpretation of inferences derived through observation, and by purposeful nursing intervention.

A psychiatric nurse accomplishes her functions by engaging in activities which will create a therapeutic milieu in which the ill person can develop as a human being: by intervening appropriately, for example, in assisting the ill person to respect self and others; by aiding him to derive enjoyment and pleasure from socializing and becoming a part of the human community. The nurse also protects the ill person, if need be, from self and others by setting limits when necessary and by helping to maintain physical health and integrity, while striving to identify and solve (when possible) problems of a somatic nature. She may participate in group therapy or other programs, in the one-to-one relationship (or intensive counseling sessions with one patient), and in many other activities. There is no *one* role or *one* function for the nurse, just as there is no *one* setting for the practice of nursing.

The psychiatric nurse also works collaboratively with members of the other health disciplines, i.e., with physicians, psychologists, social workers, occupational and recreational therapists, and can direct and supervise psychiatric aides and attendants. She also works with the clergy, legal authorities, legislators, and members of lay organizations.

PART IV—THE MYSTIQUE OF PSYCHIATRIC NURSING

Although it is less common now than previously, there still remains an aura of mystery surrounding the nature of psychiatric nursing. Perhaps this stems from the ancient cultural views of mental illness as being caused by sin, demons, or other "forces of evil."

The terminology used by psychiatric nurses and psychiatrists has compounded the problem. Psychiatric nursing, as is true in many other clinical area specialities, has tended toward "special area provincialism," a tendency to focus on the clinical area in which one is primarily interested instead of on nursing as a whole. Commonalities with other clinical areas are not stressed—rather, differences are expounded ad infinitum.

One cannot speak of the mystique of psychiatric nursing without considering what is, in many cases, a humorous situation, but is actually the failure to clarify the role and function of the psychiatric nurse. This is the problem of "imbued omnipotence"—a term which refers to a complex of unrealistic beliefs held about psychiatric nurses by others, i.e., colleagues from other clinical specialty areas, behaviorally ill persons and their families, lay people, friends, relatives, and acquaintances. One of these beliefs is that psychiatric nurses possess certain esoteric knowledge which enables them to read minds, interpret dreams, foresee the future and perform other feats of magic. Another widely held belief is that psychiatric nurses constantly "psychoanalyze" others. That psychiatric nurses do not, and are not prepared to, "psychoanalyze" anyone has not seemed to penetrate—neither has the fact that psychiatric nurses are not in the least interested in psychoanalyzing others. If they were they would have been psychoanalysts, not psychiatric nurses.

Another still-prevalent belief is that psychiatric nurses are in some ways peculiar or, as the less charitable state: "They must be a little crazy or they wouldn't work with mentally ill individuals." A variation on this theme is that the longer a nurse works with the mentally ill the more like *"them"* she becomes.

One might question the reason why the above-mentioned beliefs are still widely held in this day and age. It is probably true that psychiatric nurses themselves are partially to blame for failure to interpret their role and function to others. Psychiatric nurses may deliberately (or by their silence) foster such beliefs and in a sense "play upon them." It is humorous to have others assume one possesses infinite wisdom and insight; it is also, on another level, quite flattering to one's ego. There is an old saying among psychiatric nurses and others working with the mentally ill that they are "expected to be a little peculiar." This is viewed by some as a fringe benefit—and in some strange ways it is.

There is a less frivolous aspect to this problem; the perpetuation of a mystique also has its drawbacks. Colleagues in other clinical specialty areas do not gain a clear understanding of the nature of psychiatric nursing or of the teaching-learning process inherent therein, or know the difficulties of identifying and applying theory in a field so fraught with ambiguities. This mystique also perpetuates the search for the mythical "golden answer"—the *one* phrase a nurse can utter to an ill person which will magically reduce his anxiety and help him solve his problems.

The practice of psychiatric nursing is a searching, tiring, sometimes tedious but always interesting process. It involves disciplined observation, a skill derived by applying theory to practice —a skill most difficult to learn. Observation of behavior must be based on knowledge—not intuition—and must be validated, whenever possible, with the ill person. Nursing intervention is based on this application of theory and observation of the human being in his totality.

One does not "work with" an ill person in the sense that one manipulates an object. The interpersonal process requires that the nurse possess knowledge of self, humility and courage to identify and cope with personal feelings and motivations in the interpersonal situation. It is much easier, of course, to focus exclusively on the behavior of a patient and to deny or ignore one's own feelings in the interpersonal situation.

The ability to observe, to develop inferences about self and patient, and to intervene appropriately implies the ability to apply and test theory—not arcane knowledge. This ability is the sine qua non of psychiatric nursing.

Psychiatric nursing is difficult to learn. It involves continual searching for and studying of new ways to apply, evolve and test theory in practice. It is time that the crystal ball concept of psychiatric nursing be shattered. The search for the "golden phrase" must be abandoned for the needed search for theory applicable to, and derived through, research of the psychiatric nursing process.

N.B. References used in this chapter are in the footnotes. These are not repeated.

Chapter II

THE PROCESS OF PSYCHIATRIC NURSING

To achieve the functions of psychiatric nursing the practitioner engages in an interpersonal process consisting of overlapping stages: observation, interpretation, decision making, action (nursing intervention) and appraisal (or evaluation) of one's actions. These stages of the interpersonal process may also be considered as basic skills needed by all nurses. The abilities to communicate purposefully and to make practical use of theory are prerequisites to the interpersonal process—a process which takes place regardless of the setting or clinical specialty area.

DEFINITIONS AND DISCUSSION OF PROCESS IN PSYCHIATRIC NURSING

The term *process* in its broadest sense is defined as the experiential aspect of nursing, i.e., what transpires between nurse and patient(s). *A major assumption is that many aspects of the interpersonal process are reciprocal,* i.e., the nurse is not only the observer but is also observed by the patient. Both nurse and patient develop interpretations about the meaning of the other's behavior, both make decisions, both act, both may evaluate their own and each other's actions. The difference hopefully lies in the purposefulness of the nurse's activities, as well as in the theoretical or content background she draws upon to understand, plan, give and evaluate results gained in the interpersonal process.

Process and Content

In professional nursing, theory and process are inseparable. Theory, i.e., facts, concepts and principles comprising the fund of knowledge used in nursing practice, is applied to and emerges from process.

> Process also influences content since it is from nursing practice that concepts and principles are abstracted; the reverse is also true, in that concepts and principles are applied to nursing practice. The relationship between content (theory) and process is a circular-oscillating one, each influencing and affecting the other.[1]

Process as Ability and Skill

In this work, the terms ability and skill are used synonymously. An individual who possesses ability or skill:

A. Possesses the knowledge underlying the skill(s), i.e., understands and can apply theoretical concepts
  1. Understands the reasons for and nature of the task(s) to be performed
  2. Knows methods or means of accomplishing the task(s)
B. Performs the task effectively and safely and with appropriate sense of timing
C. Evaluates the performance

An individual who possesses the knowledge underlying the skills —i.e., a person who can apply theoretical concepts—is able to identify and communicate these concepts to others. It is possible to act intuitively in nursing situations, but the fact remains that the nurse must possess the facts and concepts needed to form a basis of action.

An individual who understands the reasons for, and the nature of, the task to be performed is also able to substantiate this knowledge on a theoretical basis. For example, a nurse who knows *why* there is a need to interpret observation will be more likely to engage in this activity than a nurse who views this task as unimportant and unnecessary. Knowledge of the nature of the activity to be performed also provides the nurse with an opportunity to view the task from the standpoint of an ethical code or value system. For example, a nurse may understand the reasons for assisting a physician to perform a prefrontal lobotomy or electric shock therapy and have no ethical problem, but giving direct assistance in some instances may violate her moral or ethical code.

Knowledge of the means of accomplishing the task(s) implies a knowledge of alternative methods of achieving goals. There is no *one* way of interpreting observations; there are many methods. A

---

[1] Travelbee, Joyce: Interpersonal Aspects of Nursing. F. A. Davis Company, Philadelphia, 1966.

nurse with such knowledge is not limited in terms of methodology but can creatively envisage and design means of achieving a goal.

To perform a task effectively the nurse must possess some degree of expertise which enables her to be goal-directed and purposeful in action. It might be said that she possesses "know-how"—the ability to know what to do and how to do it well and safely. Safe performance means that the nurse does not harm self or patient by actions used, and implies that she acts within the legal framework of nursing practice. She also needs an appropriate sense of timing; in interpersonal situations the nurse comprehends and anticipates patient needs and proceeds at the patient's pace, and is able to recognize when to speak and when to be silent, when to act and when not to act. Developing a sense of timing is difficult and little is known about how to teach "timing" to others.

To evaluate performance, in its most general sense, the nurse must assess whether or not the activity was helpful to the patient. To be more specific, evaluation centers around achieving the particular objectives of nursing care; the extent to which the nurse is able to achieve these objectives is the criterion used to evaluate nursing actions.

Whether or not a learner possesses any of the skills discussed above may be ascertained by use of various devices, tests or measurements, or by validated observations.

Process in Psychiatric Nursing and Other Clinical Specialty Areas

The emphasis on process in psychiatric nursing, as compared to other clinical specialty areas, seems to lie primarily in priorities placed on certain functions, or work roles, assumed in psychiatric nursing as compared to those in other specialties. Peplau states: "Medical-surgical nursing emphasizes technical care; pediatric nursing emphasizes the mother-surrogate role. . . . Psychiatric nursing emphasizes the role of counselor or psychotherapist."[2]

Although nurses in all areas must know how to observe, interpret observations, and intervene, the psychiatric nurse engages in these practices within the total context of the work role of counselor. It is probable that *what* the nurse observes, interprets or decides in a nurse-patient situation is partially determined by her own past experiences which may affect understanding, acceptance and knowledge of priority work role or clinical emphasis.

---

[2] Peplau, Hildegard E.: Interpersonal techniques: the crux of psychiatric nursing. Amer. J. Nurs., 62:50, 1962.

PART I—OBSERVATION

Observation is important because it is the first phase or step leading to nursing action. From observation the nurse develops interpretations or inferences, and decides to act, or withhold actions, according to these interpretations of what has occurred in the nurse-patient situation. It is not possible to plan, structure, give, or evaluate nursing actions without being a skilled observer; neither is it possible to develop any kind of a helping relationship. *One aspect of observation is experiencing, and a major assumption in this text is that experiencing should precede interpretation or analysis of the data.*

DEFINITION OF OBSERVATION

Observation, as used in this text, refers to collection of raw sensory data prior to interpretation. Observation includes the content of the data, i.e., what is seen, heard, smelled, etc. To observe is to notice, be mindful of, or focus on what is happening in a situation; it implies intentional scrutiny or concentrated attention. Observation is an active process, a meaningful as well as a purposeful process.

PURPOSES OF OBSERVATION

To observe accurately, the nurse's attention must be focused on what is being sought. Observation is not an end in itself.

What are the purposes of gathering raw data? From a survey of basic nursing textbooks in various clinical areas the purposes of observation may be grouped broadly as follows: to "infer" patients' needs and problems in order to plan appropriate nursing action, to assist the physician in diagnosing the patient's illness, to assess the efficacy of therapies prescribed by the physician, to gather information about the patient in order to share these findings with other members of the health team, to prevent complications and sequelae, and to observe signs of illness. As can be inferred from the above, the importance of separating sensory data from interpretation of the data is *not* stressed or implied.

While it cannot be denied that the purposes of observation as stated in the texts surveyed *are* important and therefore should be given priority, one gets the impression that the human being who is the patient is not viewed in his totality during the search for signs and symptoms of illness.

The professional nurse practitioner does not "observe signs of illness"; the nurse observes an ill human being who may (or may not) be experiencing symptoms of a particular illness, and validates (with the ill person if at all possible) the subjective experiences he is undergoing.

In psychiatric nursing, as in other clinical specialty areas, the purposes of observation are many and varied. However, it is *always* the ill human being who is observed, not signs of illness.

However, the individual is not an *object* in the sense one observes protozoa through a microscope; neither is he a "specimen" to be analyzed, scrutinized or "watched" with a view to reporting his deviant behavior. Observation is *not* spying—nor is it usually engaged in for the sole purpose of information gathering, although this may be the case if one is participating in certain types of research projects.

What are the purposes of observation in psychiatric nursing? Observation is a process used to get to know the ill individual(s) as unique human being(s). This is a necessary first step in a working nurse-patient relationship. A more specific purpose is to collect raw data in order to interpret and validate its meaning (whenever possible with the ill individual), and then to decide on a course of nursing action. Collecting raw data is a necessary prerequisite in planning, structuring, and evaluating the nursing care given a specific individual or group of individuals. Whatever reason a nurse may have for observing an ill person—whether it is to assess the effect of a particular drug on an individual's behavior, to watch for signs of somatic illness, or to detect signs of increasing anxiety—she goes through the same process. The practitioner begins by collecting raw data.

Should the nurse conceptualize what she is planning to observe before interacting with an ill person? The answer is "no," since she cannot know in advance *what* will be observed. The nurse *can,* however, have certain tentative objectives in mind, based on knowledge of the patient and his needs. For example, she may wish to assess the ill person's anxiety level. Assessment of anxiety level then will be a tentative objective conceptualized in advance of the interaction— tentative since there may be a need to modify or change objectives during the interaction. (Such changes or modifications may be brought about by changes in the ill person's behavior which necessitate a shift in emphasis.) Knowing, in part, what one hopes to accomplish *does* help the nurse to focus attention. In assessing anxiety level, the nurse's attention would be directed toward observing behavioral manifestations of anxiety should these emerge during the interaction, but it should be remembered that the very fact of "looking for" certain aspects of behavior may bias the observer. The observer may "see" behavioral manifestations and infer that these are manifestations of anxiety, whereas the behavioral manifestations do not, in fact, exist except in the mind of the observer. Knowledge of this proclivity, careful scrutiny, and validation of the meaning of the data with the ill human being and others are means of eliminating some of the bias in observation.

THE PROCESS OF OBSERVATION

Observation begins with an external event or phenomenon and the stimulation of a sense organ and its receptors, followed by formation of a percept which gives meaning and clarification to what has been perceived and leads to the development of concepts. All of man's knowledge comes through, or originates in, the senses. Proper functioning of the sense organs is therefore essential to make accurate observations.

It may seem simplistic to state that one of the first prerequisites in developing skill in data collection is for the nurse to spend time with the ill person(s). It is, of course, naive to assume that spending time with an ill person is an indication that the nurse is focusing attention on what is happening to the ill person, or between the ill person and self. This may, or may not, be true.

Data Collection

The data the nurse collects consist of what is seen, heard, smelled, touched, i.e., everything taken in via the sense organs. It is important to identify and collect raw data prior to interpreting their meaning. For example, a person frowns. The raw data—"wrinkling of the brows" or "frowning"—may be interpreted as indicative of worry, pain, depression, preoccupation, daydreaming, etc. The nurse has no way of knowing whether or not the interpretation of the data is correct unless the interpretation is validated with the patient or with others. What *is* important is that the nurse be able to notice and report what *was actually seen and heard* prior to interpretation. Discussing one's raw data with others is an important means of verifying or substantiating the probability of correct interpretation.

In addition to the purposeful collection of raw data there is another important aspect of observation, that of experiencing. Experiencing precedes analysis, dissection or interpretation of the data.

Experiencing As an Aspect of Observation

Experiencing as an aspect of observation is difficult to define; it is probably akin to a mosaic-like structure composed of various elements. Experiencing includes collecting data using all sense modalities, while holding interpretation of the data in abeyance. It means focusing on the individual within the total context of his setting and environment, not parts or aspects of the whole One reacts as human to human and allows the other's personality and uniqueness to become real, on a level other than what is known *about* him. There is a vividness to experiencing—an immediacy and a sense of confronting a real person rather than an individual whose behavior we have scrutinized, categorized or dissected.

There is a difference, for example, between experiencing a sunset and analyzing or categorizing the event. *Experiencing precedes interpretation, analysis or dissection of the experience.* A work of art, a statue, may be pulverized and ground into pieces, its components subjected to microscopic scrutiny, its various parts identified chemically, but in the process its wholeness and integrity are destroyed. If this be true of inanimate objects, how much more so of human beings? The analogy may seem a bit farfetched, since nurses do not pulverize human beings or reduce them to their basic elements, but there is a danger that—in segmenting the human being by focusing exclusively on nursing problems, pathological behavior, or signs and symptoms of illness—one will fail to perceive or experience the human being and to relate to his uniqueness. Experiencing is an active as well as a relatively passive process—active in the sense that one collects raw data and holds the interpretation in abeyance, and passive in the sense that one strives to "be still" in order to appreciate the unfolding of the uniqueness of the other person. Experiencing is akin to appreciation, rather than to intellectual comprehension or knowledge, of the individual.

Experiencing is not a one-time event, as, for example, something which occurs during an initial interaction with a person; *it is a continuous process.* Experiencing the uniqueness of another is not an esoteric art confined to the practice of psychiatric nursing. In personal as well as in professional relationships, whenever one strives to appreciate the uniqueness of another prior to interpreting his behavior, experiencing is occurring.

BARRIERS TO DEVELOPING SKILL IN OBSERVATION

Although observation is a skill which can be taught and learned, there are many barriers to its development. In addition to improper functioning of the sense organs, some of these are: familiarity, inability to separate sense data from interpretations, inability to use all of one's sense modalities, and a high anxiety level.

Familiarity As a Hindrance

The individual tends to observe that which he is accustomed to observing, while discounting other perceptual data. While familiarity may or may not breed contempt in interpersonal situations, it cannot be denied that what is familiar in an interpersonal situation, event, or setting may be either discounted or not noted at all; only extremes or deviations from the familiar may be noticed. Underlying this tendency seems to be the fallacious assumption that what is familiar is known and need not be noted. The familiar becomes a baseline, and while deviations may be observed sameness is not. This sameness is an illusion—it does not exist. For example, a nurse may assume an ill person's condition *today* is the same as it was *yesterday* because she does not "notice" any difference in the patient's condition. The nurse does not notice any difference—not because there is none—but because the deviation from the baseline may be so slight, or so familiar, that it is not perceived. *Individuals, however, are always in the process of changing.* To stretch a point it might be said that the ill person observed one day ago is not the same person seen today. The observer also has changed in the interim and is not the same person she was one day ago. How may this problem be surmounted? Awareness of one's tendency to ignore the familiar—to take it for granted and focus only on deviations from a fictitious baseline—is a beginning, but it is not enough. One must begin to look at it anew and, to use an old cliche, "see with fresh eyes" and from a different perspective. What does this mean? It means to look at familiar objects or persons as if "seeing them for the first time"; it means to be still and experience again the familiar as the unfamiliar. It means to be truly open to sensory input and experience, as opposed to a stultifying, ossified, unchanging manner of perceiving objects, people or events. It means to shift perspective and to open up dimensions in which one truly reacts as the *involved* and not as a detached (or even as a participant) observer or analyzer of an event or phenomenon. This is why one of the necessary steps in observation is first to experience the object of inquiry before dissecting, categorizing or analyzing its components or elements. To see with fresh eyes is not merely to be concerned with perceiving the familiar as unfamiliar, it is also to recognize that experiencing is a prerequisite to analysis.

It is probable that the problems of discounting the familiar, or the failure to experience before interpreting or analyzing, cannot be completely eliminated; however, they can be kept in mind. By diligent disciplined practice the nurse can learn to observe and interpret the behavior of another without obliterating the uniqueness of the human being whom she is striving to help.

Inability to Separate Raw Data and Interpretations

In addition to the tendency to perceive what we are accustomed to perceiving (the expected or familiar) while discounting other data, another major difficulty in developing skill in observation seems to be the inability to separate what is seen, heard, smelled, touched, etc., from personal interpretations regarding the meaning of the phenomenon, event or situation. For example, a nurse will report that an ill person "looks worried." Worry per se *cannot* be seen or heard since it is an interpretation derived usually from something either seen or heard during the interpersonal encounter. What is important is that the nurse identify *what* was seen or heard, i.e., collect the raw data which led to the interpretation of worry. Data must first be elicited before one can interpret it, much less validate it. *An interpretation is not raw data.* Learners in psychiatric nursing (the term "learner" includes every nurse practicing in the clinical area field) have varying degrees of difficulty in identifying and separating raw data from interpretations, or conclusions, about the data.

The inability to separate raw data (what is seen, heard, etc.) from personal interpretations (or conclusions as to the meaning of the data) is a widespread problem. One may test this hypothesis by trying an experiment. For example, play a situation in pantomine and ask the group to describe what is occurring in the situation. Most, if not all, of the responses will be interpretations; few, if any, respondents will report raw data. Following one role-playing session (in pantomine) during which the actress moved her lips twice (without uttering a word), a large percentage of the student-group interpreted the lip movements as indicative of hallucinations. The actress was not hallucinating but the group did not attempt to validate the inference until the lack of supporting evidence was pointed out to them. What *was* seen by group members was an individual who moved her lips twice; movement of the lips comprised the raw data. Hallucination is an interpretation or conclusion as to the meaning of the lip movement. What is ultimately involved here is the ability to think clearly and logically. The quick leap from data to interpretation (without validation) is the cause of inappropriate, ineffective, and sometimes harmful nursing action. It is also a probable cause of much friction, dissension, and difficulty in interpersonal relationships in everyday life.

Inability to Use All of One's Sense Modalities

Another barrier to developing skill in observation is the failure to use all of one's sense modalities—not just sight and hearing—in collecting raw data. Many observers use only one or two sense modalities primarily. One may test this hypothesis by trying the following kind of experiment. Give each individual in a group an object and ask each person to describe the object fully and completely. This may be a paper clip, a match, a leaf, a stone, a blade of grass, etc. Responses to such an experiment are interesting. Usually individuals will first classify or in some way categorize the object, i.e., "it is a paper clip"; "it is made of steel" (or some metallic substance) ; some will describe the uses to which it may be put. When learners are asked to take the object home and study it before writing their descriptions, the nature of the descriptive data varies more. Some individuals weigh the object; others measure it carefully and report its length, width, height, etc. Few persons will make any reference to the "feel" of the object— its softness, coldness, etc.—or in any way refer to the tactile sensation of handling it. Fewer persons still will refer to its odor (or report the absence of odor) and even fewer will refer to the taste of the object (assuming it is something which can be tasted).

Inability to Shift Perspective

Another interesting outcome of "object study" is that apparently no individual observed the object (the paper clip, for example) from any other perspective than that of a flat surface and in one-dimensional terms. There were no reports, for example, of how the object was "seen" when suspended by a thread. Neither were any descriptions included of perception of the object as seen from a distance and up close or from above and below. No directional descriptions were given, such as differences in perceiving the paper clip from a northerly, southerly, easterly direction. These experiments, the findings of which are unsubstantiated at present, may possibly be used with modification of research design to explore the extent to which individuals can shift perspective in working with people.

Following the writing up of these experiments in collecting raw data, the author's attention was called to an article by I. A. Richards on "The Secret of 'Feedforward' "[3] which seems, in part at least, to substantiate some of these speculations.

It is quite possible that a prerequisite in helping others to observe will be to provide opportunities whereby learners will be taught (actually retaught or reintroduced) to use all of their sense modalities and not limit themselves to sight and hearing.

ANXIETY AND OBSERVATION

Some degree of anxiety is useful, and may well assist the learner in observing. Too much anxiety lessens one's capacity to "take in" what is occurring in the interpersonal situation and may cause the observer to focus on details rather than to perceive the situation as a whole. There are research findings in the literature validating the effect of anxiety on the individual's capacity to focus on, and make sense of, perceptual data.

PART II—INTERPRETATION

Collecting significant raw data is no easy feat; it is even more difficult to draw valid interpretations about the meaning of raw data. To interpret data requires a fund of knowledge and understanding concerning the nature of the data perceived. To acquire this knowledge it is necessary to develop various cognitive skills and the ability to use and apply concepts to data—and here lies much of the difficulty encountered on the interpretive level.

DEFINITION OF INTERPRETATION

Interpretation consists of explanation of raw data and the attempt to place what was observed into a meaningful whole. A wide variety of conclusions of the meaning of data is possible, i.e., interpretations may range from an unsubstantiated "opinion" to a tentative working hypothesis which is related to a body of theory (hypothesis meaning a proposition which is capable of some degree of validation; the term is not used in its strictest connotation).

---

[3] Richards, I. A.: The secret of "Feedforward." Sat. Rev., February 3, 1968: 14.

THE PROCESS OF DEVELOPING INTERPRETATIONS

The ability to interpret sensory data begins at birth and progresses as the individual proceeds through the various phases of growth and development. Almost immediately the human being strives to organize raw data—to label or in some way categorize data. This necessitates the use of concepts. A concept is an abstraction or an idea, as compared to a percept. Interpretations or conclusions regarding raw data necessitate the use of concepts at varying levels of abstraction and complexity.

The ability to think logically and use concepts develops slowly over a period of time as the individual grows and acquires facility in the use of language and the capacity to communicate with others. The reader is referred to Bruner, Goodnow and Austin's work on the process of concept attainment for in-depth discussion of these processes (see Appendix I, Bibliography, Chapter II).

Concepts may be considered as being of varying degrees of complexity ranging from lower-level abstractions such as objects or things to more highly abstract ideas lacking a visible external referent. Lower-level concepts are more readily amenable to consensual validation than are higher-level abstractions.

For example, the concept "chair" is a lower-level concept and is consequently validated when a majority of individuals in a group agree that it will be used to refer to a particular object constructed in a certain manner, its express purpose being that of seating a human being. It must be stressed that the term "chair" is a concept. "Chair" per se cannot be *observed* and hence is not, strictly speaking, raw data but rather a concept used to apply to certain sensory data. "Chair," while considered a lower-level concept, in another sense may be considered a high level of abstraction within the low-level concept category. The term "chair" is used to designate a generalized class of meanings but in no way is there any differentiation between chair 1 and chair 2, or between types or kinds of chairs. However, compared to more abstract concepts, it is relatively easy to validate concepts related to objects and things having a visible external referent; for example, one can point to a chair and say, "this is what I mean when I say chair." It is not possible to point to the external referent of such high-level abstractions and constructs as justice, humanity, honesty, love, depression, happiness or anxiety. One cannot, for example, see anxiety as one "sees" an object such as a chair, a glass or a lamp. One observes behavioral manifestations which are interpreted as indicative of the presence of anxiety. However, to conclude that certain behavioral manifestations indicate anxiety in another individual presupposes that the observer "knows" the effects of anxiety upon behavior and is able to discriminate between observable indicators of anxiety and indicators of some other affective state.

What is the relationship between a theoretical basis for understanding anxiety and the ability to observe behavioral manifestations of anxiety in another person? In other words, is it necessary to "know" much about anxiety in order to infer its presence in another person? While it is true that lay persons, lacking a theoretical knowledge of the nature or causes of anxiety, *can* and *do* make valid inferences regarding the presence of anxiety in another individual, there are differences between the lay person's interpretation and that of the professional nurse practitioner. The difference primarily lies in the wealth of theoretical data the practitioner brings to the interpersonal situation and her ability to apply this knowledge to assist the ill person. Hopefully, a professional nurse practitioner can identify not only the gross but the subtle behavioral manifestations of anxiety, through receiving the type of preparation which enables her to assess the level of anxiety the ill person is experiencing, and can make a clinical judgment as to the nature of the intervention needed.

In addition to knowledge of observable indicators of a feeling state and possession of a theoretical base upon which to make clinical judgments, what else may determine the extent to which an individual can develop valid inferences regarding the subjective experiences of another person? It is, for example, interesting to speculate whether or not it is possible to infer a feeling state in another person if one has never personally experienced the state (or a similar state). Studies on empathy seem to indicate that it is not possible to comprehend the experience of another unless one has personally undergone a similar experience. It would also be valuable to know the extent to which theoretical understanding can compensate for a dearth of experiential background. The answers to these questions are not known at the present time, and research in these areas is needed.

KINDS AND LEVELS OF INTERPRETATIONS

Four kinds of levels of interpretations will be defined and discussed.

Assumption level. Assumption is here defined as the act of taking for granted that something is true without critically examining the data to determine whether or not the statement or "fact" has any validity. When one assumes, there is no question regarding the validity of the assumption; the assumer "just knows" but is unable to supply supporting data to substantiate the assumption. The assumer is usually defensive when questioned as to the validity of his assumption.

Opinion level. Opinions are defined as highly subjective conclusions about data. The conclusions may be true or false, valid or invalid. A characteristic of the opinion level interpretation is that the holder of the opinion usually "substantiates" the validity of his beliefs by recourse to "personal experience." He generalizes from one or more of his own experiences and applies these generalizations to other experiences and events as explanations. The interpreter, on this level, fails to understand the limits of generalization. The opinion holder views each new experience or event as a replication of some past experience or event in his own life. Opinions are considered a higher level of interpretation than assumptions because the opinion holder does attempt, however inappropriately and ineptly, to transfer his "knowledge" to another situation. Opinion holders believe that "everyone has a right to his opinion" and usually have the incorrect idea that all opinions have equal validity. Actually, an opinion on physics by the late Albert Einstein obviously should be given different weight than a lay person's "opinion" on the same subject. As in the case of the assumer, the opinion holder tends to become defensive when questioned as to the validity of the opinion.

Supposition level. A supposition is defined as a conclusion or interpretation which is considered by the holder to be tentative and open to question, since suppositions may or may not be theoretically correct. The individual can, however, substantiate his interpretation to some extent. The difference between this level of interpretation and those of assumption and opinion is that the interpreter *is* willing to admit to possibilities or alternatives other than his own supposition. The interpreter on this level is not apt to become defensive about his interpretations; he is willing to admit uncertainty and to tolerate ambiguity.

Hypothesis level. An hypothesis is defined as a gradation or higher level supposition, a proposition which is capable of some degree of validation. Hypothesis is not a fixed conclusion about what has been observed; it is tentative, fluid, and may be changed as new data emerge or new relationships are envisaged. The formulation of a useful working hypothesis is dependent upon one's theoretical framework and ability to verify the working hypothesis.

Discussion of Levels

Any conclusion regarding the meaning of raw data may be interpreted on any of the levels discussed. For example, the conclusion that "the patient is anxious" may be an assumption, an opinion, a supposition or an hypothesis. It is important, in terms of nursing action, to identify the level of interpretation being used. If the interpretation is on the *hypothesis* level the observer will be able to:

a) describe what was seen, heard, smelled, etc., and identify the raw data from which the conclusion was tentatively formed

b) communicate to others *why* "anxiety" was inferred rather than some other conclusion (i.e., the observer can compare and contrast)

c) state clearly the theoretical framework used in explaining the concept of anxiety

d) explain how the conclusion or interpretation can be tested or validated

e) use validated interpretations as a basis for planning, giving and evaluating nursing actions.

Hopefully, the professional nurse practitioner will interpret raw data on the hypothesis level and not on the lower levels of interpretations. As stated previously, it is necessary to validate conclusions regarding raw data.

THE PROBLEM OF VALIDATION OF INTERPRETATIONS

Validation is defined as verification or substantiation, by at least one other person, of raw data obtained during a particular experience or event. Interpretation of the meaning of raw data is also validated.

Psychiatrists make use of interviews, case presentations, and the findings of psychological tests, etc., to validate conclusions regarding a patient's problems or to gain insight into the patient's perception of himself and others. Psychiatric nurses may, of course, make use of these findings, but they are not necessarily a meaningful guide in the here-and-now validation of the meaning of behavior. *The psychiatric nurse, in the one-to-one relationship, is concerned with the present reality—i.e., with the here-and-now interpretation of the possible meanings of the patient's behavior and the relevancy of these meanings for nursing intervention.* Specifically, validation requires checking or sharing data with another individual to approach as high a degree of accuracy in interpretation as is possible. Ideally, in nursing situations, the individual with whom the nurse checks or shares data is the source of the data—namely, the patient. For example, during the one-to-one relationship the nurse may conclude that "the patient is anxious." A "simple" solution would be to ask the patient if he is anxious, but using a term depending on the patient's level of comprehension. A difficulty in using this approach to validation is that many ill patients are not aware of their anxiety level and hence cannot always corroborate the nurse's conclusions. Sharing perceptual data with the ill person is another means of validating conclusions; for example, one might say to the patient, "Your hands are trembling —tell me why." It is not, however, feasible or desirable to share perceptual data with all patients. Judgment is required here.

Interpretation of the meaning of raw data should be validated with the individual involved if at all possible; if this is not feasible, then validation of other observers can be sought. Other clinicians can be asked to observe the patient. Additional raw data are collected and interpretations may, to some extent, be verified and validated. This is not to say that if two clinicians observe behavioral manifestations of a patient and both arrive at the same conclusions their interpretations are necessarily correct. Each may be wrong. As has been stated, many factors affect one's ability to observe and interpret accurately. Sharing one's conclusions with someone else *does* afford the opportunity to think through and explore alternate possibilities or interpretations regarding the situation. It is through sharing and exploring that thinking can be clarified and synthesized. Use of the supervisory process affords the clinician another opportunity to share raw data, and to discuss and explore plans for nursing intervention.

The professional nurse strives to validate conclusions or interpretations of the meaning of what was seen, heard, etc., in the nurse-patient situation. It is a reciprocal process in that the nurse not only gathers raw data about the patient and attempts to arrive at meaning but also collects data about self, i.e., what she is saying, doing, thinking, feeling. The nurse's knowledge of self is important. It is quite possible to project to a patient the nurse's own feeling state. A system of checks and balances, and the validation of conclusions, is important from this aspect alone.

Validation is difficult—there is no doubt about it. Further, although a practitioner may be able to identify the raw data from which conclusions were drawn, to communicate to others the process through which a conclusion was reached, and to state how to test both the hypothesis and its conclusion—thereby using validated conclusions to plan, give and evaluate nursing care—there is still another quality that is needed. This quality, which is almost a prerequisite for successful nursing intervention, is *humility*. An individual possessing humility knows how very little is understood through personal awareness as compared to what there is to learn; she realizes that conclusions about the behavior of others, despite the most critical scrutiny, may be incorrect because attainment of absolute certitude and wisdom is not possible.

PART III—DECISION MAKING AND NURSING ACTION

In decision making the nurse observes, develops interpretations as to the meaning of data, tries to validate these conclusions, and then decides what action (if any) to take as a result of investigative inquiry. Conclusions and interpretations necessitate judgment, and decisions are made depending on correct use of investigative inquiry in any given situation.

A decision is a judgment made as to the ways of solving a problem or testing an hypothesis. *Decisions are on a cognitive and not an action level.* The judgments made are directly concerned with nursing care and are therefore within the scope of the legal definition of nursing practice. Decisions are action indicators, action proposals, or actions of a directional nature. Nursing action implements the decisions made. Action is what the nurse *does* as a result of decisions and includes methods, techniques, and ways of intervening, as well as the intervention itself.

DIFFERENTIATION

Interpretation is differentiated from decision making on the basis that an interpretation is the identifying of the problem or hypothesis to be tested, but does not include judgments as to ways or means of solving the problem or testing the hypothesis.

In actuality, decision making and nursing action are inextricably intertwined, since decisions can be, in and of themselves, considered action. For purposes of discussion, however, each will be considered separately. There is, as can be noted, an overlapping of various aspects of the interpersonal process. These aspects are difficult to separate, since each phase emerges from and flows into another.

DETERMINANTS OF DECISION MAKING

The quality of decisions reached regarding the ways of solving a problem or testing an hypothesis in a nursing situation is determined by many factors. Some of these are: the nature or content of raw data; the nurse's ability to separate raw data from interpretations; the kind or level of interpretation made; and the ability to validate interpretations or conclusions. Affecting these factors is the ability to apply theory to observation, interpretation and decision making.

A decision as to ways of solving a problem or testing an hypothesis is also dependent on one's knowledge and understanding of the possible alternatives available in a given nursing situation. This, of necessity, requires not only a theoretical background but imagination, creativity, and the possession of cognitive flexibility.

DISCUSSION OF DECISION MAKING

A decision, in many instances, is ultimately a choice among possible alternatives. Each is reflected upon and scrutinized and then a choice is made—one alternative is given priority over the others. The nurse strives to foresee the consequences of the choices made. It is, of course, not always possible to foresee the result of one's decision-making process; a certain degree of ambiguity may be involved. The practitioner may consult resource people, the literature, or supervisors in trying to decide the best possible ways of resolving patient problems. The nurse in the one-to-one relationship, however, does not always have time to do this and many times must make on-the-spot judgments and decisions. This is one reason for the importance of developing tentative objectives for working with patients, and to conceptualize in advance, as far as is possible, some methods of achieving these goals.

A "wrong" choice or decision is always possible, since human emotions are also involved in decision making. Decisions, in some instances, are made by the nurse on the basis of what is personally the least stressful solution; the nurse's psychological comfort—or lack of it—may determine the choices made. Some nurses who make decisions on the basis of their anxiety level are aware of their problem; they can conceptualize it, discuss it with supervisors or others, and strive to find means of coping with anxiety, instead of communicating it to the patient or withdrawing physically, or psychologically, from the patient. Other nurses are not aware that the "decisions" they make about patients are almost entirely predicated on their own discomfort or comfort index. In both instances nurses need assistance in coping with feelings of discomfort and in "seeing" the effect their own anxiety has on their ability to make sound judgments in nursing situations.

Even the most competent practitioner will make a wrong decision at one time or another. Hopefully, instead of being a discouraging experience, this can be used as a learning opportunity. The nurse is given a chance to develop hindsight and foresight. With the development of foresight she is able, to some extent, to transfer what was learned in a previous situation to a similar situation in the future.

In planning and structuring nursing care the professional nurse practitioner is responsible for the decisions made. While members of other disciplines can be consulted as resource people they are *not* qualified by education, experience or competency to plan and structure nursing intervention. Nurses need to be and *must* be free to make decisions relating to nursing care. They cannot relinquish this responsibility to a member of another discipline. This point cannot be emphasized too strongly and, at the risk of engaging in polemics, it must be categorically stated that *only nurses can speak for nursing*. The implementation of doctor's orders is *not* the sole criterion of "nursing care" although some nurses still operate on this untenable premise. Hopefully, the day will soon arrive when nurses will refuse to attend meetings or subject themselves to listening to members of other health disciplines give lectures on "The role of the nurse in . . ."

At the risk of sounding redundant it must be emphasized that only professional nurse practitioners are qualified by their education and competency to make decisions regarding nursing action.

NURSING ACTIONS

Nursing action, as stated, is the implementation of decisions. Action refers to nursing intervention—to *what* the nurse does and *how* she accomplishes her goals. Nursing action implies performance. Assessment of nursing actions, although considered separately in this chapter, is a continuous process during the nurse-patient relationship. The phase in the interpersonal process following observation, the development of interpretations, decision making, and nursing action is the evaluation or appraisal of one's intervention.

PART IV—APPRAISAL OF NURSING ACTIONS

Appraisal or evaluation of nursing actions is one of the hallmarks of professional nursing practice. Competency in nursing practice cannot be developed, much less improved, without a continual appraisal of one's nursing intervention.

DEFINITION OF APPRAISAL

Appraisal of nursing actions is the process of judging, assessing, estimating, or evaluating the quality and efficacy of the intervention.

DISCUSSION OF APPRAISAL IN NURSING SITUATIONS

Some salient questions are: What is being appraised or evaluated? What criteria are to be used? By whom? Why? How is "successful" nursing intervention to be estimated? What constitutes "success" or "failure" in nursing intervention?

Criteria must be established by the nurse practitioner before appraisal is possible. These criteria may vary, depending on what the nurse wishes to accomplish in the nurse-patient interactive process. Goals, then, may be general or specific—short- or long-range. Goals should be formulated in such a way that assessment or evaluation is possible.

Appraisal centers about the achievement of particular objectives of care. The extent to which the nurse is able to achieve these objectives is the criterion used to evaluate nursing actions. Again, objectives of care should be stated in such a way that the extent to which the behavioral change has occurred can be readily ascertained by means of various evaluative devices (for example, validated observation). The construction and validation of objectives are discussed in greater detail in Chapter VII, "Process Recording."

It is important to identify not only *what* is appraised but *who* is appraising, i.e., the patient, the nurse, or both participants in the relationship. Is "patient progress" (however this dubious term may be defined) the criterion for evaluating nursing intervention in psychiatric nursing? If the patient does not "improve" can it be said that lack of improvement is due to "faulty" nursing intervention and, conversely, that patient "progress" is a sign of "successful" nursing intervention? It would seem that neither stance is defensible or justifiable as the sole standard by which nursing actions can be evaluated. Too many variables are involved. Patient progress in psychiatric situations may become discernible within a relatively short period of time or over a period of many months or years. Nurses practicing in clinical areas other than psychiatry are not held solely accountable for lack of improvement in patient progress *if* they have skillfully, conscientiously, and effectively performed all of the nursing measures possible, and the same is true in psychiatric nursing situations. Not all practitioners in psychiatric nursing share this viewpoint, nor need they. However, it is believed that nurses should reflect on this matter and decide for themselves the extent to which, and the conditions under which, they should be held responsible for "patient progress" or its lack.

This is not to say that nurses are never accountable for lack of patient improvement. Too many examples and instances can be cited to prove the contrary. Nurses *are* responsible for trying in every possible way to assist ill persons toward social recovery. They are responsible for fulfilling the professional obligations incumbent upon them. Nursing is a lifelong commitment to service.

In educational programs the appraisal or evaluation process, of necessity, focuses on the abilities or skills gained by the learner as a result of the learning experiences provided. Here again, "patient progress" is not a deciding issue. Hopefully, the ill person will improve as a result of the learner-patient interactive process but the evaluation or appraisal is in terms of *not* how much the ill person improves but *how much the student learns,* i.e., the extent to which the student is able to achieve course objectives. The course objectives include those abilities needed to plan, structure and evaluate nursing intervention.

Chapter III

ASPECTS OF THE ONE-TO-ONE RELATIONSHIP

The purpose of this chapter is to examine and assess directives, assumptions and myths which affect nursing intervention in psychiatric situations. A critical examination is necessary because assumptions, beliefs and myths guide and direct behavior in some nursing situations.

There are assumptions, written and "unwritten" laws, or directives regarding "appropriate" behavior in nursing situations. Some of these approach the status of myths. A famous myth is that "the patient is the most important person in the hospital." That this is a myth is obvious to any thinking human being. If this were a fact how differently ill persons would be treated than presently in hospitals, clinics and other facilities! There would be no need to improve care. By fiat, or wishful thinking, the patient is already the most important person in the hospital. Who can improve this ideal situation? The patient is important by definition only, and this particular myth has little if any basis in reality in most institutions and settings. To say the patient *should* be the most important person in the hospital is quite different from declaring, without any substantiating evidence, that he *is*.

What is the origin of these assumptions, beliefs, or directives which influence nursing action? Probably they are a legacy from nursing's militaristic past. Pronouncements from authority figures regarding appropriate behavior (such as the "noninvolvement with patient" policy) are accepted without question, repeated throughout the years (and indeed the centuries) and, in time, assume the status of eternal verities. There is probably no clinical area in nursing so permeated with platitudes, maxims, and unrealistic assumptions as the field of psychiatric nursing.

Directives and pronouncements often become "word-facts" or "phrase-facts." For example, nurses are urged to give "emotional support" to patients without any clear understanding of what this somewhat unscientific concept implies. Nurses "believe in" emotional support and assume they understand what is meant by this phrase without being able operationally to define the behaviors involved. If a nurse is able to "emotionally support" patients it is probably because she is sensitive and intuitive rather than because she knows what is involved in emotional support.

Directives tend to widen the credibility gap between what a nurse is "taught" to believe and what she actually sees. A nurse taught to believe the patient is the most important person in the hospital soon becomes aware of the discrepancy between the professed belief and the reality as seen in practice.

It is not for the sake of engaging in polemics that these assumptions, myths and directives are discussed. It is because they need to be subjected to critical inquiry, not blithely accepted. It is the writer's hope that the discussion which follows will be critically assessed and tested for validity in practice. It is *not* the author's intent to substitute one set of myths and assumptions for another. Nurses are urged not to accept as true any statement regarding aspects of, or guidelines for, the one-to-one relationship that *they* cannot validate in practice.

Assumptions regarding four major concepts will be discussed. These are emotional involvement, acceptance, the nonjudgmental attitude, and objectivity.

PART I—EMOTIONAL INVOLVEMENT

Emotional involvement is necessary if the nurse is to establish a relationship with a patient or any other human being. Emotional involvement is both cognitive and affective. It is the ability to transcend self and to care for, and about, another human being—and to do this in such a way that one is not incapacitated by one's caring and concern.

There are probably many factors which affect one's ability to become emotionally involved. Prerequisites include a recognition and acceptance of one's self as a distinct entity and the concomitant ability to perceive others as unique human beings. The ability to express, or control the expression of, one's feelings when interacting with a patient—and to do this on a conscious level with an appropriate sense of timing—is also essential.

Emotional involvement on a mature level assists the human being who is the patient to experience the concern and caring of the human being who is the nurse. The ill person is not overwhelmed by the nurse's caring. Emotional involvement requires knowledge, insight and self-discipline on the part of the nurse but it also requires that she possess the openness and freedom to expose self as human being to another human being—namely, the patient.

Emotional involvement takes place within the context of a nurse-patient relationship. It cannot be planned, ordered or prescribed. Some physicians write "orders" on a patient's chart for "T.L.C." (tender loving care). Loving care cannot be "ordered." It must be freely given. The degree or kind of emotional involvement depends on the character structure or personality of the individuals in the relationship. If a relationship *is* established it is because each participant becomes emotionally involved with the other. The ability to become emotionally involved with patients, on a *mature* level, is the hallmark of a professional nurse practitioner and of a mature human being.

THE POLICY OF NONINVOLVEMENT

The directive "Do not become emotionally involved with patients" is well known. This particular admonition has almost acquired the status of a nursing principle (using the term *principle* very loosely). The hypothesis underlying this is: the greater the degree of emotional involvement the more "unprofessional" the relationship and, conversely, the greater the lack of emotional involvement the more professional the relationship. Noninvolvement is thus elevated to a characteristic of the "professional nurse-patient relationship."

Proponents of noninvolvement usually focus on the negative connotations of immature involvement and stress the effects as "overidentifying" with patients. In general the picture presented is one of the ineffective, bungling, inept individual who "feels too sorry for patients," is too sensitive, and hence cannot be truly helpful. If this is one's definition of emotional involvement, then one can readily agree that such behavior is not only nontherapeutic to patients but destructive to the growth of the human being who is the nurse and is not to be encouraged. Advocates of noninvolvement propose, as an antidote, that the nurse not become involved at all and thus eliminate any risk of unprofessional conduct. The antidote, however, is worse than the disease. The antidote is successful—of this there is no doubt—for certainly no one will be accused of unprofessional conduct if she adopts noninvolvement as a policy. Neither will the nurse be "accused" by patients of being a helpful, concerned, knowledgeable human being, i.e., possessing wisdom of the human heart, mind and spirit.

If strictly followed, the doctrine of noninvolvement means that the nurse should not experience happiness or joy when a patient recovers, should not feel sad when a patient dies, and should not experience the satisfaction of helping a human being in time of emotional turmoil and crisis. In effect nurses are taught to deny their humanity. There are, of course, avenues of escape from this dilemma. One is to give lip service to the noninvolvement policy because it is expected. In this case a nurse who becomes involved despite exhortations to the contrary may try to hide her involvement and may experience guilt feelings for transgressing the directive. A nurse torn with the desire to become humanly involved with patients despite "rules" against involvement is in the situation of a mariner trapped between Scylla and Charybdis. Another, unfortunately more frequent, solution is to take the path of least resistance, i.e., follow the directive, exhibit a carapace of detachment, and eventually become a little less of a human being.

One cannot help but wonder why prohibitions against emotional involvement have been clung to for so many years by so many nurses. Why is it that this doctrine has not been seriously challenged or even questioned until quite recently? Obviously the directive met a need, and still does. Some nurses must "protect" themselves from discomfort and anxiety. This protection is afforded by maintaining distance from the source of the anxiety—namely, the patient.

The real antidote to immature types of emotional involvement is learning to become involved on a mature level. Professional status is not diminished; it is enhanced, and the nurse grows as a human being to the extent that she permits herself to become involved with other human beings.

The policy of noninvolvement has far-reaching effects in schools of nursing. It denies learners the opportunity to be truly helpful to patients. Students who learn the doctrine of noninvolvement as appropriate behavior, prior to psychiatric nursing, tend to have great difficulty in establishing meaningful relationships with emotionally ill individuals. Such students must unlearn in order to learn, and this goal cannot always be accomplished in the short period of time allotted for a psychiatric nursing course. This is not the only effect of noninvolvement. If learned in a school of nursing, it can become a policy which guides one's behavior in other areas of life. Closeness with other human beings is avoided. Distance becomes a goal and alienation a way of life.

PART II—ACCEPTANCE AND THE NONJUDGMENTAL ATTITUDE

Accepting the patient as he is is another directive suggested as a guide for nurses. But what is acceptance? Why is it necessary to accept a patient as he is?

"Acceptance seems to be more akin to forgiveness in the sense that one weighs or judges the behavioral characteristics of another and, while acknowledging the 'undesirable' or 'negative' aspects of another, glosses over them, blurs them, while bringing into sharper focus those characteristics most pleasing and reassuring to one's self."[1] Acceptance may, or may not, be an automatic process. It is probable that we automatically accept individuals who tend to meet our needs. It is also postulated that we do not accept individuals who threaten our self-esteem, or in some way fail to meet our needs. If these assumptions are valid then it follows that acceptance, if not an automatic process, is a goal to be accomplished.

Nurses will neither automatically accept nor like all ill persons. The human being is not capable of automatically accepting every individual he meets, and the nurse is no exception. It is not possible to accept every patient or his behavior because he *is* a patient. What nurse can automatically accept a patient who slaps her, spits, curses, uses vulgar and obscene language, taunts, or crudely makes fun of her? It is unrealistic to expect *any* human being automatically to accept such behavior, or even excuse it, on the basis that the person is mentally ill and hence cannot control his behavior. Nurses are creatures of the culture in which they live and cultural views regarding deviant behavior *will* affect the nurse's perception of behavior despite her intellectual understanding of pathology. Intellectually the nurse may understand *why* the ill person is behaving as he is. This intellectual understanding, however, does not negate the fact that the nurse, at the time of such an experience, usually does feel anger toward the patient. This is not meant to imply the nurse reacts in a

---

[1] Travelbee, Joyce: Interpersonal Aspects of Nursing. F. A. Davis Company, Philadelphia, 1966.

punitive manner. It does mean the nurse cannot, at that time, "accept" or like either the patient or his behavior.

It is suggested that the nurse admit feelings of nonacceptance, dislike or anger and decide what, if anything, she intends to do about these feelings. If a nurse cannot accept a patient, it is better for both nurse and patient that this be admitted and that the nurse seek assistance from the supervisor in order to resolve the problem. To fail to do this is less than honest. A frank admission that one is human and reacts on a human level is far better than denying one's feelings and taking out one's anger on the ill person by rejecting or ignoring him or in some other more subtle way "punishing" him for his behavior.

ACCEPTANCE AS A DIRECTIVE

According to an old adage nurses are supposed to like and accept all patients. Acceptance, however, like emotional involvement and T.L.C., does not occur by fiat, neither can this experience be "prescribed." Acceptance either occurs automatically or remains a goal to be achieved.

What is the logical outcome of "accepting a patient as he is"? If a nurse accepts a patient as he is then the nurse does not strive to effect changes in the patient's behavior. *In reality nurses do not accept patients as they are. They continually strive to effect changes in the patient's condition and engage in purposeful activities in order to do so.* Behavioral problems are identified and the nurse strives, through purposeful intervention, to effect a change toward social recovery. At the risk of creating a new directive, it is suggested that nurses not accept patients as they are but purposefully and deliberately strive to change them.

There are many unanswered questions in relation to the process of acceptance. Research is needed to clarify the meaning of the concept and to differentiate acceptance from other similar concepts. If acceptance is not an automatic process how can nurses be assisted to accept particular patients? Is acceptance a reciprocal process? Is acceptance of patients as important and necessary as we tend to believe at this time?

For an operational definition of the concept of acceptance see the work of Caroline Wallace.[2] (See Appendix I, Selected Reading Refer-

---

[2] Wallace, Caroline Ogilvie: "Acceptance" *in* Conference on Teaching Psychiatric Nursing in Baccalaureate Programs. Conference Materials. Southern Regional Education Board, Atlanta, January 23-25, 1967: 10.

ences, Chapter II, for references on the concept of acceptance and other related concepts.)

THE NONJUDGMENTAL ATTITUDE

In nursing situations the term *nonjudgmental* means that the nurse does not make moral judgments about the patient or blame the patient for his behavior. Nurses "are not supposed to be judgmental." However, deciding to be nonjudgmental is, in a sense, a judgment, since the nurse decides on some basis not to blame the patient for his behavior. The directive to be nonjudgmental may have a deleterious effect on the nurse-patient relationship. *It is suggested that nurses do not try to be nonjudgmental.* The nurse should strive to become aware of the judgments she has made about the ill person and his behavior. Only by awareness of these judgments—whatever they may be—can she consider their effects on the nurse-patient encounter.

The nonjudgmental attitude, it is believed, is an unrealistic directive and a myth. It does not exist. The human being always makes judgments. The nurse, as a human being, needs to know *what* judgments she has made about the patient in order to intervene effectively.

PART III—OBJECTIVITY AND THE NURSE-PATIENT RELATIONSHIP

Objectivity is often cited as an attitude to be developed by nurses in all clinical specialty areas. Objectivity is usually defined as the ability to view what is actually happening without being biased by personal feelings.

One gets the impression, from nursing literature, that a nurse who is objective is a detached person who is able to view experiences as external events and is unaffected by any subjective feeling state. Yet one's personal feelings affect *what* one perceives and *how* one interprets what is perceived.

Complete objectivity is not possible. A reasonable degree of objectivity is a goal in nurse-patient interactions. It is probable that the degree to which an individual can separate sensory data from interpretations about the data is a major determinant affecting ability to be objective. However, factors affecting the extent to which a nurse can be objective have not been reported in nursing literature and offer a fertile field for research. There are many unanswered questions about objectivity which require careful scrutiny and scientific inquiry. Some of these are: How does one know when he is being reasonably objective? How important is reasonable objectivity? Is objectivity a synonym for honesty or is it rather a particular way of perceiving another human being? How can the nurse be a participant yet stand outside and apart from an experience shared with the patient? Does not the nurse's involvement in the interaction hinder her ability to be reasonably objective?

There is another important aspect of objectivity which must be considered. Like the doctrine of noninvolvement, objectivity is an attitude which *can* and *does* spread into other areas of the individual's private and professional life. The desire to be objective is used, by some nurses, as a reason for not becoming involved with patients. One nurse gave as her reason for not interacting with a patient: "I knew I couldn't help him (the patient) if I got emotionally involved and besides I was trying to be objective." Unfortunately noninvolvement has been considered a prerequisite for objectivity.

The nurse's understanding of the concept of objectivity may affect the manner in which she relates with the patient. To some nurses being objective means having a "neutral attitude" toward all patients. Other nurses interpret objectivity as meaning the nurse should at all times exhibit a bland, expressionless facial countenance. Nurses should become aware of their nonverbal mannerisms, as this is essential in establishing and maintaining a relationship. We deplore the encouragement, by educators and others, for nurses to appear frozen-faced and communicate nothing but a total lack of affect or feeling. An ill person seeking warmth and contact with another human being will scarcely experience the humanity of the nurse when interacting with a bland expressionless automaton.

Reasonable objectivity is a goal which can be achieved by the nurse. It is not, however, achieved by a cold, detached, expressionless creature who relates with patients as if they were specimens to be dissected and analyzed. It is probable that overemphasis on superficial aspects of a relationship has produced the frozen-faced, technique-oriented nurse whose intervention is limited to a series of stereotyped questions and answers culled from a particular school of thought. Objectivity, in the sense of detachment and coldness, is a barrier to a meaningful relationship with another human being.

Chapter IV

INTRODUCTION TO THE ONE-TO-ONE RELATIONSHIP: A GENERAL FRAME OF REFERENCE

The one-to-one relationship between nurse and patient is not a new concept introduced by psychiatric nurses. Effective nursing care in all settings has always been given within the context of a relationship. However, it is only within the past two decades that the purposeful use of the one-to-one relationship in psychiatric nursing has become the subject of scientific inquiry and scrutiny. Papers relating to relationship therapy by such pioneers as Hildegard E. Peplau, Gwen E. Tudor, June Mellow, Mary Redmond and Dorothy Gregg are considered, by many psychiatric nurses, as classics in the field of psychiatric nursing.

A general frame of reference for the one-to-one relationship will be introduced in this chapter. Assumptions underlying the one-to-one relationship are discussed and purposes and goals in the relationship are explored.

PART I—ASSUMPTIONS UNDERLYING THE ONE-TO-ONE RELATIONSHIP

There are six major assumptions underlying the one-to-one relationship. A discussion of these follows.

1. *Establishing, maintaining and terminating a one-to-one relationship are activities which fall within the province of nursing practice.* The nurse-patient relationship is not a watered-down or diluted

doctor-patient relationship, neither is it a social worker-client relationship. The goals in nursing differ distinctly from those in other health disciplines. Members of various health disciplines share the major overall goal of relationship therapy, namely, to assist the ill person toward social recovery. However, the specific methodology used to accomplish these goals varies. It needs to be emphasized that the one-to-one relationship lies within the province of *nursing* and that the nurse does *not* require the permission of the psychiatrist to practice nursing any more than the psychiatrist needs the permission of the nurse to practice psychiatry. This is not to deny the importance of professional collaboration; it stresses that *only* nurses are prepared to decide the purposes, roles, activities and functions of nurses.

Members of other health professions are qualified neither by education nor experience to direct nursing activities. This point is emphasized because the "handmaiden-to-the-physician" viewpoint still guides some nurses in the practice of their professional activities. Nurses have many independent functions but only *one* dependent function, namely, the execution of legal medical orders. Aside from this one dependent function, a physician cannot "order" nursing care any more than a nurse can "order" medical care. *Only professional nurses can, and should, decide and guide the destiny of nursing.*

2. *A relationship is established only when each participant perceives the other as a unique human being.* Strictly speaking, a nurse and a patient cannot establish a relationship. It is only when the roles of nurse and patient are transcended, and each perceives the other as a unique human being, that a relationship is possible. The term *nurse-patient relationship* is a misnomer and is used in this text only for purposes of communicative economy.

3. *Only qualified psychiatric nurses are prepared to supervise nurses in the practice of psychiatric nursing.* The nurse who begins interacting with a psychiatric patient for the purpose of establishing a one-to-one relationship should have at her disposal a qualified psychiatric nurse supervisor. By *supervisor* we mean an individual who holds at least a master's degree in the field of psychiatric-mental health nursing; she may be a clinical specialist in psychiatric nursing or a prepared psychiatric nurse faculty member. The supervisor is a resource person with whom the nurse shares data relevant to the one-to-one relationship. The supervisor guides the nurse in clarifying data regarding the relationship and holds regularly scheduled conferences with the practitioner. The supervisory process is discussed in greater detail in Chapter X.

4. *The major learning experience provided in the psychiatric nursing course is to provide students with the opportunity to establish, maintain and terminate one-to-one relationships.* It is believed that group work skills should be taught on the graduate level. Psychiatric nursing is an upper-division nursing course. The concepts used to explain psychiatric nursing intervention are ambiguous and abstract. Time is required for students to understand and apply these concepts meaningfully in a nurse-patient situation. It is recommended that the psychiatric nursing course, on an undergraduate level, extend over a semester. The maturity level of students is also important in determining the extent to which they will be able to establish relatedness with mentally ill individuals. It is recommended that psychiatric nursing be the *last* clinical nursing course offered in the program of study. (Behavioral concepts of course should be taught in all clinical nursing courses, not just in psychiatric nursing.)

Students enrolled in a baccalaureate program should, prior to the psychiatric nursing course, possess a basic understanding of major concepts from the natural, physical, biological, medical, behavioral and nursing sciences. Content related to psychiatric nursing is taught concurrently with field experience. Students, through the group reconstruction process, are taught to apply theory to practice. Ways of implementing the goal of applying theory in practice are explored in Chapter X.

5. *Nurses need to know how to use library facilities and how to search the literature for needed information.* It may seem somewhat simplistic and self-evident to state that nurses need to know *how* to use library facilities and how to search the literature for needed information and data. It cannot be assumed, however, that nurses or faculty members know how to use library resources to find reference materials. The author has encountered students in graduate programs who have never heard of the Index to Nursing Literature, the Index Medicus, Excerpta Medica and other sources. Source materials pertinent to psychiatric nursing are listed in Appendix II.

6. *The knowledge, understanding and abilities needed to plan, structure, give and evaluate care during the one-to-one relationship are necessary prerequisites for developing competency in group work.* Some nurses object to learning skills required to establish a one-to-one relationship on the basis that most nurses in psychiatric settings are required to work with large groups of patients, not with individuals. They maintain it is more "realistic" for psychiatric nurses to be prepared to work with groups of patients. However, it is believed that

group work is best taught on the graduate, not the undergraduate, level. It is further believed that the abilities developed in learning to establish, maintain and terminate the one-to-one relationship can be readily transferred and applied to group work. It is more difficult to transfer the knowledge and abilities needed for group work to the one-to-one relationship.

PART II—DEFINITION OF THE TERM ONE-TO-ONE RELATIONSHIP

The one-to-one relationship is a goal to be achieved. It is the end result of a series of planned purposeful interactions between two human beings, a nurse and a patient. It is also a series of learning experiences for both participants during which they develop increased interpersonal competencies. In this chapter, and throughout the text, the terms *one-to-one relationship* and *relationship* are used synonymously.

DISCUSSION OF DEFINITION

A relationship does not "just happen"; it is deliberately and consciously planned for by the nurse. A relationship is more than "just talking" with an ill person for a specified period each day, or having a series of interactions with a patient. The number of interactions added together do not necessarily constitute a relationship. One of the characteristics of a relationship is that *both* patient and nurse change and modify their behavior. Both learn as a result of, or because of, the interactive process. If changes do not occur in either or both participants, then it is assumed that a relationship has not been established.

As a result of the relationship the ill person grows in his ability to face reality, to discover practical solutions to problems, to become less estranged from the community, and to derive pleasure from communicating and socializing with his fellow human beings.

The nurse grows as a human being as a result of the encounter with the emotionally ill person. The practitioner learns new ways of assisting the ill person to move toward meaningful participation in the human community. She learns more about self and, over a period of time, develops the ability to audit and change her behavior. The nurse grows in ability to face and confront reality situations and to cope with expectations of self and others. Sometimes this involves facing unrealistic goals she may have established. It is never easy to compare what one wishes to accomplish with what one has accomplished and to live with the hiatus between the two.

The nurse becomes increasingly aware of her strengths and—what is harder to assimilate and use constructively—her limitations. It is hard to admit that one is human and fallible, lacks knowledge and wisdom, and makes mistakes in judgment. It is also hard to accept the fact that, while all patients can be helped, not all patients will recover; social recovery may be an unrealistic goal for some patients. But who among us possess the wisdom to know beyond a shadow of a doubt that a patient will not recover? Too many factors are involved to know this with any degree of certainty. The nurse therefore strives to assist *all* patients. Few patients show dramatic changes and improvement in their behavior; most exhibit slow changes and gradual improvement. The nurse learns that change takes place slowly over a period of time and that the relationship develops in uneven stages. In the beginning progression is evident; this is followed by a period of retrogression and then a period of stagnation before a period of progression occurs again. In the period of stagnation there is no discernible movement in the relationship and the nurse learns to appreciate the necessity of waiting. There is a tempo to all human relationships. This tempo, once comprehended, enables the nurse to wait for the next stage without becoming discouraged.

As a result of establishing a relationship, the nurse learns how little she knows, how much there is to learn, and how wide the gulf is between the two. The nurse learns to respect and appreciate the uniqueness of the individual patient. She realizes in a concrete way that a patient is not a label or an illness; each is a human being in his own right—a human being who does not easily fit into a diagnostic mold. This appreciation and insight are not easily gained. They are earned by the nurse who possesses courage and perseverance, and who has a profound understanding of the human condition.

A relationship is purposeful and goal directed. It is helpful to have a frame of reference with general guidelines to assist one in structuring and maintaining a relationship. This is proposed in Part III.

PART III—THE GOALS OF THE NURSE

Nine general goals of the nurse in the one-to-one relationship are explored. A discussion of each follows.

1. *The nurse helps the ill person to cope with present problems.* The nurse is concerned with "here-and-now" problems as perceived and defined by the ill person. She is *not* concerned with uncovering unconscious content or with tracing present problems back through the patient's earliest formative years. This is not to deny that such information is useful (or interesting)—it *does* imply that the nurse's primary aim is to help the patient conceptualize his *present* problem. Knowledge of the ill person's past history as obtained from the chart, resource people and others, is helpful insofar as what is learned guides the nurse in structuring nursing intervention; however, the nurse does not probe or request this information from the patient. If the patient reveals it, then the nurse uses this knowledge to help her understand his present problem. It is well to remember that there may be a discrepancy between problem(s) as perceived and defined by the patient and the patient's problems as perceived and defined by nurses, psychiatrists, etc.

2. *The nurse helps the ill person to conceptualize his problem.* As stated previously, one of the goals in the interactive process is to assist the ill person to identify or conceptualize problem(s) as *he* perceives them. This is the primary focus of inquiry throughout the series of interactions. Problems identified by patients *will* and *do* change as the relationship progresses.

The practitioner elicits information from the patient and helps him to conceptualize his problem(s). Various communication techniques, including planned inquiry, are used. The nurse listens carefully to the patient or may ask direct questions. Many types of problems may be conceptualized by patients; these may range from the very vague to the very specific. Some patients will deny the existence of problems requiring psychiatric or nursing intervention. However the patient defines his problem, whether the nurse believes the patient or thinks the problem is unrealistic is unimportant at this point. It *is* important that the nurse elicit a complete account of the problem(s) as the patient perceives them. A patient may maintain he is in the hospital because the doctor wants to find out why he is having trouble sleeping. This is the patient's conception of the problem and the logical starting point for discussion in the nurse-patient interaction.

After the patient has identified the problem the nurse begins to collect data regarding it. She does not necessarily limit inquiry to the problem as defined by the patient; however, it is recommended that clarification of the problem as defined by the patient be given precedence in the interaction. Actually, anything having relevance to the problem is a subject of legitimate inquiry.

3. *The nurse assists the ill person to perceive his participation in an experience.* The nurse strives to assist the patient to see himself as an active participant in life and its events. For example, a patient has insomnia. Obviously this behavior is caused by something. The patient is helped to focus on his behavior. What is his explanation for the insomnia? When did the insomnia begin? What does the patient think caused him to develop insomnia? What helps him to sleep? What hinders him? *What can the patient do to help himself?* The emphasis is on helping the ill person to realize that he is an active agent, i.e., that something he does, thinks, or feels will play a part in producing or alleviating the problem.

The practitioner strives to assist the patient to gain (or regain) a sense of immediacy—of aliveness—and an appreciation of the uniqueness of his individuality. The nurse's message is that the ill person is an *active*, not a passive, participant in life experiences. With the help and support received in the relationship hopefully the patient will begin to perceive this, although it is probably one of the most difficult goals to accomplish in working with patients. It is not easy for the hypothetically normal individual to identify and acknowledge his participation in an experience, and it is even more difficult for a mentally ill person to do so.

As the relationship progresses, it becomes easier for the patient to acknowledge that he *is* an active participant in life experiences and that what he thinks, feels, and does elicits a response from others. The patient begins to realize that *he* affects the behavior of those about him. The patient also learns that the individuals he encounters will react toward him on the basis of his behavior toward them. This knowledge is gained slowly and over a period of time as the patient begins to develop an appreciation of cause-and-effect in behavior.

4. *The nurse assists the ill person to face emerging problems realistically.* Problems, as initially conceptualized by the patient, frequently undergo a change. The initial presentation by the patient of a somewhat "superficial" problem gradually changes, and deeper problems begin to emerge as the relationship progresses and the patient is able to perceive his participation in life experiences. For example, the

patient whose initial problem was insomnia may now define his problem as a fear of sleeping "lest he lose control of himself" or as a fear of recurrent nightmares. A patient whose initial problem was "crying spells" may now be able to disclose her sense of loss, anger and depression following the death of her husband. This process takes place over a period of time as the patient begins to trust the nurse and gains the support needed to reveal himself.

5. *The nurse assists the ill person to envisage alternatives.* Many ill individuals resort to stereotyped means of solving problems, i.e., their thinking tends to be of a dichotomized either-or variety. The nurse assists the ill person to consider alternative means of solving problems in living. It may not occur to an ill person that choices are possible in relation to his particular problem or, if choices do exist, he cannot picture himself acting any differently than he has in the past. The ill person's ability to envisage alternatives is a legitimate subject of inquiry. The nurse may elicit this by asking: What can *you* do to solve this problem? Is there anything else *you* can do? The nurse does *not* make choices for the patient. She *does* assist the patient to understand that there is usually more than *one* solution to a problem.

6. *The nurse assists the ill person to test new patterns of behavior.* Another general goal in interacting with ill persons is to assist them to test new patterns of behavior. A patient who has difficulty conversing with others is helped by talking with the nurse. The nurse then assists the patient to interact with another patient on the unit. A patient who has difficulty in approaching authority figures is helped by the nurse to approach the psychiatrist. Nurse and patient together develop the plan and the patient tests the new pattern of behavior. The extent to which the plan is successful is discussed during the nurse-patient interaction. The aim of testing new behavioral skills is to help the patient to gain confidence in himself as a person who *can* plan, test, envisage alternatives and face the outcome of the testing. As the result of gaining this ability the patient gains a deeper appreciation of himself as an active participant in life experiences.

The nurse needs to appreciate how very difficult it may be for a patient to test a new mode of behavior. For example, a patient wished to test whether she could approach a stranger. The stranger she selected was another patient on the unit. She planned to approach the patient and say: "Good morning, how are you?" The patient was successful but later stated that she "trembled and shook" as she approached the "strange lady." Afterwards she was very pleased and had gained confidence in herself as a result of having been able to engage in this relatively simple activity. The activity was, of course, not simple to the patient; it was a trial about which she experienced a veritable agony of anxiety. Success does not always occur. The inability to test new behavior may be quite discouraging to a patient, as may the failure to carry through a plan to test a new pattern. In such situations nurse and patient explore what occurred and identify any factors which may have hindered the patient.

7. *The nurse assists the ill person to communicate.* Mentally ill individuals generally have difficulty in sharing their thoughts and feelings with others. A general goal in the nurse-patient relationship is to assist the patient to communicate logically and clearly with others and to become aware of what he communicates. The concept of communication is discussed in Chapter V.

8. *The nurse assists the ill person to socialize.* Mentally ill individuals generally have difficulty in socializing with others. The term *socialize* means more than the ability to talk with others. An individual who has the ability to socialize derives pleasure and enjoyment from interacting with others and is attentive to the needs of others. Socialization is a reciprocal process.

The goal of socializing has been construed by some nurses to mean that the nurse is to get patients involved in group activities such as playing cards or engaging in games. Some patients are helped to socialize by engaging in game-type activities, but this is by no means true of *all* patients. It is quite possible for a patient to engage mechanically in game-like activities without socializing or being interested in the activity or in the people with whom he is in enforced contact. Judgment is necessary to select the type and kind of socialization experience best suited for a particular patient. Judgment is also required, on the part of the nurse, to decide the appropriate time to initiate such activity.

9. *The nurse assists the ill person to find meaning in illness.* The nurse assists mentally ill individuals to find meaning in their suffering and distress. "Meaning is the reason given to particular life experiences by the individual undergoing the experience."[1] It is the *why* of Nietsche's often quoted comment: "He who has a *why* to live for, can bear almost any *how*."[2] "The term 'meaning' is used in a restricted

---

[1] Travelbee, Joyce: Interpersonal Aspects of Nursing. F. A. Davis Company, Philadelphia, 1966.
[2] Frankl, Viktor E.: Man's Search for Meaning: An Introduction to Logotherapy. Washington Square Press, New York, 1963.

sense and refers only to those meanings which enable the ill individual not only to submit to illness, but to use it as an enabling life experience . . ."[3]

The goal of finding meaning in illness is based on two assumptions: (1) Every ill person seeks a reason, or meaning, for enduring his illness, and (2) illness and suffering can be self-actualizing experiences provided the ill individual perceives some meaning in his suffering. It is believed that illness *can* and *should* be a learning experience, i.e., an experience that can help the person grow and develop as a human being as a result of his suffering.

The mentally ill and the physically ill both attempt to find reasons for their suffering and distress. Individuals in both groups may blame themselves or others for causing the illness. They may blame God, bad luck, fate, relatives, friends, acquaintances or co-workers for causing, or contributing to the development of, their illness. Some mentally ill persons, through lack of insight, may not blame others because they do not believe they are ill.

Most patients seek, and find, a blame object. The search for a blame object is probably a necessary initial phase in the patient's attempt to find meaning in illness or to discover possible reasons why he is suffering. The blame phase can become a formidable barrier. One of the first obstacles the nurse encounters in helping the mentally ill person find meaning in illness is this blame barrier. The nurse must assist the patient to surmount or rise above it.

It is not only patients who remain fixated at a blame level—nurses and other health workers may also have this problem. Because of certain theories regarding the etiology of the major functional mental illnesses it is quite possible for the nurse to "blame" the patient's relatives—usually the mother—for "causing" the patient's illness and to "absolve" the patient from any responsibility for his behavior. Whether the parents were or were not the "cause" of the patient's illness is not so important as the effect this belief has on the nurse's attitude. Nurses and other health workers can and do convey to the patient the message that he is not responsible for his behavior. An unfortunate consequence of this attitude is that the patient is led to believe he is an irresponsible individual who cannot change his behavior or affect his future destiny.

Under the best of circumstances it is difficult to perceive meaning in illness and suffering. It is impossible if the individual cannot rise

---

[3] Travelbee: op. cit.

above the blame level and if this behavior is reinforced by those whose task it is to help and comfort.

The blame barrier can, through relatedness with a helping person, be surmounted. How does the nurse assist the patient to use mental illness as a meaningful learning experience? The emotionally ill person requires a "why to live for" in order to somehow endure the "how." The "why to live for" varies with each patient. The nurse, through relating with the patient, helps him to search for and find a "why" which has meaning for him. The nurse cannot give meaning to an ill person but she can assist him to find a basis for meaning. It is probable that meaning can be found only to the extent a patient is able to perceive his participation in life experiences and to accept his human condition. The ability to accept the human condition implies that the individual does not exempt himself from suffering—whether this suffering be primarily mental, physical, or spiritual in origin.

The nurse strives to understand the patient's attitude toward suffering and his manner of dealing with it. Mentally ill persons are generally handicapped by the ineffective means they use to cope with life problems. The nurse attempts to identify these ineffective methods and to assist the ill person to develop methods which are more effective.

Nine goals of the nurse in the one-to-one relationship have been discussed. Many factors will affect the nurse's ability to achieve these goals. Some of these are: the nurse's knowledge and ability to use it, the degree or kind of pathological behavior exhibited by the patient, the character structure of both nurse and patient, and such variables as the sex, age, color, ethnic background, religious views and social class of both nurse and patient. Common problems encountered in establishing and maintaining a nurse-patient relationship are discussed in detail in Chapter IX, "Problems in the One-to-One Relationship."

N.B. For a more detailed discussion of ways of assisting patients to find meaning in illness see Travelbee, Joyce: Interpersonal Aspects of Nursing, Chapter X. F. A. Davis Company, Philadelphia, 1966.

Chapter V

COMMUNICATING WITH PATIENTS

The ability to communicate enables the human being to relate, reach out, give and share of self with others. He is known by what he conveys about himself to others. To be acknowledged, hated, liked, loved or considered an object of indifference or ridicule by others is contingent, in part, on what one communicates to others. Whatever one communicates is invariably assessed and evaluated by the recipient of the communication. Judgments and opinions about the sender of the communication are formed. Judgments made about others, however, invariably reflect judgments about self and are drawn from and filtered through the background of one's own life experience. How easy it is to misconstrue the motives of another human being—to attribute to others feelings and thoughts they have not expressed. How difficult it is *not* to jump to conclusions or assume one understands what another person is saying without asking the other person what he is trying to convey. How easy it is to misunderstand other human beings; thought is not required—an emotional reaction born out of defensiveness or oversensitivity suffices. To hear, understand and accept a message one does not wish to receive—a criticism—is even more difficult. Perhaps the more arduous task—one requiring great courage and humility—is to receive these messages, critically examine them, learn from them and be grateful that other human beings cared enough to share truths about ourselves. Whether the intent of the criticism is constructive or not (and one's judgment is not always to be relied upon in relation to this point), the fact remains that one is offered an opportunity to "see oneself." Such experiences, though in many ways stressful, can be helpful provided one recognizes the opportunities inherent in them for personal growth. If nurses cannot look at their behavior and how it affects and influences others

—if they lack the capacity or desire to examine their habitual pattern of communicating with others or the manner in which they receive the messages of others—then it is doubtful that they can help those individuals whose life problems may stem from the inability to communicate and form meaningful relationships with other human beings.

PART I—DEFINITION OF THE TERM COMMUNICATION

Communication means the sending and receiving of messages by means of symbols, words (spoken or written), signs, gestures or other nonverbal means. Communication is divided into two major categories —*verbal,* which includes messages sent and received by means of written or spoken words, and *nonverbal,* which includes messages sent and received by means of signs, gestures, facial expression, gait, posture, tone of voice, groans, etc. It is possible to communicate nonverbally without the use of verbal messages; however, it is unlikely that an individual can communicate verbally without the use of nonverbal messages. It is hypothesized that nonverbal communication invariably accompanies verbal communication in every nurse-patient interaction.

DISCUSSION OF DEFINITION

Communication implies that the message is understood by both sender and receiver. If the message is not understood it is assumed that communication has not taken place. Understanding of course does not mean agreement. The receiver of the message does not have to agree with the content of the message in order for communication to take place. This is a common misconception of the nature of the communication process. For example, the sender of a message may think that communication did not take place because the receiver does not agree with the message. The sender, in such instances, must verify whether or not the message was understood by the receiver. This point is being stressed because some individuals assume that if a message is understood the contents of the message must be agreed upon by the receiver. One has only to listen to such statements as "I can't communicate with him" or "I don't believe I communicated" to realize the extent to which this assumption has been accepted. Communication may well have occurred. The problem may be that the receiver does not agree with the contents of the message.

Communicating with another person can be a meaningful experience or one completely devoid of meaning to one or both participants. Communication may help a person to get to know another human being or it may have the opposite effect. Communication, in and of itself, is important, but equally important is *what* is being communicated. Dislike and indifference are as readily communicated as are respect and concern, and the message is as readily received.

PART II—RATIONALE

Why is communication of such importance? Communicating with ill persons is one of the primary methods used by nurses to accomplish the specific as well as the overall goals of nursing intervention. Specific goals are those focused on particular problems, and, as such, change as the individual's behavior is modified. Overall goals of nursing intervention are more-or-less unchanging. The extent to which these goals are accomplished will vary depending on the many factors affecting the nurse-patient interactive process.

The overall goals of nursing intervention were previously discussed in Chapter IV, Part III. They are restated here for purpose of review. The nurse assists the ill person to cope with present reality problems, conceptualize his problems, perceive his participation in an experience, face emerging problems realistically, envisage alternatives, test new patterns of behavior, communicate and socialize with others, and find meaning in illness. Skillful use of the communication process by the practitioner is essential if the goals of nursing intervention are to be accomplished.

The accomplishment of these goals, however, is not the sole reason why ability to communicate with ill persons and to assist them to engage in meaningful communication is being stressed. The ill person's inability to communicate often prevents him from forming social relationships with others. The ability to communicate with other human beings—to understand and be understood—is an essential interpersonal competency, a competency which is usually developed as the individual progresses through various phases of growth and development. Whatever interferes with the individual's ability to develop this competency has far-reaching effects. The inability to share experiences, to correct one's faulty impressions, or to have one's thoughts and feelings validated results, not merely in disordered thinking, feeling and acting, but in a life of unrelieved loneliness and mental anguish. Specifically, disordered communication may be a reflection of an underlying disturbance in thinking. It is recognized that disturbances in thinking are, in many instances, symptoms of mental illness. These disturbances in thinking are reflected in the individual's behavior, i.e., in his actions as well as in his speech.

Some nurse-clinicians hypothesize that correction of speech behavior can effect a change in thinking, which in turn will effect changes in feeling and acting. What is this hypothesis based upon? A brief review of the relationship between thinking and language behavior follows.

Language skills are learned as the individual progresses through the various phases of growth and development. A child learns to speak and develops linguistic habits peculiar to the culture in which he is raised. There is some evidence in the literature to support the belief that thinking abilities develop concomitantly with learning to speak.

Prior to the development of the ability to speak the human infant operates primarily on a preverbal level. As the child begins to speak he also begins to use symbols. The symbols used in speech and in thinking may have highly subjective personal meanings to the child or, in other words, may be the product of autistic invention. Autistic thinking, as evidenced in speech behavior, is characterized by the use of words (or sounds) which are highly subjective in meaning and when heard seem ambiguous, illogical or even unintelligible to others. Some of the babbling sounds made by the child may be understandable to the mother (or mothering person); however, such sounds are meaningless as tools of communicating with others. Gradually the child, usually with the help of the mother, begins to replace autistic invention with consensual validation. That is, the child learns that in order to communicate with others he must use the words agreed upon, accepted and understood by other individuals in the society. As a result, the child can understand and be understood by others. He can share experiences with others and be a recipient in the sharing process.

What occurs when a child is blocked, thwarted or not assisted in changing from the autistic level to that of consensual validation? There are, of course, many factors involved. A child who receives some (but not enough) assistance in using consensually valid symbols may develop the ability to think fairly clearly and to communicate with others. However, later in life in anxiety-laden situations, the individual may be unable to use logical rational thinking to solve problems and may, as a result, revert to the use of autistic invention and display signs of a thought disorder. Some examples of disordered thinking as reflected in language behavior include circumstantiality, scattering, a loosening of thought associations, inability to focus attention, varying degrees of vagueness, a tendency to overgeneralize, the use of global pronouns lacking specific referents (such terms as "they" and "them"), and an inability to describe one's participation in an experience.

The mythical normal person also may display various signs of disturbances in thinking, especially when undergoing anxiety-laden experiences or encountering crisis situations. However, the normal person usually can—with, and sometimes without, assistance—realistically assess the situation and make tentative plans to resolve or in some way to cope with it. Individuals encountering a crisis situation may seek the help of friends, relatives, clergymen or members of the health disciplines. It is through communicating thoughts and feelings regarding the problem, being assisted to clarify the problem, receiving corrective feedback, obtaining information regarding resources, and being helped to envisage possible alternative ways of dealing with the stress that the normal person is helped to diminish his anxiety. The disturbance in thinking is therefore usually transient and self-limiting. In contradistinction, the individual who has not been given the opportunity of, or has for various reasons been incapable of, sharing his problems with others is unable to ask for and receive assistance during times of crisis. He is "forced" to cope with these stressful life situations alone. Without corrective feedback from others, and without the sharing of problems and experiences, the individual eventually becomes unable to clarify misconceptions or to view his life experiences from any perspective other than his own. This results in a more-or-less stereotyped, rigid approach to problems. The individual can use only whatever inner resources he possesses. The inability to form meaningful relationships with others eventually results in impoverishment of personality, diminished sensitivity, and a deterioration of social skills.

Communication thus is important because of its effect on the formation of the individual's personality and character structure. The foundation of the person's perception of self, the world and his place in it, is in part developed as a result of all of the communicated messages directed toward him by individuals significant in his life—when, by whom, and for what purpose. A child who continually receives verbal and nonverbal messages that he is unloved, unwanted, of little value, stupid, or malicious obviously develops a different concept of self than the child who receives messages that he is loved, wanted, needed and is a capable worthwhile person. A child subjected to inconsistent messages about himself or given love and approval by parents only under certain conditions develops another concept of self. According to Bateson, et al., a child subjected to a recurrent pattern of contrary or opposite messages sent by parental figures is caught in a "double-bind" situation.[1] The result of repeated experiences may be schizophrenic symptoms.

The way in which an individual perceives self and others is learned behavior. Behavior is also "unlearned" or new behavior patterns relearned within the context of communication with others in an interactive framework. Through skillful use of the communication process the nurse can assist the individual suffering from disturbances in thinking by helping him to correct language behavior. Correction of language behavior, however, is but a means to an end. The desired result is to increase the individual's capacity to identify and cope with problems, to perceive his participation in life experiences, to envisage alternative ways of acting and to test new patterns of behavior. The task is by no means an easy one. It is a time-consuming process requiring knowledge of the nature of thinking, ability to identify the presence of a thought disorder, and ability to intervene appropriately. This last is, in part, determined by the nurse's understanding of the communication process. In the section which follows communication patterns are discussed and their relevance in nursing situations is explored.

PART III—COMMUNICATION PATTERNS AND THE INTERACTIVE PROCESS

A communication pattern is a relatively consistent network of messages sent and received in a short- or long-term interaction. A pattern may also be defined as the individual's more-or-less habitual mode of communicating with others.

Why is knowledge of one's habitual mode of interacting with others important? There are rules, whether one chooses to acknowledge them or not, governing appropriate behavior in various life situations. It is important to know when, how, to whom and under what circumstances one is required, permitted or expected to behave or communicate in one manner rather than another. The ability to be

---

[1] Bateson, Gregory, et al.: Toward a theory of schizophrenia. Behav. Sci. 1:251, 1956.

flexible and to move from one level or type of communication pattern to another is essential.

Ideally, the human being learns how to communicate with others through meeting and sharing experiences with individuals from diverse backgrounds. He learns (often through trial and error) how to conduct himself appropriately, i.e. what to stress or not mention when conversing with others. One's learning, however, is always limited in that it is never complete enough, or thorough enough, and there is more to learn than can ever be accomplished in one lifetime. All people do not learn how or what to communicate to others at the same rate or speed; neither are all people afforded (nor do they create) the opportunity to seek out individuals from cultures and subgroups other than their own. Hence all individuals probably have some deficiencies in terms of ability to shift from one communication pattern to another as circumstances change. There are, for example, some individuals who cannot engage in "small talk" or "social chit-chat"; others seemingly can engage in no other kind of communication. Some individuals do not care about listening to the interests of others because they find them boring and without meaning. There are those persons who "come alive" when ideas and issues are discussed yet evidence no interest in discussing such topics as clothes, recipes, or house furnishings. People who are interested in particular hobbies or sports tend to seek out kindred souls with whom they feel free to converse. Whatever one's idiosyncratic typical communication pattern, it is a meaningful experience to encounter another person with whom one may share one's thoughts and feelings.

Two common patterns and one relatively uncommon pattern will be discussed. They are: the social amenity pattern, the informational or utilitarian pattern, and the less common relating pattern.

THE SOCIAL AMENITY PATTERN

The ability to engage in social amenities is, in our society, an essential interpersonal competency. Social amenities may be subsumed under the broad category of etiquette, i.e., the conventional rules and ceremonials observed in a given society. Social amenities are prescribed by custom or by what is considered proper behavior under given circumstances or in certain settings. In order, therefore, to engage in the behavior decreed by custom or convention the individual needs to know the rules or ceremonials observed within the society and must be able to implement this knowledge. The facility with which an individual learns and can engage in the proper behavior is termed social skill.

Social amenities dictate the language one should use in various life situations, as what to say when being introduced to a stranger. One says, "Hello" or "How are you?" to casual acquaintances. The message, by common cultural consensus, is not to be taken literally and hence the standard reply "Fine, and how are you?" is considered socially appropriate. Communication takes place—a message is sent and received—but such communication is seldom meaningful in the life of the average person. Not being acknowledged or asked "How are you?" would be more meaningful (in a distressing sense) to the individual than going through the standard, conventional, social amenity ritual.

If one person habitually maintains a social amenity pattern with another, the most probable interaction produced would be superficial and shallow. The social amenity communication pattern, unless transcended, does not enable either participant to begin to know the other as a unique human being. Instead, each remains uninvolved—a peripheral marginal figure in the life of the other. The conventional statements each directs to and at the other obscure what each is experiencing. If neither person maintaining the social amenity pattern begins to test the receptiveness of the other to moving toward the more meaningful sphere of relating, then the interaction remains frozen, static, stagnant and superficial.

"Small Talk"

Small talk or "social chit-chat" is generally not subsumed under the category of etiquette; however, such behavior is at times engaged in and expected under certain circumstances and in various life situations. Small talk encompasses such mundane areas as the weather, various aspects of the immediate environment, and other trivial comments. Small talk may have many purposes. It may be a "time-killing" device (though why time needs to be "killed" is a subject open to much speculation) or a tentative testing of another person to assess the desire of the other to engage in more meaningful conversation. Small talk or social chit-chat, like social amenities, may serve as a means of transcending a communication pattern plateau and enable the participants to move toward the more meaningful pattern of relating.

Relevance in Nursing Situations

The social amenity pattern as accepted in society as a whole influences behavior in nursing situations, although the rules deviate somewhat. However, even in nursing situations social amenities are prescribed by what is considered to be proper social and professional behavior. Actually, in nursing situations, the social amenities might properly be called "professional amenities" (defining the term *professional* quite loosely). There is, however, little that is professional or social in the use of such amenities. Professional amenities are used not only by health workers but by patients as well and both groups are expected to know the rules and engage in the appropriate behavior. In a psychiatric setting the intensity of a patient's illness is sometimes measured by the degree of deviance from expected "patient amenity" behavior. Although some leeway is allowed, the expectations of the staff are almost invariably communicated to the human being who is the patient and some patients very quickly "learn how to act" and what to say in order to be discharged from the psychiatric unit.

The professional amenities, to some extent, determine the language the nurse uses when talking with a patient. Whether or not the nurse is interested in the ill human being (or in his reply), she is expected to ask such stock questions as "How are you feeling?" "Did you sleep well last night?" "Did you eat your breakfast?" etc. The questions asked by the nurse, according to the "rules," are to be taken literally by the ill person and answered on the literal level. Nurses frequently receive stock answers to these questions for many reasons, the primary one being that the social amenity pattern influences the answers patients give to conventional questions. This is not always true, but generally the more conventional the question the more conventional is the reply to the question—the more meaningless is the response. Ill persons fairly quickly learn the "expected and correct" replies to conventional questions. Both nurse and patient learn the rules of the game; they learn them too well, in fact. Neither communicates with the other although some pseudocommunication is taking place.

Nurses engage in small talk and social chit-chat for many reasons. Small talk is one way to avoid becoming involved in the ill person's life or in his problems. It is also a guarantee that the interaction will be on a superficial level. The nurse may enjoy small talk and hence engage in it for this reason, or she may do so because she believes ill persons should become interested in areas other than their own problems. Social chit-chat and small talk are automatic in that little or no thinking is involved. This fact, in and of itself, may explain the attraction of these habitual modes of communicating with others and nurses are not immune to this attraction.

What is the effect on the patient if the nurse habitually utilizes social amenities or small talk as a mode of communicating? As stated, remaining on a social amenity level is a guarantee that neither nurse nor patient will move toward knowing the other as a unique human being. The same is true at the social chit-chat or small talk level. The only possible type of interaction is an automatic one devoid of meaning for both. Each remains a stranger to the other or, at best, becomes an acquaintance. Neither gives of self during the act of communicating; each participates in a ritual.

If the nurse remains on this level of communication, does this necessarily mean that she cannot assist the ill person toward social recovery? It is probable that if the ill person improves it is in spite of, and not because of, the nurse's "assistance." In fairness it must be stated that there are some few nurses who commit every possible communication blunder but who, because of their deep and abiding interest in the welfare of each ill human being they encounter and because of their "well-meaningness," *do* help patients toward social recovery. Such nurses, however, are rare. It is well not to consider oneself as belonging to this select group unless one has overwhelming evidence to support the assumption. Most nurses *must* learn how to communicate with others, and most nurses need assistance in developing skill in this most difficult art.

It is the nurse's responsibility to break through the stultifying effect of expected behavior and stereotyped stock questions and answers to assist the ill person to reveal himself. Conventionality is a barrier to self-disclosure. Some ill persons, however, may feel more comfortable in beginning interactions by talking with nurses on a professional amenity level or by using small talk. The nurse can deliberately use nurse-isms or stock questions and answers as a bridge to a more meaningful interactive pattern. She cannot, however, remain at this level or permit the patient to do so if she desires to establish a meaningful relationship with the ill human being.

THE INFORMATIONAL OR UTILITARIAN PATTERN

The informational or utilitarian pattern of communication differs from the social amenity and small talk pattern. It is used when an individual requests information or gives instructions, directives or "orders" to others. The pattern is utilitarian in the sense that the communication given or received is useful to the sender or the recipient. Some examples of informational communication patterns in everyday life are requesting directions to a specific locale, instructing a cab driver as to one's destination, telling a saleslady what it is one wishes to purchase, phoning in a grocery order, etc.

Relevance in Nursing Situations

The informational-utilitarian communication pattern is used in nursing situations and, in some instances, overlaps with the professional amenities pattern. The distinction between the two can be made in terms of purpose or intent. For example, a nurse may ask a patient "How are you feeling?" because this question is an expected professional amenity or because the information is needed in order to write something on the patient's chart. In the latter instance the nurse is operating on an informational communication pattern level.

The utilitarian communication pattern is utilized by nurses when orienting newly admitted patients to a unit or when giving instructions or directives to patients. Some "health teaching" attempts unfortunately seem to be characterized by an informational unilaterally directed communication chain.

The messages inherent in the informational pattern of communication may, or may not, be helpful or meaningful to the recipient. The manner in which the nurse communicates informational messages to an ill person may determine the extent to which a patient will cooperate with the instruction, directive or "order." For example, it is the custom in some psychiatric units for the nurse to dispense medications from the nursing station. The nurse many times shouts "Time for medicine." She expects patients to queue up in single file in front of the nursing station to receive medication. Some ill persons do not follow the nurse's directive. Is it logical to assume that the only possible reason for a patient's failure to follow directions is based on his illness? Could it be that the patient is well enough to resent being shouted at and made to stand in line like a supplicant beggar? A similar example of the effect of the manner in which a nurse communicates informational messages follows. It is still the custom, in some psychiatric units, for a nurse or attendant to announce "Time for electric shock." The effect of this type of directive on patients scheduled for electric shock treatment, and on those who are not, is best left to one's imagination. Are these examples exceptions? One would like to believe such occurrences are rare, but unfortunately they are all too prevalent. The ill person is not an animal to be herded; he is a human being. It is deplorable that such incidents occur in any setting; it is especially deplorable that they occur in psychiatric settings. Such practices are often condoned or engaged in by professional nurses—nurses whose aim should be to provide a humanizing milieu and all that this implies. A humanizing milieu cannot exist in institutions where such tactics are commonplace.

It is the professional nurse's responsibility to identify those things which dehumanize the patient and change them. To fail to speak through timidity, indifference, or respect, or because one does not wish to be considered a "trouble-maker," to fail to register complaints through the proper channels, is to condone and approve such dehumanizing tactics. It is interesting to speculate how much improvement in patient care would result if nurses, en masse, refused to give consent to or condone (by commission or omission) any acts, or to become active members of any institutions, that dehumanize the ill person or permit ineffective, unsafe or untherapeutic care. There are times when the nurse is obligated by conscience to speak out against conditions and institutions which degrade the human being. Precipitous action is *not* suggested. It *is* suggested that the nurse collect facts and present these to the proper authorities. To fail to protest or speak out when one *knows* one should is to begin a slow and inevitable process of corrosion of basic integrity. Material possessions, loved ones, health may be lost throughout one's life, but to lose one's integrity is by far the greatest loss a human being can encounter. Without integrity life can have no meaning; with it meaning can be found in whatever may befall us. Let there be no mistake about it. The nurse who *does* protest dehumanization may find herself very much alone. It is quite possible that the professional nurse who protests will be misunderstood, maligned and in some instances persecuted by others. But when one measures what is really at stake it soon becomes clear that there is no choice. The decision to be made is clear.

The nurse as an agent of change has been discussed in some detail because the author believes that nurses must become more actively involved in bringing about needed changes in agencies and institutional settings in order to render safe, effective and humane care to patients.

Nurses who habitually utilize the informational utilitarian approach—whether its effects be constructive or dehumanizing—are unable to get to know the ill human being and are incapable of establishing meaningful relationships. It is the nurse's responsibility to transcend the informational utilitarian level to a more meaningful in-depth type of communication in which each participant is free to disclose himself as a unique individual to the other. Neither the social amenity nor the informational pattern is a goal to be attained in nursing situations. What is the desired pattern? *It is hypothesized that relating is the desired communication pattern in the establishment of a nurse-patient relationship.*

RELATING AS COMMUNICATION PATTERN

Relating is an experience, or series of experiences, characterized by meaningful dialogue between two human beings—a nurse and a patient—wherein each is aware of, and experiences openness, closeness and understanding of, the other. Relating is more than intellectual awareness or knowledge of abstract concepts; it is more than the ability to communicate. When human beings relate both are affected and irrevocably changed, and the experience is not readily forgotten by the people who participate in it.

Relating is an Experience . . .

As experience, each participant, to a greater or lesser extent, is aware of what is occurring, or what it is he (or she) is encountering, although the elements of the experience may not be known or clear at the time of the encounter.

Meaningful Dialogue . . .

Meaningful dialogue is characterized by purposeful reciprocal communication between both participants in the interaction. What is discussed is pertinent, relevant and appropriate. The content of the communication is directed toward the "here-and-now" problems of the patient. Timing—the art of knowing when to speak, when to be silent, what to say and how to say it—is vitally important. One ill person stated in reference to a nurse assigned to establish a relationship with her:

> I was so depressed and worried about my children and how they were I could have cried—yet the nurse kept asking me about the basket I made in O.T. I wanted to talk about my children but she (the nurse) was more interested in basket-weaving.

In this example the nurse was too focused on self to pay attention to the patient. There was no meaningful dialogue because there was no sharing and the conversation was not appropriate to the ill person's need at the time.

Necessary prerequisites to meaningful dialogue on the part of the nurse are knowledge and the ability to use it for the good of the patient, sensitivity, and an exquisite sense of timing in the interpersonal situation.

Meaningful dialogue is reciprocal. Although the focus is primarily on the ill person's needs and problems, dialogue is meaningful to the extent that the nurse is able to share and to give of self in the en-counter. Both nurse and patient grow as human beings as a result of the experience of relating.

Each . . . Experiences Openness, Closeness . . .

Openness to experience is characterized by the capacity to allow opposing problems or feelings to coexist without succumbing to the need to avoid discomfort by seeking premature closure or the immedi-ate "solving" of the problems. It is the ability to hold in abeyance the problem-solving process while mulling over and seeking ways of as-sisting the patient to cope with the problem, to be accessible, and to convey this accessibility to the ill human being. It is the nurse's role to structure the interaction in such a way that the patient can experi-ence this openness.

The capacity to be open to experience is probably, on the part of the nurse, one of the necessary prerequisites to helping the ill person to a sense of closeness. Individual nurses vary in their ability to develop closeness with other human beings. Because of the long-standing prohibitions in nursing about "becoming overly friendly with patients" and exhortations about "being professional," some nurses may have great difficulty in attaining closeness with patients. The ill person, because of his sickness or life problems, may have difficulty in developing trust and confidence in the nurse—also necessary to the attainment of closeness.

An element of risk is inherent in developing closeness. Closeness implies caring about another individual. To care about someone, in turn, implies the threat of losing, or of being hurt by, the object of one's caring. But it is only to the extent an individual can experience closeness with others that he can develop his human potential. The kind of closeness suggested in the nurse-patient relationship cannot easily be categorized. The development of a personal friendship with all of its connotations is *not* the goal in nursing situations, but rather a type of closeness for the purpose of freeing the patient to experience other objects of caring. It is hoped that the patient will experience warmth and develop confidence and trust in the nurse and then, in turn, in other human beings. Such closeness transcends the roles of nurse and patient; each participant relates to the other as human to human. The patient as a human being relates to the humanness and uniqueness of the nurse. The nurse as a compassionate, knowledgeable human being guides the interaction in such a way as to enable the ill person to test patterns of closeness and to experience trust and con-fidence.

The nurse is only the guide on the journey. The ultimate goal is for the ill person to be free to seek and find for himself the kind of closeness which has meaning for him. Closeness thus on the part of the nurse is not a possessive "holding on"—it is rather a striving to enable the ill person to find ways of relating with individuals other than the nurse.

And Understanding of the Other

To understand is to acknowledge the uniqueness of the other and to feel comfortable in doing so. Understanding is more than having knowledge about another person; it is more than being able to put knowledge to use or to transfer that which is learned to new situations. Hopefully the nurse will enable the ill person to accomplish these goals during the nurse-patient relationship. Understanding includes, but is more than, the testing or learning of new interpersonal competencies or new patterns of interpersonal behavior. It is a reciprocal process wherein both nurse and patient perceive and interact with each other on a human-to-human basis.

Understanding is a force which can provide the ill person with the necessary endurance and courage to face the inevitable problems which lie before him. The experience of relating can be a healing force as well as a source of strengthening the healthy aspects of the ill person's personality.

The ability to relate seems to be contingent on the nurse's possessing and being able to make use of various attributes. Her character structure, i.e., her life experience background, the knowledge she brings to the situation as well as the ability to use this knowledge wisely for the good of the patient, and her commitment to help others without expecting gratitude are three major components of this ability.

In addition to communication patterns, other factors affect the communication process in the one-to-one relationship. Seven of these are explored in the section which follows.

PART IV—FACTORS AFFECTING THE COMMUNICATION PROCESS

Seven factors which influence the communication process are presented for review and to assist nurses in diagnosing communication distortion and breakdown.

1. *The perceptions, thoughts and feelings of the sender and receiver immediately prior to message transmission, i.e. the intrapersonal framework of each participant.* What occurs *prior* to an interaction may determine the readiness of the receiver to accept, i.e., to listen to, the sender's message. It may also determine to some extent the way in which the message is transmitted by the sender.

2. *The relationship, if any, between sender and receiver.* Are they strangers, acquaintances, friends, co-workers, subordinates, authority figures, peers? The type of relationship existing between sender and receiver prior to communication may determine what message is transmitted and how it is transmitted.

3. *The intention(s) of the sender.* Is more than one message intended? What does the sender want, expect, desire, or wish the receiver to do or say in response to the message? It is assumed that some kind of response is expected by the sender of the message.

4. *The content of the message.* What is actually being conveyed? Can the sender's purpose(s) or intention(s) be determined by the content of the message? Is the language used by the sender clear and precise? Is the language understandable to the receiver? Technical jargon and the use of words and terms not within the vocabulary of the recipient may block reception or interpretation of the message. What level of interpretation is necessary to comprehend the content? Can the message be interpreted literally or must it be desymbolized in order to be understood? Is there a disparity between what is said and what is meant? Is the sender transmitting one message verbally and a contrary nonverbal message?

5. *The context in which the communication takes place.* Context includes physical environmental factors (the setting) and psychological factors related to readiness and timing. What is taking place in the setting when the sender transmits the message? What is the receiver doing, thinking or feeling? Was the receiver interrupted from a task in which he was engaged in order to pay attention to the sender? Readiness, timing and appropriateness are all aspects of context.

6. *The manner in which the message is transmitted.* In verbal communication this includes vocal tone, rate of delivery, emphases, nuances and other aspects of the acoustic dimensions of the human voice. The vocal tone or rate of delivery of the message may offer cues for interpretation of the sender's feeling state at the time of the interchange as well as of the message. This dual cue system poses a dilemma for the recipient. To which aspect of the message is the

receiver expected to respond—to the feeling state, to the content of the communication, or to both?

7. *The effect of the message on the receiver.* Depending on the intentions of the sender, did the message elicit the desired response (s) from the receiver? Did the sender have to rephrase the message or try in some other way to communicate his intentions in order to bring about the desired response? Does the message affect the receiver personally? Does it, for example, cause the receiver to react emotionally to the message or to the sender? Does the message threaten the receiver? Does it enhance his feelings of self-esteem? To what extent is the message meaningful, pertinent, or relevant to the life experience of the receiver?

All of these factors affect the communication process but are by no means to be considered all-inclusive. Communication is also influenced by culture, the roles of sender and receiver, status, expectations and other factors.

In addition to knowledge of the nature of the communication process, the practitioner must also possess knowledge of the communication techniques. The judicious use of communication techniques will assist the nurse to achieve the goals of the one-to-one relationship.

PART V—THE COMMUNICATION TECHNIQUES

Communication techniques are methods used to accomplish the specific as well as the overall goals of nursing intervention. As such, the communication techniques include not only the use of verbal interchange with ill persons but also all nonverbal means used by the nurse to influence the patient. Techniques are used to guide the flow of communication into goal-directed channels in order to assist the patient to clarify circumscribed areas of content.

Communication techniques are means to an end and not ends within themselves. Nurses are encouraged to use *any* technique whereby they are assisted to accomplish the specific and overall goals of nursing intervention, but to avoid their repetitive, stilted, or inappropriate use. Not all nurses will feel comfortable in using some of the techniques discussed in this chapter. Therefore it is suggested that they creatively design techniques which will enable them to feel comfortable while achieving the goals of the interaction.

Techniques are not magic phrases; they do not always elicit a response or the desired behavior. Too much focus on techniques may well inhibit the nurse in achieving relatedness with the ill human being. Guidelines can be suggested, but communication techniques should not be used indiscriminately without regard for the patient with whom one is attempting to interact.

GUIDELINES IN COMMUNICATING WITH PATIENTS

The guidelines in communicating with patients are predicated on the assumption that it is the nurse's—*not* the ill person's—task to guide, direct and structure the interactive process. Abdication by the nurse of responsibility in this area will seriously affect the quality of assistance she can offer. Guidelines concerning communication techniques are stated in terms of tasks to be accomplished by the nurse in order to achieve the overall goals of nursing intervention.

Encourage the Ill Person to Verbalize

Encouraging the ill person to verbalize serves many purposes. The ability to verbalize, in and of itself, may be helpful to an ill person. Further, it is partially through sharing of self in the verbalization process that individuals get to know each other. So it is in nursing situations that each participant becomes known through the sharing inherent in conversing with the other. Verbalization also provides the ill person with a method of releasing tension and anxiety other than acting out these feelings. Through talking with a skilled practitioner the ill human being is enabled to identify problem areas, face them realistically, envisage alternatives and test new patterns of behavior. The communication process gives the patient needed emotional support and assists him to develop the interpersonal competencies inherent in problem solving.

The ill person may be encouraged to verbalize by the judicious use of some of the following questions or statements:

"You were saying?"
"And after that you . . ."
"Continue."
"Tell me more about . . ."
"And then what happened?"

The nurse may also encourage the ill person to verbalize by using nonverbal means such as head or hand movements which convey the message "continue" or "keep talking." In some instances nonverbal methods may be more effective than verbal methods in assisting patients to talk.

Assist the Ill Person to Clarify

The nurse assists the ill individual to clarify the meaning and the nature of the message he is conveying. Because of disordered thinking, ill persons many times may have difficulty in stating clearly what they are trying to convey, or may assume that others know what they are thinking or feeling without any effort on their part to convey the message. Communication under such circumstances may become an onerous burden to the ill person rather than an enjoyable sharing experience.

The nurse is encouraged to interrupt the individual's flow of verbalization whenever she does not understand the meaning of a patient's comments or questions. For example, the nurse should not assume she knows to whom an ill person is referring when he uses such pronouns as "he," "she," "ours," "them," "you," or "it." If the meaning of a statement or question is not clear the nurse may use any of the following statements or questions to seek clarification:

"I don't follow you. Tell me about . . . again."
"I don't understand what you are saying . . ."
"To whom are you referring when you say he (or she, ours, etc.)?"
"To whom are you referring when you say everybody or all of the people?"
"What do you mean when you say it helped? What helped?"

In seeking clarification the nurse assists the patient to become less vague and more specific. The following is an excerpt from a process record:

Patient: Everybody here hates me.
Nurse: To whom are you referring when you say everybody?
Patient All of the patients here.

At this point in the interaction the nurse may decide to confront the ill person and cast doubt on the assumption that "all of the patients hate me" by asking: "Is it possible that *all* of the patients here hate you?" Or she may choose to assist the ill person to become more specific by saying: "Give me one example." The nurse strives to assist the ill person to describe one specific experience and to identify one specific individual to whom he is referring. Many times ill individuals arrive at conclusions based on insufficient or distorted data and then generalize from one experience to all like experiences.

Some ill persons are unable to express themselves on a literal level and use metaphors, similes or other figurative expressions. The following patient's statement is from a process record:

"Life is a balloon floating off into space buffeted by every wind current that comes along."

At this point the nurse needs to decide what aspect of the patient's statement to focus upon; she develops inferences as to the probable meaning of the statement. For example, the nurse may decide the patient is referring to himself and his own life experiences and may seek validation by saying: "Tell me what your statement—'life is a balloon floating off into space'—means in terms of *your* life."

Depending on the nurse's skill and judgment, she may decide to confront the individual with her inference to seek validation. For example, the nurse may say: "You feel helpless?" "You feel helpless?" is the nurse's decoded interpretation of the patient's statement. Sharing decoded interpretations may be helpful to a patient. However, it is possible that the nurse may encourage the patient to use figurative language by sharing decoded interpretations with him if this is done too early in the interactive process, whereas her ultimate goal is to assist the patient to communicate on a literal level.

Vagueness in language behavior may be more subtle than the figurative example just described and may be characterized by the use of global adjectives or by the more-or-less continuous use of conventional (social amenity) statements. An example follows:

> "I went out yesterday with my husband and we had the nicest time. It was just swell."

On the surface it may appear as though there is nothing to question the patient about. Upon further examination, however, it becomes apparent that the patient has not actually described her experience. "Nice" and "swell" are conclusions reached by the ill person on the basis of some data. The nurse needs to assist the patient to describe the experience(s) leading to these conclusions. The nurse may say: "Tell me more about your visit" or may choose to focus on clarifying the meaning of the word "it." The ultimate goal of the nurse is to assist the ill person to supply the data upon which the conclusions were based.

Another example of vagueness and the use of global adjectives follows:

> "Everybody here is just wonderful to me . . . I have the best doctor in the whole world and I love all of the nurses."

The nurse first decides what aspect of the patient's statement to investigate. She may ask: "To whom are you referring when you say everybody?" or she may ask the patient to describe one particular experience which led to the assumption that " everybody here is just wonderful to me."

Some patients exhibit "scattering," i.e., a behavior in which the connection or association of one idea with another is not readily apparent. The result is language behavior that is useless as a tool for communicating in normal social situations. An example follows:

> Patient: Like I said, A. J. is the key that unlocks the idea. I'm not too sure about the idea but it has something to do with A. J. and the sun setting in the west. I wish I was sure about it but I'm not—not really—not yet.

To assist the patient to clarify, the nurse decides what aspect of the patient's statement to investigate. Some responses she may choose are:

> "I don't understand what you are saying. Please restate it."
> "Who is A.J.?"
> "Tell me more about the key."
> "I don't understand the connection between: the key and the idea?" the idea and A.J.?" A.J. and the sun setting in the west?"

Assisting such patients to clarify will take time. The ill person must unlearn the scattering and then relearn how to communicate clearly and intelligibly to others. Depending on her relationship with him, the nurse may confront the patient with his language behavior in an attempt to help him clarify. For example, she might say: "You're not making sense" or "I don't understand you at all." Above all, time and patience are essential. A year of intensive counseling may be required before some ill persons will be able to communicate clearly with others.

Assist the Ill Person to Focus

Many patients have difficulty in focusing their attention on one topic of conversation for any period of time, and may mention several different topics or subjects within a relatively short time span. An apparent inability to focus may be a result of anxiety level or it may also be a defense against involvement, i.e., a conscious desire to avoid disturbing topics and to remain on a superficial social amenity level.

An inability to focus may be exemplified by rapid changing of subject within a short time span. One idea immediately prompts an association with another idea. The following excerpt is from a process record:

> Patient: It's hot today—even the chairs are hot—like a hot seat—an electric chair—I've read about them. Do you know who my favorite detective is? [Doesn't wait for a reply] I like Philo Vance. I used to go steady with a boy named Vance. He was from my home town. His family ran a grocery store. With the price of food the way it is they must make a mint of money. They are putting brass in the money and taking out the silver. I read about it in the paper. I don't get a chance to read the paper the way I did at home. I enjoyed my paper and my cup of coffee in the morning."

How may the nurse best assist the individual who scatters to this extent? She can interrupt the patient's stream of conversation to make inquiries. For example, the nurse may wish the patient to clarify the connection with hot weather, hot seats and the electric chair. Depending on the nonverbal cues communicated by the patient, she may ask the patient to tell her more about Vance. The nurse then strives to get the patient to remain on one topic—for example, Vance —for a period of time without digressing or bringing in another related subject. Once the nurse manages to get the patient to remain on the topic she should not change the topic. A patient cannot learn to focus if the nurse keeps changing the subject of conversation.

There may be many reasons why a nurse chooses to change the subject of the conversation. She may wish to focus on more meaningful data, to decompress the patient's anxiety level by a less stressful topic, to make herself more comfortable—or she may simply not know what else to say.

A device used by some patients to avoid focusing on themselves is to focus on the nurse. For example the patient says: "My, you look nice this morning. I like the way you fix your hair. What did you do over the weekend?" A simple statement by the nurse such as "Tell me how *you* are" soon refocuses the interview. If the patient continually strives to focus on the nurse, then the nurse may share this impression with the patient by saying: "I get the feeling you are trying to avoid talking about yourself" or "Tell me why you keep bringing the conversation around to me and my life?" The nurse under such circumstances should communicate in a kind, gentle manner and if possible try to avoid making the patient feel guilty for transgressing a rule.

In the following excerpt from a process record, on which aspect of the patient's statement should the nurse focus? Patient: "My mother came to see me today. She brought me some ice cream." The nurse might choose to focus on the mother's relationship with the patient and may say: "Tell me more about your mother's visit" or, more specifically, "Tell me what you and your mother talked about." The nurse strives to elicit data re the patient's thoughts and feelings prior to, during, and following his mother's visit. The nurse may also say: "Tell me about your mother. What is she like?" Her intention here is to help the patient describe his thoughts and feelings about his mother. It is quite common, however, for patients to respond to such questions by giving a physical description of the other individual instead of describing the relationship between the other person and themselves.

The following questions are less valuable because they are on the informational or social amenity level and do not assist the patient to describe his experience.

1. "How long did your mother stay?"
2. "When was the last time you saw your mother?"
3. "Has your mother been to see you before?"
4. "Has your mother brought you ice cream before?"
5. "What kind of ice cream did your mother bring you?"
6. "Were you glad to see your mother?"

The first five questions are classified as informational. The reference to ice cream in questions #4 and #5 may lead the patient to believe the nurse is more interested in ice cream than she is in his mother. Question #6 suggests the answer "yes" because in our culture an individual is supposed to be "glad" to see his mother. It is suggested that in all instances when a patient is talking about an experience between himself and another person the nurse focus on the interaction rather than upon incidental details. The kind of ice cream the mother brought is not so significant as the interaction between the patient and his mother.

Assist the Ill Person to Identify Cause and Effect

When the ill person can verbalize, clarify, and focus, he is then assisted to identify cause and effect. The nurse helps him to identify what he did or said prior to, during, and following the experience. An excerpt from a process record shows a nurse striving to assist a patient to identify cause and effect.

Patient: I felt bad all day yesterday.
Nurse: Tell me about feeling bad.
Patient: There was a fight on the ward. Myrt and Wanda had an argument. I don't know what it was about but it scared me.
Nurse: You said you felt bad *all day yesterday*. When did you start feeling bad?
Patient: It was after . . . no . . . when they were fighting.
Nurse: You started feeling bad when Myrt and Wanda were fighting?
Patient: Yes, that's when it started. I got to shaking all over . . . I got weak. I went to my room and put my hands over my ears.
Nurse: You weren't feeling bad before the argument started?
Patient: No, I guess I just can't stand squabbles. Come to think about it I used to act that way at home when Mom and Dad got to fighting . . .
Nurse: You used to leave the room when your mother and father began fighting?
Patient: It was the only thing I could do. I stayed away—then I felt better.
Nurse: And how did you feel yesterday after you went to your room?
Patient: I was shaking but then I felt better. Like I said, it's the same thing as when Mom and Dad used to fight.

In this example the nurse helps the patient to identify cause and effect, to focus on one specific problem, and to identify the method(s) used to reduce anxiety.

Assist the Ill Person to Perceive his Participation in an Experience

Many mentally ill individuals have difficulty describing their participation in life experiences. An outcome of assisting a patient to verbalize, clarify, focus and identify cause and effect is his increased ability to perceive himself as an *active* participant in life experiences. The nurse helps him to understand that he is a thinking, feeling human being who elicits responses from others and affects the behavior of others. An excerpt from a process record is an example:

Patient: They don't like me here.
Nurse: To whom are you referring when you say *they?*
Patient: The patients.
Nurse: Give me an example.
Patient: All I did was go and sit at the card table and everybody left.
Nurse: Who left?
Patient: Paula, Sam, Jane and Mike.
Nurse: What happened?
Patient: Well, I sat down and lit a cigarette. Paula and them were playing cards. I said, 'Good morning—isn't it early to be playing cards?' They just looked at me. So I thought they're not going to give me the cold shoulder. Then I said 'Can't anybody be decent?' Finally Mike said 'Good morning.' Paula, Sam and Jane just glared at me. Then Paula said 'Don't blow smoke in my face. I don't like it.' Well I just let her have it. I told her off. Jane is *her* friend—she's meek and mousy and didn't open her mouth. Sam just glared at me. Then they all left me sitting there.
Nurse: Everyone got up and left?
Patient: Well, Miss X (the aide) called out breakfast time. But that's not why they left. They just don't like me.
Nurse: Let's go back to your statement 'Isn't it early to be playing cards?' Why did you say this?
Patient: Well, it just was, that's all. Oh, you think maybe my saying that caused the reaction I got?
Nurse: Is it possible?
Patient: I guess so. I don't know why I said it. That's not true. I do. I was mad at Paula for not waking me up and asking me to join them and I just took it out on everybody.
Nurse: You were angry at Paula, then at the group?
Patient: Yes, I was. I wanted to hurt them.
Nurse: Your behavior then affected everyone at the table?
Patient: Yes, I did upset them. I'll have to apologize.
Nurse: What will you do if this happens again?
Patient: If I had to do it all over again I'd tell Paula I was mad because she didn't wake me up.
Nurse: Then what?
Patient: Well, (laughs) I hope I wouldn't make such a big production out of it—but, you know, I really was mad.

Nurse: Are you mad now?
Patient: No, but I feel foolish.

In the foregoing the nurse assisted the patient to clarify ("To whom do you refer when you say *they?*"), to focus ("Give me an example . . ."), to identify cause and effect, to perceive her participation in the experience and to envisage alternatives ("What will you do if this happens again?").

The tasks to be accomplished by the nurse, as discussed in this section, are by no means all-inclusive. The communication techniques are not rules to be rigidly adherred to but are rather suggested ways to assist the nurse in accomplishing her tasks; they are means to an end and are not ends within themselves. General goals, purposes or objectives should be conceptualized prior to the interaction. However, one must never overlook the person for whom the goals are designed. The human being who is the patient is more important than the techniques used to help him.

Knowledge of goals and techniques, however, is no guarantee that communication breakdown and distortion will not occur.

PART VI—COMMUNICATION BREAKDOWN

As stated, communication is the sending and receiving of messages by means of symbols, words (spoken or written), signs, gestures and other nonverbal means. For communication to take place, the message must be sent, received and understood by both sender and receiver. Communication breakdown, i.e., failure to communicate, may occur when the message is not received or when it is distorted, misinterpreted or not understood by the recipient.

MAJOR CAUSES OF COMMUNICATION BREAKDOWN AND DISTORTION

Failure to Listen

Failure to listen is probably one of the most common causes of communication breakdown. A message is sent but the intended receiver does not pay attention to or hear the message. There may be many reasons for failure to listen, on the part of patient or the nurse, ranging from willful intent *not* to listen to a desire to listen but being prevented by certain factors operating in the situation.

In the interpersonal process listening is a skill which must be developed by both nurse and patient. Hopefully, the nurse will have developed some degree of expertise in this most difficult art. Individual patients possess listening skills of varying degrees. It is the nurse's responsibility not only continually to develop her listening skills but to assist the patient to pay attention to and hear the messages communicated to him. A patient's anxiety level may hamper his ability to heed incoming messages. It is the nurse's obligation to assess the patient's anxiety level, to help him reduce his anxiety level, and thereby to enable him to listen to and heed communicated messages.

As mentioned previously, it is expected that the professional nurse will have developed some degree of skill in listening. Like patients, nurses develop this interpersonal competency in varying degrees of depth. Why do some nurses have difficulty in listening? A nurse may not wish to hear a patient's comments, requests or questions. The speech behavior of the patient may hinder the listening process. If a patient uses broken English, mumbles, or speaks in a low monotonous tone, the nurse may "tune him out." This is not to condone the nurse's behavior but, being human, she is quite apt to fail to listen to an individual whose speech habits make it difficult for her to hear, much less understand, the person's comments. The nurse, being human, may also fail to listen to a patient who irritates her or who subjects her to an endless litany of complaints. If the nurse believes she knows what the patient is going to say before he says it, she tends not to listen. A patient who uses long prefacing remarks before saying what he wants to say or who "beats around the bush" before coming to the point may also be subjected to not listening on the nurse's part.

Nurses who converse with an individual patient for fifty to sixty minutes daily, during the one-to-one relationship, well understand the strain of focusing attention during this relatively short span of time. Nurses who work eight hours a day conversing with numbers of patients are, in many ways, under a far greater strain. Is it possible really to listen to each and every ill person with whom one comes in contact with during an eight-hour period of time? It *is* possible but it is also difficult. Nurses are often helped to focus on the patient's conversation if they are allowed to retreat to a quiet place to reflect upon and think through what it is they are trying to accomplish. Time to recoup one's forces and energies, to examine one's behavior in relation to patients, to look into one's motives, and to plan ways of meeting patients' needs is of the utmost importance in psychiatric nursing. A nurse is a human being and tires under the strain of listening, planning, structuring and attempting to evaluate the quality of care given. This is not to recommend withdrawal as a means of avoiding patients. *It is recommended that nurses be given an uninterrupted period of time in which to think.* The professional nurse practitioner *will* use this time to plan, structure and evaluate nursing intervention.

There are many reasons other than those previously mentioned why nurses may fail to listen to patients. A nurse may not listen because she is indifferent toward the patient's needs. Dislike of a patient may foster not listening. The nurse may be preoccupied with her own problems to the extent of being incapable of focusing on the comments of others. The anxiety level of the nurse may cause her to shut the patient out. A nurse may fail to listen because of pressure to perform other tasks to which she has given higher priority. Paper work, for example, may be given precedence over the people for whom the paper work is being done. Some nurses operate on the premise that if something is not heard one doesn't have to do anything about it. Hence, in order to avoid doing anything about the patient's requests the nurse simply doesn't hear the patient or, if she does, the message "goes in one ear and out the other," making no impression whatsoever on the brain. Some nurses simply have never developed the habit of listening.

It is probable that most nurses want to listen to patients and that patients want to communicate with health workers. Granted the well-meaningness of most health workers, why do these individuals have difficulty in listening to each other? Is it that good intentions are not enough? Well-meaningness is helpful, good intentions are fine, but unfortunately neither will assist nurses who lack the perseverance required to strive continually to improve their ability to listen. Listening is an art which can be developed—a skill which can be learned, cultivated and nurtured—but one must actively engage in the listening process. That *listening is an active process* has become almost a cliche, but it is nevertheless true. A person who listens is "caught up," so to speak, in the interpersonal exchange. *Listening requires total involvement.* It is more than hearing. One may hear a message but not really listen to it, extract meanings from it, or use the encounter as a means of communing with another human being.

What of those situations wherein the recipient of the message is bored or irritated by listening to the comments of the other person? Are there not occasions when one is not obligated to listen? In social situations one is not strictly obliged to become actively involved in the listening process; there is no professional obligation to pay attention to a person who is trying to convey a message, but there is the ever-present human obligation of one person to the other. In such situations each person must decide for himself, in terms of his own conscience, the extent to which he will become involved.

In the nurse-patient encounter one has a clear professional obligation to pay attention, to hear and to listen. Whether the patient's comments are boring, uncouth, distasteful or irritating to the nurse in no way relieves her of this obligation. And who needs to be listened to more than those patients whose language repulses rather than attracts? Who needs to be *spoken* to by nurses more than those patients who are relatively mute? The nurse does not listen to the patient, since he does not speak; she *does*, however, convey to the patient a readiness to hear, to listen and to help.

What is the result of a nurse's failure to listen? The nurse conveys to the ill person the message that he is not worthy of her time and interest. To be listened to, to have someone truly understand what one is trying to convey despite ineptness, social awkwardness or uncontrollable language behavior, is to be treated as a human being— as a person whose existence means something.

Failure To Interpret a Message Correctly

To understand a message the receiver must often interpret it. If it is not correctly interpreted, communication has not taken place.

Comments made by ill persons and others cannot always be accepted at face value and interpreted literally. A single statement made by one individual to another may contain several intended messages or levels of meaning and be prompted by various motives. For example, a wife says to her husband: "Supper is ready." The husband replies: "I'm not hungry." The husband's reply may be interpreted by his wife on any of the following levels:

1. "I have no appetite." (I am not experiencing physiological hunger.)
2. "I am not hungry now." (I may be hungry later on.)
3. "I don't like what you prepared for supper." (Why didn't you fix something I like?)
4. "I am too tired (worried, concerned, etc.) to eat." (Ask me what's wrong.)
5. "You have spoiled my appetite." (It's your fault I'm not hungry.)

If the wife knows her husband usually looks forward to their evening meal together, she will inquire why he is not hungry. If she knows her husband well, it is probable she will be able to interpret the intended message correctly. The wife will probably "get the message" implied if she pays attention to her husband's tone of voice, his facial expression, etc. It is probable (but not always true) that individuals who know each other quite well are more apt than strangers to interpret each others' comments correctly. Each knows if a remark is to be taken literally or not.

The wife who interprets her husband's comments on levels #1 and #2 may inquire why her husband is not hungry and has no appetite. She may ask what he ate for lunch, if he had something to eat before he came home from the office, etc. If the wife interprets her husband's comment on level #3, she may become defensive and explain why she is serving these particular foods. If, however, the wife interprets her husband's comments on level #4, she may ask why he is tired, worried or concerned in order to help him resolve the problem. An interpretation on level #5 will obviously elicit a different kind of response from the wife.

Knowledge of an individual and the ability to pay attention to the accompanying nonverbal communication often lead to correct interpretation. However, one cannot automatically assume he understands what another person means by a comment unless he verifies the meaning with the other individual.

In the initial stages of the interactive process the nurse usually does not know the patient. She may have great difficulty in correctly interpreting the message the patient is trying to convey or may jump to conclusions about its meaning. The meaning the nurse attributes to the patient's comment may, or may not, be accurate. The result of failure to interpret a message correctly is inappropriate nursing intervention, or none at all. Unless the nurse asks the patient what he means by his comment, she has no way of knowing whether or not the message has been interpreted correctly. The comment "I am tired of everything," for example, may mean *any* or *none* of the following:

1. "I am bored."
2. "I feel drained."
3. "No one is meeting my needs."
4. "Do something to help me."
5. "I am annoyed."
6. "I feel useless."
7. "I feel hopeless about the future."
8. "Nothing gives me pleasure or satisfaction."
9. "There is nothing to look forward to."
10. "I am depressed."
11. "I am sick and tired of living."
12. "I wish I were dead."
13. "I am tired of you."

The nonverbal communication accompanying the patient's verbal comment may provide cues for interpreting the message. However, the nurse cannot automatically assume she understands what the patient is trying to convey. At the risk of sounding redundant, it must be reemphasized that the nurse's task is to elicit from the patient the meaning(s) he attributes to his comments or responses. Unless the nurse understands *what* the patient is trying to convey, appropriate intervention cannot occur. It is obvious that interventive measures will be quite different if the patient really means "I am bored" than if he means "I wish I were dead."

Failure to interpret a message correctly is caused, in part, by the nurse's lack of knowledge of the patient conveying the message, by her inability to identify nonverbal cues, and by her failure to verify the truthfulness of her interpretation with the patient.

Jumping to conclusions may affect the patient's recovery. For example, some nurses believe that because a patient is labeled "psychiatric" every remark made by him is either untrue or indicative of a deep underlying disturbance. Hence, if a patient complains of a headache the nurse assumes automatically that the headache is psychogenic in origin. A patient complaining of pain in the abdomen is accused of "putting on" in order to gain attention. That psychiatric patients can, and do, suffer from organic illnesses does not seem to occur to some psychiatric nurses. Strict attention *must* be paid to every physical complaint made by a patient. The complaint should be reported to the physician and recorded on the patient's chart. Psychiatric patients *can* and *do* die from ruptured appendixes, bleeding peptic ulcers, pneumonia, heart attacks and other illnesses.

The fact that a nurse may jump to the conclusion that a patient's behavior is indicative of psychological disturbance when this is by no means true is illustrated by the following two examples. A patient sitting in the day room suddenly laughed aloud. The nurse observing this behavior assumed the patient was hallucinating, but asked him what he was laughing about. The patient said he was thinking about a funny joke another patient told him and related the joke to the nurse, who laughed with him. At a private psychiatric hospital, a student was assigned to care for an elderly female patient. After her first interaction with the patient the student told the instructor: "Mrs. X. has delusions of grandeur." The instructor asked the student what led her to this conclusion. The student replied: "The patient says she is a millionairess." The instructor said: "Mrs. X. *is* a millionairess. She owns four shoe factories." These examples illustrate failure to interpret a message correctly. If the nurse in the first example had not verified with the patient the fact that he was laughing at a joke, she well may have reported the incident as evidence of nonexistent hallucinatory behavior. In the second example, the patient's comment was true; the nurse's interpretation was false. This point is stressed because it is important and has serious implications. Whether or not a patient is committed to a psychiatric facility may depend, in part, on the nurse's recorded observations of his behavior. It therefore behooves the nurse accurately to interpret the speech or nonverbal messages of her patients.

Failure to Focus on the Ill Person's Problems

The patient's problems are the focus of the one-to-one relationship. The nurse's failure to identify and help the patient cope with the here-and-now problems of living will inevitably result in communication breakdown or in a superficial meaningless type of vocal interchange. There may be many reasons for a nurse to fail to focus on the patient's problems. Ignorance may be a cause, i.e., the nurse may not possess the skill needed to identify problems or to assist patients to explore these in depth. Hence, patients are not given an opportunity to resolve the difficulties. Lack of experience, with consequent anxiety engendered during the one-to-one interaction, may be another causative factor. Beginners in psychiatric nursing often fail to see the patient's problems because they cannot "get themselves out of the way." The learner is focused on self rather than on the ill person. Usually this inability to focus on the patient is temporary and diminishes as the learner develops skill and confidence in her ability to assist the patient. As the learner becomes less concerned about self her energies are freed to focus on the other individual in the interaction. The beginner also may be hampered because she is too concerned with trying to remember what the patient said for the process record. Another barrier may be overconcern with "correct" communication techniques; instead of concentrating on the ill human being, the student concentrates on techniques.

Of all of the barriers mentioned, probably the most important is immaturity, i.e., the inability to get beyond and outside of self in order to focus on the human being who is the patient. Some nurses in psychiatry are never able to overcome this deficit. The ability to focus on another human being, to give of self to others without expecting gratitude in return, is vital to psychiatric nursing.

The nurse who is unable (or unwilling) to focus on the patient's problem may demonstrate this deficiency in a number of ways. Some of these are discussed below.

Failure to Remain on the Topic Under Discussion

It is the nurse's task to guide, direct and structure the interactive exchange in such a way that the ill person feels free to reveal himself and communicate on a meaningful level. In order to accomplish this goal, it is necessary that the nurse help the patient to verbalize and focus, in depth, on problem areas. If the patient is allowed to direct the interview, it often results in conversation on a superficial, social amenity level. Once the nurse permits such a pattern to be initiated by the patient, it is difficult subsequently to assist the patient to discuss problem areas. There is, instead, a tendency on the part of the patient or the nurse to shy away from them and change the subject when problem areas emerge. The inevitable results of failure to focus on the patient's problems are breakdown in communication and ineffectual nursing action.

A nurse may purposefully change the topic under discussion. Many times she may do so because she is uncomfortable talking about a particular topic; she reduces her anxiety level by changing the topic to a "safer" one. Probably one of the most common reasons why beginners in psychiatric nursing change the subject is because they do not know how to respond to a patient's comments, or believe that they must respond to everything said by the patient. In assisting learners in psychiatric nursing, it becomes apparent that some learners are seeking the "golden phrase"— the magic words a nurse can utter which will help the patient and will reduce the anxiety levels of both patient and nurse. Verbal reassurances, by the supervisor, that there are *no* magical methods or golden phrases are not always helpful. Sooner or later beginners must learn this basic truth for themselves.

There are other reasons why nurses change the subject. The nurse may be more interested in certain aspects of the patient's illness than in others. A patient, for example, may wish to discuss the difficulties he is experiencing in accepting the role of patient in the hospital. The nurse may be more interested in listening to a discussion of the hallucinations he experienced prior to his admission to the hospital, and may change the subject in order to elicit information about the hallucinations. Changing the subject may not be helpful or meaningful to the patient but it is *interesting* to the nurse. The nurse's need is met; the patient's need is not.

One may expect a patient to switch topics if a nurse's comments make him uncomfortable, but changing the subject is not necessarily the way to reduce the patient's anxiety. Often an acknowledgment by the nurse that the patient appears uncomfortable when talking about his problem(s) may suffice to reduce his anxiety level and open up channels of meaningful dialogue.

Talking Too Much

A patient's problems may never be identified, much less explored, if the nurse talks too much; the overly verbal nurse may never even give the ill person an opportunity to discuss his problems. Nurses may be encouraged by some patients to talk too much about themselves. The patient may do this because he wishes to see if the nurse is more interested in him than in self. Or the patient may use this maneuver as an avoidance technique, i.e., if he can keep the nurse talking about herself she is not apt to ask the patient to talk about himself. The patient may thus subtly encourage the nurse to carry the bulk of the conversation while he sits back and listens. Roles are reversed in the interaction, with the patient guiding and directing the interview.

A nurse who is afraid of silence may also talk too much. There are all kinds of silence, some of which may be necessary and helpful to the patient. Knowledge of the patient, and of self, is required in order to know the values of the different kinds of silence one encounters in a nurse-patient interaction.

Talking Too Little

Some nurses never focus on the ill person's problem because they do not talk *enough* during the interview. The nurse must encourage the patient to communicate, direct the flow of verbalization, and help the patient to focus. She must guide and direct the patient in order to accomplish these goals.

The nurse cannot say to a patient: "Tell me about yourself" and then sit back and expect the patient to give a complete account of his life and difficulties without her *active* support and assistance. The nurse is a participant in the interaction, not a spectator or an entomologist peering at a specimen to observe its reactions. The ill person requires her active assistance and support if he is to discuss painful life situations. The nurse who "sits by the sidelines" will not be told anything of significance by the human being who is the patient.

Responsiveness on the part of the nurse must be communicated to the patient. The nurse by her behavior conveys to the patient that she is listening, is interested in assisting him, and is an active participant in, as well as the director of, the interview. The nurse with a frozen, "deadpan" facial expression who never smiles or gives any indication that she has ever experienced an emotion, much less expressed one, is hardly a model of mental health to the ill human being. The nurse who seldom speaks, nods her head or engages in any nonverbal mannerisms often appears to patients not as a warm living human being but as an automaton. This is *not* to advocate that the nurse engage in emotive behavior or register every feeling or smile all of the time. It *is* suggested that she become aware of her verbal and nonverbal modes of behavior and carefully examine the effects of this behavior.

There are times during the nurse-patient interaction when the patient *needs* a response from the nurse. The mentally ill person who must interact with a silent nonresponsive nurse is indeed burdened. The nurse who does not talk enough blocks communication as effectively as does the overly verbal nurse. Talking too little, giving the patient too little structure and guidance, is probably more prevalent in the one-to-one interaction than is overtalkativeness on the part of the nurse.

Ineffective Reassurance

To explore the meaning of ineffective reassurance, it is first necessary to examine the concept *reassurance*. Reassurance is an unscientific concept with an assumed meaning. A concept with an assumed meaning is characterized by the fact that everyone "knows" what the term implies yet no one can define it. The term *reassurance* has not been operationally defined in the literature to the extent that one can observe the behaviors implied in the term.

Reassurance implies that assurance has been lost and hence reassurance is necessary. Assurance also is a concept with assumed meaning. It is probable that an individual who has been assured believes the statements made by the assurer and has confidence in his truthfulness and sincerity. A person who has been assured then presumably would experience encouragement, trust and confidence. Depending on the problem and the nature of the assurance, one can speculate that the assured individual would also experience hope.

Reassurance then is the act of assisting an individual to regain the lost state of assurance. In this text reassurance is defined nonoperationally as any behavior by which the nurse attempts to identify the problem and purposefully (with great sensitivity) attempts to diminish or allay the distress caused by the problem. The nurse cannot always assist the patient to solve the problem, since not all of life's problems are solvable; however, she does try to help him to develop the courage needed to cope with the difficulty. The outcome of reassurance is the restoration of a sense of assurance, especially a reexperiencing of hope.

Since each human being is unique, each act of reassurance has its own uniqueness. What is reassuring to one individual may not be to another. The knowledge that a nurse is technically expert and knows what to do in case of emergencies may be reassuring to some patients, but is not to others who cannot judge the expertise of a practitioner. It is probably the way in which the nurse ministers to him which conveys (or does not convey) reassurance to the human being who is the patient. The nurse who appears as a knowledgeable human being who cares and will do everything possible to assist the ill person is the type of individual most likely to demonstrate the behavior termed reassurance.

The reassuring nurse opens channels of communication. She is a sensitive individual with an astute sense of timing, i.e., she knows when to speak, what to say, when to say it, and when to be silent and use nonverbal means to convey caring. Such a nurse's behavior is *consistent*. In the area of reassurance it becomes apparent that the nurse who cares demonstrates this attitude by her behavior. Human beings are known to others by the behavior they display. Reassurance cannot be equated with the total of words spoken to a patient by a well-meaning nurse. If a nurse speaks with the tongue of angels and lacks the quality of caring she is as a machine. If the practitioner possesses all nursing knowledge and theory and lacks the ability to care, knowledge and theory are to no avail. Without the ability to care *for* and *about* another, it is not probable the nurse will assure, much less reassure, a fellow human being.

What is meant by ineffective reassurance? Reassurance is ineffective if it does not assist the individual to regain the state of lost assurance. A nurse may engage in ineffective reassurance through lack of knowledge and experience, anxiety, not knowing what to say or a desire to be liked and appreciated. Reassurance is ineffective when the patient either does not need to, or cannot, believe what the nurse is trying to convey. The nurse may, through lack of sensitivity and knowledge, attempt to reassure a patient when he is not ready to, or capable of, utilizing reassurance. A lack of necessary information may lead to ineffective reassurance, as shown in the following excerpt from a process record:

A patient who had been hospitalized for seven months asked: "Nurse, when am I going home?" The nurse, who did not know *when* the patient was to be discharged, replied: "Oh, I'm sure you won't be here much longer. After all, you've been here seven months already, haven't you?"

The nonreassuring statements listed below, included for purposes of emphasis and review, are probably familiar to most psychiatric nurses. They have achieved the status of platitudes, maxims, or at best nurse-isms. The ill individual who escapes exposure to at least one of these platitudes is indeed fortunate.

"All you need is a nice long rest."
"Get your mind off yourself."
"Get out and mingle with the other patients."
"Cheer up."
"You're not alone. Everyone has problems."
"You're not mentally ill, you are just a little nervous."
"There is nothing to be afraid of."
"You're a little upset today, aren't you?"
"Why don't you develop a hobby?"
"If you will cooperate we'll all get along fine together."

Many more nurse-isms could be added to this list. Although some of them may seem humorous they are not in the least bit funny to the recipient. They do not reassure and heal and may deepen the patient's sense of hopelessness when attempting to communicate with a nurse who does not, and cannot, understand—much less help.

Pep Talks

A nurse fails to focus on a patient's problems when engaged in giving pep talks and inspirational exhortations. Nurses who "mean well" may, in their desire to be helpful, subject ill persons to talks designed to inspire, encourage and motivate. Such pep talks usually consist of advice relative to the necessity of the ill person's helping himself before anyone else can help him. What the nurse has obviously forgotten is that if the ill person could help himself he would not need psychiatric assistance.

Some nurses, because they have had to cope with many problems unaided and have surmounted obstacles unassisted by others, may adhere to the "pull-yourself-up-by-your-own-bootstraps" school of thought and believe others should do likewise. What they fail to remember is that not every human being is fortunate enough to have "bootstraps" with which to pull himself up.

Patients with particular problems are usually subjected to the pep-talk approach. Individuals with drinking problems are quite apt to be selected as targets for such "helpful conversations." Ill persons suffering from depressions are also likely candidates for "cheery" pep talks. Pep talks are used by nurses who believe that patients will be cured if they develop *will power*. The purpose of the pep talk is to encourage the patient to "pull himself together," "make up his mind," etc. The ill person inundated with pep talk cannot focus on his problem; the nurse is too busy solving it for him and setting him "on the right track." Pep talks are not useful, meaningful or in any way helpful to ill persons. They block the ill human being from discussing problems as he perceives them. Being subjected to pep talks may increase a patient's sense of hopelessness, loneliness and despair.

Failure to Adapt Communication Techniques

The nurse's inability to adapt or change habitual ways of conversing with patients is another major cause of communication breakdown. Rigid adherence to *one* approach or set of communication techniques may block the interactive process. For example, a nurse who consistently uses the nondirective reflecting technique when communicating with a patient, and who does not, or cannot, change as the patient's condition merits it, may block him from proceeding to the higher level of relatedness. One of the major criticisms by patients subjected to the reflecting technique is that they "can never get a straight answer from the nurse." One patient stated: "You never say anything. You just repeat everything I say." This is not to single out one approach for critical comment. Any approach or technique can be adhered to so rigidly by the nurse that the patient reacts with anger and frustration. There are times when a patient asks a nurse a question and *needs* the information; he does not need to have the nurse reflect the statement or say: "Why do you ask?" This is *not* to imply nurses should answer any question a patient asks without reflecting. It *is* suggested that the nurse use discretion and judgment and provide the patient with the specific information he needs at the time he needs it.

Another problem related to failure to adapt communication techniques is that of the "overly goal-directed" nurse who is so determined to achieve the objectives of the interaction that she neglects the person for whom the objectives were designed. There is nothing sacred about objectives; they can and should be changed during the course of the interview if necessary. Further, some nurses in their desire to gain knowledge about an ill person engage in intensive premature probing. Such nurses forget that ill persons must be *ready* to reveal themselves. Premature probing of sensitive problem areas may block the communicative flow between nurse and patient.

Flexibility in approach, technique and methodology is essential in the practice of psychiatric nursing. Nurses are encouraged to test a variety of approaches, techniques and methods. Repetitive, stilted and inappropriate use of communication techniques is to be avoided. A communication technique is a tool. A tool is useful *only* when it achieves the purpose for which it was designed. When the tool does not fulfill this basic requirement it should be discarded and another tool used. It is suggested that nurses creatively devise and design communication techniques and approaches which will enable them to achieve the goals of the interaction, and that they share these approaches and techniques with their colleagues.

Chapter VI

THE SELECTION OF PATIENTS

Psychiatric nurse supervisors, head nurses, instructors or others may request, or assign, nurses to interact with particular patients in a one-to-one relationship. These assignments or requests are generally based on inferences made about the patient's behavior, i.e., the requester believes that the patient, or the nurse, will benefit as a result of the interaction. The reasons for selecting a particular patient for the one-to-one relationship then are to improve the patient's condition, to provide the nurse with a learning experience, or both.

Undergraduate nursing students are most frequently assigned to establish a one-to-one relationship with patients whom it is believed will show some signs of improvement in a relatively short period of time. The usual rationale given for this practice is that students "need to see the results of their labors and will become discouraged if they don't see patients improve." Many instructors and supervisors assign learners and practitioners to care only for those patients about whom the psychiatrist, head nurse, instructor or supervisor feels "therapeutically optimistic." These are young "first-admission" patients, patients diagnosed as "reactive depressive" or patients in the acute phase of a psychiatric illness. In the excluded category are patients with many readmissions to the psychiatric unit, individuals diagnosed as "sociopathic personality," patients receiving electric shock therapy, and all chronically ill psychiatric patients and patients with organic brain damage. Such selection practices are understandable if one accepts the premise that beginners become discouraged if "patients don't improve." The author does not accept this premise. To do so would be to stereotype *all* beginners. Learners, with assistance and guidance, *can* and *do* establish relationships with patients in the excluded categories. Much depends on the instructor's or supervisor's expectation of learners. Learners who are "taught" to gain satisfaction in nursing *only* from seeing patients recover will hardly gain satisfaction in observing the slower, but just as meaningful, progress of the chronically ill psychiatric patient.

In addition to being assigned to establish a relationship with a particular patient, nurses frequently select their own patients. There are few research findings reported in the literature as to reasons why nurses select particular patients. What are the determinants of this choice? It is believed some nurses will select patients on the basis of inferences made about the patient's behavior, i.e., the patient "looks lonely" or "looks depressed" or the nurse wishes to "help" the patient. It also speculated that some nurses choose particular patients with whom to work because the patient "looks safe" or "looks friendly"; translated, this means that the patient looks as if he will meet the nurse's needs by talking, responding and being generally cooperative.

Students frequently select as patients individuals within their own age group. Given a choice, young students will rarely, if ever, select an older patient with whom to establish a one-to-one relationship. There may be many reasons for this behavior, such as the identification with individuals within one's own age group, as well as an erroneous belief that older patients, i.e., individuals over thirty years of age, suffer from organic brain damage and cannot be helped. The latter rationalization is frequently supported by nursing instructors and supervisors who approve students' choices *because* younger patients *are* apt to be first admissions and will probably improve with or without the nurse's assistance.

The diagnosis of the patient is used as a determinant for selection by some nurses, who "feel" they can best establish relatedness with individuals with certain diagnostic labels. For example, some nurses believe they can more easily establish a one-to-one relationship with a schizophrenic patient than with a depressed individual. This may be true. However, the patient's diagnostic label is not as valid a guide to nursing intervention as is the patient's behavior. The "typical" schizophrenic or depressed patient is a myth. The human being does not readily fit into a neat category of diagnostic classification, and the patient's diagnostic label is not considered as a valid criterion for selection.

Another method of patient selection (or, rather, nurse selection) occurs when the patient chooses the nurse. For example, the nurse talks individually to all patients on a unit and tells them that one patient will be selected for the one-to-one relationship. The nurse states that she will return and announce to the group the name of the "chosen" patient. What usually happens here is that the most gregarious, talkative, aggressive or manipulative patient "gets selected." In this instance the patient really chooses the nurse. Such a situation forces patients to compete for the attention of the nurse, and those patients who cannot compete are never chosen.

One wonders what students learn as a result of these kinds of patient selections. An obvious, logical learning outcome would be the assumption that only certain types of psychiatric patients can be helped. The learner does not know other patients can be helped because she is not given an opportunity to work with these ill people. While one might deplore the outcomes of these kinds of patient selection, they are nevertheless frequently necessary since the nurse cannot establish a relationship with every patient in the agency or hospital.

PART I—CRITERIA FOR SELECTION OF PATIENTS

What should guide the nurse in selecting a patient? Five major factors must be considered: purpose, availability of the patient, clearances and permissions needed, willingness of the patient, and willingness of the nurse. Each of these will be discussed individually.

PURPOSE

What does the nurse wish to accomplish by interacting with a particular patient? Patients may be selected to fulfill a specific learning need of the nurse. For example, the nurse may not have had the opportunity to work with patients displaying particular behavior problems. She may have been unable to establish relatedness with a very withdrawn patient and may desire, under supervision, to develop this ability. She may have difficulty setting limits and may desire to work with a patient who "acts out." The reasons given by nurses for selecting certain patients with whom to work are valid; however, such reasons are by no means to be accepted at face value since unconscious factors also determine patient selection.

Another purpose of selection is to help the patient toward recovery or to improve or change the patient's behavior. The nurse may have identified a problem in relation to the patient—a nursing problem which requires a solution. For example, a patient refuses to eat and the nurse wishes to investigate this problem further. The nurse identifies the cause of the patient's refusal of food, develops hypotheses about the meaning of the patient's behavior, plans, structures and evaluates nursing intervention in relation to solving this particular problem. It is well to remember, however, that a practitioner may wish to solve nursing problems or change a patient's behavior for many reasons. The practitioner "likes the patient" and desires his recovery, or the patient may be perceived as a professional challenge, i.e., the ill person may be selected because the nurse wishes to assure self or others of her professional competence. Motives for patient selection are seldom clear-cut; neither are they always consciously determined. Like Pygmalion, the nurse may desire to mold or change the lives of other human beings. The desire for power over the lives of others cannot be rejected as a possible motive in nursing intervention. As Amiel wrote: "We must distrust our instinct of intervention, for the desire to make one's own will prevail is often disguised under the mask of solicitude."[1] It is recommended that practitioners try to become as cognizant as possible of their reasons for selecting particular patients yet realize that they may also be influenced by unconscious motivations.

AVAILABILITY OF THE PATIENT

Will the patient be available? In some agencies or institutions it is difficult to establish a one-to-one relationship with patients since practically every hour of the day is taken up by such activities as occupational therapy, recreational therapy, group therapy, etc. While it is not impossible to establish a one-to-one relationship with an ill person in such a highly structured setting, nevertheless it is *very* difficult. How long will the patient remain in the hospital? The answer to this question is, at best, an inference or a guess. It is important, however, for the nurse to have some idea as to how long the patient will be available, since the time factor may determine the nurse's objectives in working with the patient. This information may be obtained from the psychiatrist or some other resource person.

CLEARANCES AND PERMISSIONS NEEDED

The clearances and permissions needed to work with patients vary with each institution or agency. A salient question follows.

---

[1] Amiel, Henri-Frederic: The Journal Intime of Henri-Frederic Amiel. Trans. Mrs. Humphry Ward. The Macmillan Co., London, 1889.

Should the nurse obtain the psychiatrist's permission before selecting one of "his" patients with whom to interact? Another question must be asked. What is the nurse's reason for asking the psychiatrist's permission? The nurse may believe it is common courtesy to request permission to work with the patient. The nurse may also be operating on the assumption that the patient "belongs" more to the psychiatrist than he does to the nurse. The practitioner may request clearance or permission from the psychiatrist because she is not convinced that the one-to-one relationship is within the province of nursing and is afraid of usurping the authority of the psychiatrist. The nurse may request permission in order to collaborate more fully with the psychiatrist in assisting the patient to recover. It should be remembered that many psychiatrists have not had an opportunity to work with nurses in a peer relationship; neither do they possess an understanding of the functions or capabilities of prepared psychiatric nurse practitioners. For these reasons it is the author's opinion that the patient's psychiatrist should be asked if he has any objection to the nurse's establishing a one-to-one relationship with his patient. The nurse should also explain to the psychiatrist the purpose of the relationship. Such practices may be a learning experience for the psychiatrist.

At the risk of redundancy, an important point should be repeated. Except for the one dependent function of nursing, namely, the execution of legal medical orders, a nurse does not require the permission of a psychiatrist to practice nursing any more than a psychiatrist requires the permission from a nurse to practice medicine. Seldom will a psychiatrist refuse to permit a nurse to establish a one-to-one relationship with a patient *provided* the psychiatrist understands the nurse's purpose and intent. In some institutions it is common practice for psychiatrists, especially those undergoing residency training, to work intensively with one or more patients. The author has heard stories of nurses who were told they could not work with these patients because they might "dilute the transference." Actually a patient may be advised not to discuss his problems with anyone but the psychiatrist. Selecting such a patient for a one-to-one relationship creates problems for the ill person and the nurse.

In summary, it is recommended that the nurse consult the patient's psychiatrist before selecting patients for the one-to-one relationship. The purposes of this consultation are to identify possible barriers to establishing a relationship, to collaborate professionally with the psychiatrist and to inform the psychiatrist about the role and functions of the psychiatric nurse practitioner.

WILLINGNESS OF THE PATIENT

Should the ill person be given a choice as to whether or not he wishes to participate in the one-to-one relationship? There are different schools of thought on this question. One view is that the patient should be asked if he is willing to participate. Using this approach the nurse explains the purpose of the relationship to the patient and asks him if he is willing to participate. If the patient refuses the nurse tries to elicit the reason for his refusal. Upon confirmation of refusal the nurse then selects another patient and goes through the same request process. There are many advantages to this approach. The very act of being asked to participate in a relationship is helpful to some patients. It communicates to the patient that he is a responsible person—one who is free to decide. This approach also communicates to the patient that he is an equal partner in the relationship and that his cooperation is essential to achieve the desired goals. The major disadvantage of this approach is that some patients who could benefit from the relationship may be unable to decide whether or not to participate. The inability to decide responsibly is a symptom of illness in some patients. Ill persons may also refuse to participate for other reasons. Patients may be unable to conceptualize the role of the nurse (or their own role) in a relationship or may be suspicious of the nurse's motives in asking them to participate. Some patients refuse because they do not understand how "talking can help." Patients lacking insight into their conditions may refuse to participate because they believe there is nothing wrong with them; participation in a relationship would, to these patients, be an admission that something *is* wrong.

Another approach is to tell the patient he *is* to participate; he is not given a choice. The nurse introduces self, tells the patient the purpose of their meetings, and indicates when and where she will meet with him for the interactions. The nurse communicates to the patient that she is there to help him, whether or not he desires her assistance. Although some patients may become frightened or overwhelmed by this approach, the very structure of the approach and the fact that there is no choice may be helpful and comforting. A withdrawn, confused or depressed patient is not likely to be able to decide whether or not to participate in a one-to-one relationship. The nurse makes this decision for him. The nurse also communicates to the patient that she cares about him and that this caring is not conditioned by the fact that he is unable to make a decision about participating. One disadvantage of deciding for the patient is that the nurse assumes the entire responsibility for the relationship and thereby bears the burden of eliciting and maintaining the patient's cooperation throughout the interaction cycle.

WILLINGNESS OF THE NURSE

Should a nurse be given a choice as to whether or not she wishes to participate in a one-to-one relationship? Students in psychiatric nursing programs are seldom given this choice. Usually they are told to establish a one-to-one relationship with a patient and their grades in the course may well depend on the extent to which they become committed to the task of planning, structuring and evaluating nursing intervention. Should students be given a choice? It is probable that not all learners in psychiatric nursing are capable of enduring the anxiety involved in structuring a relationship. Some students may be unable to "get beyond themselves" and are incapable of becoming involved in the problems of others because of their own personal problems. What is the effect on the patient "cared for" by a nurse who is incapable of, or unwilling to, become involved? If a student is incapable of learning to structure a nurse-patient relationship, should other learning experiences be offered? Sooner or later the psychiatric nursing instructor will be confronted by this problem and must solve it. The solution depends on the instructor's beliefs about the essential skills needed by the practitioner in psychiatric nursing. If an instructor believes the ability to establish relationships with patients is the crux of psychiatric nursing, then the instructor will strive to assist the learner to develop this ability and to bear the anxiety involved in reaching out to others. While a very few students will not be assisted despite the instructor's efforts and will fail to achieve the objectives of the psychiatric nursing program, most students *can* and *do* establish relationships with patients.

Before interacting with a patient for the first time the nurse must make many decisions. Some of these decisions will be discussed in the section which follows.

PART II—PREREQUISITES TO THE FIRST INTERACTION

How much information about the ill person should the nurse have before the initial interaction? Should she read the patient's chart? If the nurse does not know the ill person should she ask staff nurses and others about the patient's behavior? What effect will information received by the nurse have on the subsequent interaction with the patient?

READING THE PATIENT'S CHART

Should the nurse read the patient's chart prior to interacting with him for the first time? There are different schools of thought in relation to this question. Some clinicians believe information on the patient's chart may bias the nurse. For example, there is a notation on the patient's chart which states: "The patient seems to be hallucinating." (N.B. This is an example of poor charting, since the ill person's behavior should be described and not categorized.) The nurse may develop a bias or a mind-set, i.e., she may "read into" the patient's behavior that which does not exist and interpret certain actions of the ill person as being confirmation of hallucinatory experience when such is not the case. One might argue that *if* the ill person *is* indeed hallucinating then the nurse needs this information to structure nursing intervention. This is not necessarily true because the nurse can, during an interaction with the patient, gain this knowledge. When interacting with the ill person the nurse observes the person's behavior, shares observations with him to check the validity of inferences, and then structures the necessary intervention.

Another school of thought maintains that it is necessary for the nurse to know as much about an ill person as possible before interacting for the first time. The nurse is urged to read the patient's chart and gather as much information as possible from such resource people as psychiatrists, staff nurses, attendants, etc. The proponents of this approach believe the more a nurse knows, i.e., the more items of information or facts possessed by the nurse, the easier it will be to establish a relationship with the patient. This may, or may not, be a correct assumption. Actually what one knows about an ill person, in terms of having items of information or "facts" about him, is not as important as what one does with this information. It *is*, however, necessary to understand the physician's plan of therapy. For example, the nurse should know if the ill person is receiving electric shock treatments or is taking psychopharmacological drugs. The ill person's behavior is changed and modified as a result of the therapies. Hence, it is recommended that all nurses understand the effects and side effects of these therapies in order to render safe, effective nursing care. The nurse who establishes a one-to-one relationship with an ill person may not have the direct responsibility for giving or assisting in these therapies; she *does*, however, need to know that the ill person is receiving them. It is relatively easy, in an interaction, to infer that an ill person is "withdrawn" or is "anxious" because of something the nurse did or said when actually the behavior of the individual is caused by the effects or side effects of the medication or treatment he is receiving.

It is the author's opinion that, aside from the plan of therapy, charts contain little information of value to the nurse in planning and establishing a one-to-one relationship. Some nurses will not agree with this statement. Reading the chart can become a ritual. Reading the chart before interacting with the ill person is also many times a delaying tactic or an antidote for the nurse's anxiety; in this case reading the chart may be of value to the nurse.

DATA COLLECTION

Data collection is inherent in the one-to-one relationship. The collection of data is the first step in the process of planning, interpreting and evaluating nursing care.

There are various ways to collect data. Notes may be taken during the interaction or written immediately following the interaction. Videotape recording of the interaction between nurse and patient is another method of data collection but is still in the experimental stage. Videotape recording in psychiatry is currently primarily used for the interaction between psychiatrist and patient. It is anticipated, however, that this medium will probably be widely used in the future to record and study nurse-patient interaction. Another method of data collection is tape recording the conversation between the nurse and the patient.

Variations of the process record are most frequently used for data collection. A process record is a written account of what transpired between nurse and patient. In the teaching-learning situation the process record is used to aid the learner in developing understanding of the dynamics of human behavior and skill in observing, recording and interpreting the meaning of behavior. Process recording as a means of data collection is discussed in detail in Chapter VII.

THE SETTING OF THE INTERACTION

Should the nurse select in advance the setting in which the interactions will take place? If so, what should guide the nurse in selecting a setting? Purpose is a major determinant. What does the nurse wish to accomplish during the interactions? To what extent will the setting influence goal attainment?

Some nurses select a setting on the basis of personal preference or the desire for privacy. Some nurses, for example, prefer to meet with the patient in a private office or room. The meeting place may be on the nursing unit, if the patient is hospitalized, or elsewhere in the hospital. The advantages of interacting with a patient in a private place are obvious. There is less distraction and interruption by other patients on the unit. The private room emphasizes the confidential quality of the interaction. These advantages, however, are often offset by some disadvantages. The patient may not understand why the interactions are held in a private place. That is, the patient may believe the nurse is interested in him personally, i.e., she sees him as a love or sex object. One must remember that the one-to-one relationship is still new and most patients are not familiar with the nurse in this role. Deviations from accustomed role behavior may create anxiety in certain patients. Careful interpretation (and reinterpretation) to the patient of one's role as nurse in the one-to-one relationship is essential. Personnel on the unit must also be oriented as to the purposes of the interaction. This is especially true in those psychiatric settings where the one-to-one relationship is *not* practiced by most health workers. Personnel are as apt to misinterpret the nurse's role as are the patients. Some personnel may believe the nurse is there to "check up" on them—or on the quality of care given—the intent being to report to the director of nursing service all that the nurse observes. Meeting the patient in a private office may, under some circumstances, promulgate this belief.

A nurse should not assume that personnel in an agency understand the nature of the one-to-one relationship unless she interprets (and reinterprets) her role to them. This point is being stressed because personnel *can* and *do* undermine or sabotage the relationship. The less personnel know about the nature of the one-to-one relationship the more apt are their interpretations to be unrealistic. Another factor needs to be considered. Personnel may understand but *disapprove* of the one-to-one relationship as being valueless and time-consuming. The nurse is not bound to change the opinions of others regarding the relationship; she *is* obligated to interpret to others what it is she wishes to accomplish in the relationship.

Instead of in a private room, some nurses prefer to talk with the patient in the day room or other setting, the purpose being to observe the patient's behavior in a group situation, i.e., to observe and develop inferences about the patient's ability to communicate and relate to others in the setting. The nurse attempts to structure a one-to-one relationship within the group setting.

The author prefers meeting with patients in a corner of the day room or community room. This setting provides the patient with a reasonable amount of privacy, is not subject to distortion by the patient, and provides the nurse with an opportunity to observe and develop inferences regarding the patient's habitual mode of relating with others. There are usually, in this kind of setting, interruptions by other patients. The interruptions by patients can be reduced to a minimum if the nurse explains to the interrupting patients her purpose on the unit, namely, to interact with a particular patient. Frequently the nurse does not have to cope with this problem since the selected patient will often tell interrupting patients that "the nurse is here to talk with me." The "grapevine" soon spreads the word.

The settings thus far described have advantages and disadvantages. The nurse conceptualizes in advance what it is she wishes to accomplish and then selects the appropriate setting.

THE NURSE'S WEARING APPAREL

Many nurses working in psychiatric settings wear street clothes instead of the traditional uniform. This trend although not widespread is becoming increasingly popular. What are the advantages and disadvantages of wearing the various types of apparel? Some nurses believe that wearing uniforms identifies them as nurse and that easy role identification may be helpful and comforting, especially to a confused or disoriented mentally ill patient. Nurses wearing the traditional uniform are not apt to be misidentified as physicians or social workers. Other nurses believe that when misidentification *does* occur it can be resolved by explanation and is not a major problem. Nurses, of course, may wear the traditional garb for reasons such as hospital regulations. A less obvious reason why some nurses prefer to wear uniforms is that they do not "feel like a nurse" out of uniform. Some believe "being out of uniform" in the work setting is somehow unprofessional and that they more readily act as professional people in uniform.

Other psychiatric nurses prefer street clothes on the basis that wearing a uniform emphasizes the traditional role of the nurse and perpetuates distance in the nurse-patient relationship. Wearing a lab coat over street clothes seems to be a compromise between either extreme. It is the author's opinion that—provided the nurse identifies herself, interprets her role to the patient, and explains the purposes of the interactions—it does not matter whether she wears street clothes, a lab coat over street clothes or the nurse's uniform.

If the nurse *does* wear street clothes it is recommended that her dress be tasteful, attractive and appropriate for the occasion. Extremes in fashion, clothing and hairdress are to be avoided. It is also recommended that nurses avoid wearing jangling bracelets or other distracting types of jewelry. Needless to say, very short skirts or low-cut blouses should not be worn.

Chapter VII

PROCESS RECORDING

After selecting a patient for participation in a one-to-one relationship, the nurse chooses a systematic method of collecting data regarding the interaction in order to plan, structure and evaluate nursing intervention. The process record, or variations thereof, is probably the most frequently used form of data collection.

Process recording is a tool used to accomplish a task. Even the best-designed tool must be used by an individual who understands the purpose for which it was designed and who possesses, or is learning, the skill required to use the tool effectively. A process record, although written by one individual, is shared with at least one other person, usually the psychiatric nurse supervisor. Process recording is time-consuming both for the individual who writes the record and for the person whose task it is to assist the writer to develop the skills required to use the tool effectively for the benefit of the patient. Therefore, it is recommended that instructors or supervisors not expect students or practitioners to write process records unless they (the instructors and supervisors) are willing to invest the time, energy and effort required to assist the learner to develop an understanding of the purpose of process recording. Another device should be selected if this condition is not met. It is also recommended that instructors or supervisors who have not had the opportunity to write and analyze process records do so (under supervision) before they expect nurses under their direction and supervision to use this difficult tool.

PART I—DEFINITION OF THE TERM PROCESS RECORDING

Process recording is a systematic method of collecting data prior to interpreting, analyzing and synthesizing the data obtained. A process record is a written account of what transpired before, during and following a nurse-patient interaction.

PURPOSES OF PROCESS RECORDING

The ultimate purpose of process recording is to improve the quality of nursing care. Writing and analyzing process records are experiences which assist the nurse to plan, structure and evaluate nursing intervention. Process recording can also help nurses become increasingly cognizant of ways to improve clinical practice.

When correctly used, process recording assists the nurse (student or practitioner) to plan, structure and evaluate nursing action on a *conscious,* rather than on an *intuitive,* level. It is also a means by which the nurse gains competency in the collection, interpretation, and synthesis of raw data under the supervision of an instructor or psychiatric nurse supervisor. Process recording also helps practitioners consciously to apply theory to practice. There are other outcomes which result from the experience of writing and analyzing process records. The writer begins to develop an increased awareness of the verbal and nonverbal communication patterns she habitually uses and the effect of these patterns on others. The writer also increasingly develops the ability to identify her thoughts and feelings in relation to self and others. The items used as a guide in writing process records should assist the practitioner to increase observational skills by helping her to focus attention and awareness. Another important outcome of process recording is that learners increase their ability to identify nursing problems and gain some degree of skill in solving these.

Process recording is a means to an end, and not an end within itself. Unless the purposes of such recording are kept in mind by the learner, teacher and supervisor, the records can easily become exercises in penmanship devoid of value as learning experiences.

USE OF PROCESS RECORDINGS

Process records are written by students in psychiatric nursing courses as well as by practitioners and clinical specialists. In the psychiatric nursing program the process records provide the instructor with an opportunity to assist the learner to develop skill in observing, in communicating and in gaining the ability to apply theories and concepts to nursing situations.

Whether written by students, practitioners, or clinical specialists, the content in the record is discussed in private conference with the instructor (or supervisor) or during planned group reconstruction sessions.

PART II—THE MAJOR STEPS IN PROCESS RECORDING

Process recording consists of five major steps or phases: collection of raw data, interpretation, application of concepts to the data, analysis and synthesis. These steps may also be considered prerequisite abilities to be developed by the practitioner in order to plan, structure and evaluate nursing action. Each step or phase will be discussed.

COLLECTION OF RAW DATA

Raw data include the verbal and nonverbal communication of both nurse and patient during the interaction. Raw data are perceptual data and include all data received via the sense organs *prior* to interpretation of the meaning of the data. Raw data thus do not include assumptions, opinions, suppositions, hypotheses or feelings. Raw data are useless without interpretation. Therefore, the next step is the interpretation of the raw data collected.

INTERPRETATION

Collection of data, although problematic for some learners, is not as difficult as is interpretation of the data. To interpret, the practitioner must possess the ability to explain that which is not explicit, to comprehend the probable meaning(s) of data, and to recognize relevance to nursing action. The practitioner may begin the process of interpretation while engaged in data collection; usually, however, in-depth interpretation follows the nurse-patient interaction.

Interpretation takes place on various levels, as has been discussed in Chapter II, Part II. For purposes of review, these levels of interpretation are repeated.

Assumption level—automatically taking something for granted without examining the data.

Opinion level—unvalidated beliefs which are highly subjective and may be true or false.

Supposition level—interpretations which are tentative and open to question and scrutiny.

Hypothesis level—a proposition capable of validation.

Ideally, the professional nurse practitioner operates primarily on the supposition or hypothesis levels of interpretation. The ability to interpret data on an hypothesis level presupposes a knowledge of the concepts and principles which underlie nursing practice. It also presupposes the ability not to "go beyond the data" in developing interpretations or "read into the data" ideas, thoughts, and feelings which exist only in the mind of the interpreter. To develop interpretations on the hypothesis level, the nurse consciously strives to apply concepts and principles to the data. She must be able to use principles and concepts to explain and predict behavior in nursing situations and to identify principles and concepts which underlie or explain nursing intervention.

APPLICATION OF CONCEPTS

In order to apply concepts the practitioner must first possess an understanding of the body of knowledge underlying nursing practice, i.e., the principles and concepts used to explain and predict behavior in nursing situations. One cannot apply that which is not possessed. However, no one individual possesses an understanding of *all* of the concepts applicable in nursing situations. What *is* required is the humility to realize what one does not know and the willingness to undertake the unending task of continuously adding to one's knowledge. Willingness to learn, in and of itself, is insufficient; one must be aware of the sources of information, whether these sources be books, periodicals, research studies or people. It cannot be overemphasized that each nurse needs to know and to be able to use reference sources when needed. (See Appendix II for important reference sources in psychiatric nursing.)

What concepts are applied in nursing situations? There is no *one* list of concepts each nurse should know in order to practice psychiatric nursing. Various nurse-authors have suggested some; however, there is little, if any, general agreement as to which concepts should be learned, who should teach them or when and how these concepts should be taught. Certainly principles from the natural, physical, biological, medical, nursing and behavioral sciences may be used to explain and predict behavior in nursing situations.

What is the value of knowledge of concepts? Concepts not only explain and predict behavior but may also indicate the nursing intervention required. For example, it may be hypothesized that an angry individual exhibiting aggressive behavior may be frustrated in achieving a goal. If a nurse understands the relationship between blocking of a goal and the subsequent anger and aggression which may follow, it may be possible for her to elicit from the patient the cause of his anger, to identify the goal which is blocked, to assist the patient to cope with his feelings of anger in a socially acceptable manner, to substitute for the blocked goal another more readily attainable one, or to intervene in some other appropriate manner. An understanding of the concept of frustration is important, then, in determining appropriate nursing intervention. It is obvious that the more knowledge the nurse brings to the nurse-patient situation the more likely it is that she will be able to institute helpful nursing action. Application of concepts may take place as the nurse collects and interprets data or, in greater depth, following the nurse-patient interaction.

ANALYSIS

After collection, interpretation and application of concepts to the data the nurse begins to analyze. *Analysis means a detailed critical assessment of the nature and significance of the data.* Analysis requires a separation of the data into component parts in order to study and critically scrutinize the relationship of the parts to the whole. Analysis involves examination of parts of the data as compared to the whole. Analysis of data is discussed in greater detail in Part IV of this chapter.

SYNTHESIS

Synthesis refers to the process of putting analyzed data together in order to form a unitary whole. Following the analytic process the nurse puts the parts of the data back into a whole and examines the results of the analysis. It is through the process of synthesis that the nurse, using the analyzed data, is enabled to plan for future nurse-patient interactions. Synthesis is discussed in greater detail in Part IV of this chapter.

The above are the five major steps of process recording. In Part III the items to be included in the process record are discussed.

PART III—GUIDE TO DATA COLLECTION

The nurse has certain professional responsibilities when writing process records. Completed records contain privileged information and, as such, are to be carefully guarded. Process records should be read only by the appropriately designated individuals. As an additional safeguard, it is recommended that the patient's name not be used in the body of the process record; initials (not those of the patient) should be substituted for the name.

The patient, as a human being, has a right to know with whom the nurse is sharing information about his life. It is recommended that the nurse, during her first interaction with the patient, inform him that what is said during the interaction will be shared with others, for example the instructor, supervisor or classmates.

FORMAT

The format for writing process records varies according to the individual preferences of practitioners, supervisors or instructors. A simple descriptive narrative form may be used. In this instance a guide to writing process records is needed to assist the nurse to focus on important aspects to be included in the record. A three-column format may also be used. This includes a column for conversation between nurse and patient, a column for the practitioner's interpretation and analysis of the data (including intervention), and a column for the instructor's or supervisor's comments. A four-column format contains, in addition to the three columns described above, a column for identification of the concepts which help to explain the patient's behavior or the nurse's intervention.

In this text the descriptive narrative form is discussed in detail. The narrative form has advantages provided the practitioner uses a guide when writing the record. One major advantage is that it assists the practitioner in organizing and synthesizing data and in developing increased ability to communicate clearly and concisely what transpired during the nurse-patient interaction. A condensed version, or short form, of a narrative process record is included at the end of this chapter.

Individual preference determines whether process records are written in pencil or ink. It is easier for the instructor or supervisor to read records written with a ball-point pen. Records may be written on loose-leaf paper or in notebooks. An advantage of using a thick notebook for all process records is that notebooks are not as readily misplaced as loose-leaf paper. If, however, the instructor or supervisor has many process records to take home and read, then records written on loose-leaf paper are preferred because of weight.

ITEMS TO BE INCLUDED IN THE PROCESS RECORD

What types of information should be included in the process record? Again, purpose is the major determinant. As stated previously, a process record is not an end within itself but only a means to an end. Since the data are to be used to plan, structure and evaluate nursing intervention, it follows that the kinds of data collected must assist the nurse in achieving these purposes. If she knows beforehand what types of information to collect, the nurse is able to focus on salient aspects of the interaction.

Introductory Material

The date and time of the interaction should be recorded. Whether the interaction is the first, second, third, etc., should be stated. When recording the initial interaction the nurse should state whether the patient was assigned or selected. If the nurse selected the patient, reasons should be given for the choice. Items to be included in the process record should be numbered. When writing the record, the nurse writes the number of the item to which she is referring on the guide instead of writing a complete statement of the item.

Background Information

If the nurse reads the patient's chart prior to interacting with him, the following background information is obtained: age, sex, color, religion, admission date (if hospitalized), previous admissions to hospital or clinic, educational background, job status, marital status, chief complaint (upon admission to hospital or clinic), tentative diagnosis, physical status, mental status, predisposing and precipitating causes of illness (if known), presenting symptoms and behavior and general plan of therapy (includes somatic, social and psychological therapies prescribed by the physician). It is important for the nurse to understand the effects and side effects of specific somatic therapies.

Beginners in psychiatric nursing should resort to the literature to gain an understanding of the dynamics of the development of the patient's illness and of the rationale underlying the somatic and psychological therapies prescribed for the patient.

Background information can be secured from the patient's chart or from resource persons in the clinical area. The patient therefore should not be "pumped" for information nor should the nurse engage in probing to uncover this information. If the nurse does not read the patient's chart prior to interacting with him, it is suggested that she ascertain the kinds of somatic therapies the patient is receiving, as these will affect the patient's behavior.

There are values in obtaining background information prior to interacting with a patient. For example, a nurse is to interact with individuals from the lowest socioeconomic category or with individuals belonging to a particular ethnic minority group. The nurse may know little or nothing about the mores, customs or life problems of such individuals. She therefore has recourse to the literature and to research findings to begin to understand (even if in a vicarious way) the problems likely to be faced by her patients. There is an obvious danger in this approach; this is the tendency to assume, on the basis of research findings, that *all* poor persons are alike or all black people, Jewish people, etc., are alike. Similarities exist, but so do individual differences.

Thoughts and Feelings of The Nurse Prior to Interacting

The nurse needs to become aware of her thoughts and feelings prior to interacting with a patient to assess the effect of these thoughts and feelings on the nurse-patient interaction.

The term *thoughts and feelings prior to interacting* refers to the nurse's ideational and affective content before the interaction. The term *thought* refers to any mental content (i.e., ideas or association of ideas) of which the nurse is aware at the time of her introspection. In this work a *feeling* is considered as having two aspects: a psychological or emotional component, and the somatic equivalent to the emotional component. For example, the experience of anxiety affects one emotionally and physically. Because of the psychological component, the nurse tries to ascertain the effect of anxiety on her attention span, on perception, on her ability to remember, etc. The somatic aspect, depending on the degree of anxiety, includes the effect of anxiety on heart rate, respiration, on various body systems such as the gastrointestinal tract, etc. It is usually easier to identify the somatic component of a feeling than the psychological or emotional component.

Thoughts are generally more easily identified than are feelings. Nurses tend to have a great deal of difficulty in identifying their feelings unless these feelings are readily discernible or are of some degree of extremity. That is, the nurse realizes when she is *very* angry or *very* sad, etc. Generally, students in nursing need to learn *consciously* to identify their feelings by focusing on this particular area.

Beginners in psychiatric nursing have a tendency to give thoughts about their feelings while avoiding identification of feelings per se. There may be many reasons for this. The student may not understand the nature of a feeling, i.e., what it is he is supposed to identify, or may be unwilling to share his feelings with peers or authority figures for fear of censure or criticism. A more common cause of inability to identify feelings is the lack of practice. Through the long years of the socialization process a child may be repeatedly admonished by his parents to deny the validity of his feelings. The result is that the individual may not be able, eventually, to identify a feeling state. A parent may tell a child: "You shouldn't be angry at your sister," or "You shouldn't feel bad because I have to punish you," etc. In school children are frequently subjected to a similar education in denial of the validity of their feelings. It is therefore necessary for most individuals in our society to relearn to identify their feelings by consciously focusing on this particular area. It is only by self-observation and conscious effort that some degree of skill can be developed.

Objectives in Interacting

Before interacting with a patient, the nurse conceptualizes what she wishes to accomplish during the interaction. As an actor rehearses before a performance, so does the nurse focus attention on the tasks which lie ahead. It is recommended that practitioners identify in writing the objectives for each nurse-patient interaction and determine the methods to be used in achieving these objectives.

DEFINITION OF THE TERM OBJECTIVES. *Objectives are statements of goals to be achieved during the nurse-patient interaction.* Objectives specify the particular changes in behavior which are desired and give structure to the nurse-patient interaction. They are not permanent, unchangeable goals and should not be considered as such; objectives may have to be changed, modified or discarded during the nurse-patient interaction. Construction of objectives assists practitioners to focus attention, identify nursing problems, and set up priorities in relation to nursing practice. Objectives assist the practitioner to evaluate the extent to which she has been successful in achieving goals.

CONSTRUCTION OF OBJECTIVES. Objectives have two major aspects: a behavior and an area of life in which the behavior operates. In the objective "knowledge of the patient's anxiety level," "knowledge" is the behavior and "the patient's anxiety level" is the area of life in which the behavior operates. It is recommended that practitioners develop an understanding of the commonly accepted definitions of such behaviors as knowledge, understanding, appreciation, ability and skill.

CATEGORIES OF OBJECTIVES. Objectives may be divided into two major categories. The first consists of general (more-or-less unchanging) aims in working with patients and the second of goals specifically designed for an individual patient. For example, "knowledge of the patient's anxiety level" may be a general goal in working with any patient, while some specific goals might be "knowledge of reasons why the patient will not eat" or "knowledge of reasons why the patient has difficulty in sleeping," etc. Specific goals are changed when the particular problem is solved or the patient's need has been met.

STATING OBJECTIVES. Objectives may be stated in terms of desired changes in the patient's behavior, the nurse's behavior, or a combination thereof. However, objectives should be stated in such a way that the person who is to achieve the goal is clearly identified. For example, in the objective "ability to identify factors which increase anxiety" it is not clear who is to achieve the goal—the patient or the nurse. A prefacing statement, "objectives for the nurse" or "objectives for the patient," usually will suffice.

VALIDATING OBJECTIVES. A nurse should be able to explain the significance of objectives selected for an interaction. Some questions the nurse might answer are: Why are the goals important? What is the theoretical rationale underlying the selection of these goals? What outcomes are anticipated if the objectives are attained?

METHODS OF ACHIEVING OBJECTIVES. It is recommended that nurses conceptualize in advance the methods to be used in achieving objectives. For example, if an objective is "knowledge of the patient's anxiety level" the method(s) the nurse will use to achieve this particular objective should be stated.

In summary, objectives are meaningful guides in structuring nurse-patient interactions. They must be *more* than words written to please teachers or supervisors. Objectives should be attainable and realistic, and should be related to the needs of the patient, the nurse, or both. Objectives should be stated in such a way that the extent to which a behavioral change is occurring can be readily evaluated by means of various devices or by validated observation. It is helpful, when writing objectives, to ask oneself: Why is this objective or goal important? (validation), How will I achieve this objective? (method), and What are my plans for measuring the extent to which this goal has been achieved? (evaluation).

Activities on the Nursing Unit

In this section the nurse briefly describes the activities taking place on the nursing unit immediately prior to her interaction with the patient. What are the personnel doing? How many and what level of personnel are on the unit (or in the clinic)? What are the patients doing?

It is necessary that the nurse develop the habit of precise observation. An example of poor observation is this excerpt from a process record: "I saw three or four nurses in the nursing station." There were *either* three *or* four nurses in the station. How many nurses were actually present? One might well ask the observer on what basis she knows the individuals were nurses. Did the observer validate her impression, or did she *assume* the individuals were nurses? If the observer maintains that the individuals are nurses, one might then question whether they are professional or practical nurses.

It may seem picayune to focus on such minute points but precision in observation begins with scrupulous attention to detail. *It is also recommended that psychiatric nurses never assume anything unless they validate their assumptions.*

Physical Description of the Setting

The nurse writes a brief description of the setting in which she found the patient, and states whether the patient was alone or in a group. If the nurse interacts with a patient in his room, a brief description of the room and its contents is included. If the patient is in bed, the nurse gives a description of the condition of the bed linens and describes the articles on the bedside table. She notes the names of books or magazines, pictures, get-well cards or any other items on the table. If the nurse interacts with the patient in the day room or other area, a brief description of this setting is included.

The description of the setting in which the nurse interacts with the patient serves as one basis for evaluating the nurse's ability to observe and develop valid interpretations. Regardless of her educational level or experience background, it cannot be assumed that any nurse is a skilled observer.

Beginners in psychiatric nursing often require assistance in separating perceptions from thoughts. Note for example this excerpt from a process record: "The patient was seated on an old beat-up sofa in the day room." The terms "old" and "beat-up" are not percepts. They are conclusions based on perceptual data. These qualities are inferred from certain observations—faded slip covers, scratched paint, torn upholstery, etc. Another example of confusing sense data with interpretations or conclusions follows: "When I saw the patient she had a letter in her hand and said she was going to mail it." The nurse did not *see* a letter; she saw a patient holding an envelope in her hand.

The ability to separate perceptual input, i.e., what is seen, heard or taken in through the senses, from one's conclusions, thoughts or feelings about the data is essential to develop clarity in thinking. The value of differentiating between percepts and conclusions about the percepts is that they can be shared with others in order to seek validation. As a result, inferences or conclusions can be altered or changed if necessary. Unidentified or unshared inferences can be neither shared nor consensually validated.

Description of the Patient

A physical description of the patient is included in the first process record written. This should include such items as: approximate weight and height, color of eyes and hair, the clothing (including footwear) the person is wearing, whether or not the patient wears jewelry, eye glasses, a hearing aid, false teeth or any other prosthesis. More specific items of observation include: scars, lesions or bruises (note particularly the neck and wrist areas), the condition of the legs and feet (observe for signs of circulatory stasis or edema), and the color of the sclera of the eyes. Some tranquilizers cause an obstructive type of hepatitis resulting in jaundice, which may first be discernible in changes in the color of the sclera. One should also note the complexion of the patient. Observation of discoloration or subtle skin changes is important because some patients receiving chlorpromazine may develop a bluish or slate gray tinge on exposed skin areas. Facial expression and characteristic gait and posture should also be observed. In and of themselves, some of these items of information may seem insignificant but taken as a whole they can be helpful in developing inferences useful in planning patient care. At the risk of sounding redundant, it must be emphasized that inferences or conclusions based on perceptual data should be validated with others.

It is sometimes helpful to ask nurses to "be judgmental." The practitioner is asked to categorize the patient as if she were describing him to someone else. Would she categorize him as handsome, ugly, repulsive? Insight into the manner in which the nurse perceives the patient may be secured in this manner.

Interaction Between Nurse and Patient

This portion of the process record includes all communication (whether verbal or nonverbal) which takes place between nurse and patient. It also includes the thoughts and feelings of the nurse and her inferences (i.e., assumptions, opinions, suppositions or hypotheses) as to the meaning of the patient's behavior. A notation should be made, by the nurse, as to whether or not the inference has been shared and validated with the patient or with others.

It is also in this portion of the process record that the nurse includes behavioral concepts applicable to the specific nurse-patient interaction.

In addition to recording the conversation, it is recommended that the nurse record periods of silence and their duration. If possible, the silent period should be timed.

During the nurse-patient interaction the nurse becomes increasingly aware of any communication difficulties and of the major and recurring themes of the patient's conversation. Areas of conversation the patient does not wish to pursue, as well as those discussed at length, are noted. The nurse develops inferences regarding the patient's level of anxiety and notes when, and under what circumstances, the anxiety level tends to increase or decrease.

THE PROBLEM OF FORGETTING. A certain amount of data will be forgotten unless the nurse writes verbatim notes while talking with the patient. There is, of course, no guarantee that in so doing she will not forget, disregard or distort the data. Research is greatly needed in this area.

If a nurse does not wish to write verbatim notes while conversing with the patient, are there some steps that can be taken which will enable her to recall the conversation readily? To answer this question it is first necessary to consider the causes of forgetting in the nurse-patient interview. Inability to remember what transpired in the interaction may be due to many factors. Anxiety is a major cause. A mild degree of anxiety is helpful in that it enables the nurse to focus her attention. Too much anxiety, however, decreases her ability to receive perceptual data and to organize these meaningfully. Anxiety may be due to preoccupation with one's personal problems, to fear of the patient, to fear of "failure" in the nurse-patient interaction, or to fear that one may not remember the data and hence will have difficulty writing the process record. Another fear in relation to writing a process record is that of exposing one's vulnerabilities to the critical analysis of another person. The desire to protect oneself is strong; forgetting may be a defense against revealing one's thoughts and feelings to another person. Forgetting may be caused by the nurse's lack of commitment to the arduous task of analyzing and synthesizing so essential to planning, structuring and evaluating nursing intervention, or by lack of practice in focusing her attention. (The ability to focus attention is acquired *only* through practice.) To reduce the normal curve of forgetting it is recommended that the nurse begin writing the process record immediately following the nurse-patient interaction.

Forgetting as discussed thus far has been considered as an unconscious process and hence not intentional or premeditated. It differs from the next problem to be considered, that of skewing the data.

THE PROBLEM OF SKEWING THE DATA. Skewing the data is probably a more common problem than is forgetting. A certain amount of distorting or skewing of data is to be expected. It is usually unconsciously motivated and the reporter is not aware of it. Some data distortion, however, is on a conscious level. A practitioner who skews data *consciously* and *intentionally* does so by distorting or omitting various portions of the nurse-patient interview. She records statements never made (by self or patient) or reports nursing actions never taken.

How does one know, with any degree of certainty, that a nurse is consciously falsifying a process record? Aside from an admission by the nurse it is difficult, if not impossible (unless the interview is videotaped), to obtain concrete evidence of falsification. There are indications, however, which may lead one to suspect skewing has occurred. For example, the statements made by the nurse to the patient tend to be "too perfect," "too pat," or to follow exactly the examples of "what to say to patients" as described in well-known textbooks or articles. During group reconstruction, or in conference with the supervisor, the nurse usually does not "remember" what she said to the patient without constant recourse to the process record. She is usually unable to give the underlying theoretical rationale for statements made or action taken. If the nurse is asked to report the interview in her "own words" (without the written process record) marked discrepancies between the spoken and written accounts can usually be noted. All of these indications of skewing data, however, may be explained on some basis other than deliberate falsification. The practitioner should be given the benefit of the doubt, even if the supervisor suspects she is falsifying. Suspicion is not evidence, and unless the supervisor possesses concrete evidence the practitioner cannot be accused of lying. Rash judgment on the part of the supervisor is to be avoided. There is too much at stake, namely, the damaging of the practitioner's professional and personal reputation.

Why would any nurse deliberately falsify, distort or omit portions of a nurse-patient interview? Some individuals undoubtedly are immature or possess a lax conscience, but such labeling does not help. The basic cause of deliberate falsification is probably fear of the consequences of one's "mistakes." The nurse may have an inordinate fear of failure or of revealing her inadequacies to others. A nurse whose parents have placed undue emphasis on the pursuit of perfection may feel that mistakes are not permitted. Hence she strives never to make a mistake or, if a mistake is made, to cover it up so no one discovers her imperfections. An individual may fear competition with peers and believe that by comparison she does not know as much or is not "as good" as another practitioner. Students in psychiatric nursing may not reveal mistakes because they are more concerned about making good grades than in learning what they need to know to care for ill persons. There are undoubtedly other idiosyncratic reasons for deliberate falsification of data than those mentioned above.

What can be done in the event the instructor or supervisor suspects that a nurse is consciously falsifying information on a process record? The instructor (or supervisor) cannot ignore the situation by pretending it *cannot* and therefore *does not* exist. The possibility must be admitted and steps taken to remedy the situation. The instructor (or supervisor) has a responsibility to the practitioner as well as to the patient being "cared for" by the nurse in question. The instructor or supervisor examines the extent to which she may be responsible for the nurse's actions. Is too much expected too soon of the student or practitioner? Is the practitioner permitted to make mistakes or does the supervisor expect infallibility? Does the supervisor provide the kind of atmosphere which enable the nurse to admit mistakes and seek guidance?

There are no clear-cut recipes or easy methods for assisting nurses who falsify information on process records. One hopes that when the nurse becomes comfortable and less threatened by admitting errors eventually she will be able to relinquish such behavior. There are unfortunately no guarantees that this will be an inevitable result. Those who deliberately falsify information or data may harm the human being who is the patient because they cannot learn how to care for, or about, others. Concerned only with self-protection, the practitioner cannot help and may actually hinder the recovery of the ill human being. Further, the individual who engages in such practices slowly corrodes and eventually destroys her own sense of integrity.

Following an account of the interaction between nurse and patient, the thoughts and feelings of the nurse following the interaction are next to be recorded on the process record.

Thoughts and Feelings of the Nurse Following the Interaction

In this section of the process record the nurse examines her thoughts and feelings immediately following the nurse-patient interview. Does she experience a sense of relief that the interview is over? Is sadness or indifference experienced? To what does she attribute these thoughts and feelings? What is the significance of these thoughts and feelings?

It is suggested that the nurse attempt to answer the questions: To what extent did your thoughts and feelings prior to interacting with the patient affect the interaction? In what way? The purpose of including this information is to assist the learner to develop increased awareness of her behavior and to assess its probable effect on others. It is helpful to reflect whether or not the patient reminds the nurse of anyone from her past. If so, the nurse might ascertain the extent to which she may be relating to the patient on this basis. It is also helpful if she thinks about the total impression the patient has made upon her. If the nurse met the patient in a social situation, for example any place other than a psychiatric hospital or agency, what would she think or feel about him? Another salient question is: What did you learn about the patient that you did not know before? Each interaction should be a learning experience for both nurse and patient. The nurse might also ponder the extent to which she is able to experience the patient as a unique human being, i.e., as a presence rather than an object of study or source of data for a process record.

Length of Time Spent With Patient

The length of time the nurse spent with the patient is the next item to be included in the record. It should be noted with the nurse's reason for spending that particular period of time. If, for example, the nurse spent twenty minutes talking with the patient, she indicates why twenty minutes were spent instead of thirty minutes or an hour.

Reaction of Others to the Interaction

If pertinent and applicable the nurse states the reactions of others, i.e., patients and personnel, to her presence on the unit. Did other patients attempt to secure her attention in order to engage in conversation? Was the nurse interrupted by personnel? Was the nurse interrupted by the patient's psychiatrist?

Evaluation of the Nursing Intervention

Nursing intervention is evaluated in terms of the degree or extent to which the objectives in interacting with the patient were achieved. If the nurse has achieved these objectives she can identify the behavioral changes that have taken place and give evidence that these changes have taken place. If the nurse cannot provide evidence to support these claims then it is assumed the objectives have not been met. If the practitioner has not achieved her objectives it is important that this fact be recognized. It can be as meaningful a learning experience to realize when one has not met her goal as to give evidence that one *has* been able to achieve objectives. If the nurse can identify why the goals were not achieved she is then able to make decisions to remedy the situation. Identification of the problem is important. Why weren't the goals achieved? Were the objectives stated in such a way as to serve as a guide and goal in nursing practice? Were the goals attainable and realistic? There may be nothing wrong with an objective per se; however, the methods used to achieve the objective may be at fault. It is important that the nurse begin investigative inquiries to identify causes for failure *and* success. If she is able to achieve the objectives she should be able, on a conscious level, to account for this success.

While evaluating nursing intervention the nurse also identifies problems which may have emerged as a result of the interview. Communication difficulties (or any other nursing problems) are identified, with the probable reasons for their occurrence.

Plans for Future Interaction

Following evaluation of nursing intervention and identification of nursing problems, the nurse makes tentative plans for the next interaction. It is suggested that these plans, goals and objectives be written immediately following the evaluation.

Identification of Customary Pattern of Reacting

In this section of the process record the nurse, through a process of introspection, identifies and describes her customary pattern of behaving or reacting. For example, feeling uncomfortable during periods of silence may be some nurses' pattern of reacting to the stress of anxiety. Engaging in superficial social chit-chat may be a customary pattern of "relating" for some beginners in psychiatric nursing. Psychiatric nursing requires its practitioners to be able to audit their behavior as a step in changing or correcting habitual patterns of acting if this is necessary. Beginners in psychiatric nursing require guidance and support in order to identify their customary patterns of reacting and their strengths and weaknesses. A knowledge of one's strengths and weaknesses is essential in psychiatric nursing.

After writing the process record, which usually takes one hour, the nurse engages in the process of analyzing and synthesizing the data in the process record, which takes a longer period of time.

PART IV—ANALYSIS OF THE PROCESS RECORD

After the process record is written it is analyzed and critically scrutinized. Each item in the process record is assessed in terms of the nature and significance of the data collected. In analysis the parts are the focus of attention, whereas in synthesis the unitary integrity or wholeness of the data is the object of focus. Analysis will be discussed in relation to the items included in the process record.

How does the nurse begin to analyze the data? She rereads each section of the process record beginning with items related to *background information* and notes any gaps in knowledge or information. Plans are made to consult the literature or resource persons in order to obtain needed information.

The nurse scrutinizes the section on *thoughts and feelings prior to interacting* and ponders the degree to which she was able to identify her thoughts and feelings. Steps are taken to improve ability in this area. This may necessitate her becoming increasingly aware of her thoughts and feelings at times other than when interacting with patients, i.e., the nurse may consciously decide to practice this skill.

Objectives are carefully studied in terms of their construction and validation. Judgments are made as to the extent to which objectives truly served as guides and goals for the nurse-patient interaction. The nurse makes plans to remedy whatever difficulty was encountered, by consulting either the literature or resource persons.

The section on *activities occurring on the nursing unit* is reread to ascertain weaknesses in observing what was seen or heard. Difficulties in differentiating between perceptual data and inferences about the data are noted and plans are made to become increasingly aware of problems in this area.

Physical description of the setting is the next item examined, for the same purposes as those listed under "activities occurring on the nursing unit."

The section on *description of the patient* is then read, again for the same purposes. In all instances precision in observing and recording is stressed. Marked differences are sometimes noted between descriptions of the patient as given by the writer of the process record and descriptions given by other observers. It is sometimes helpful to request the nurse to write a second description of the patient; she is often astonished at the difference between the two accounts. The practitioner notes the extent to which she was able to separate perceptual data from conclusions about the data. For example, "The patient is neat" is a value judgment. It is not perceptual data. What did the nurse see which led to this conclusion? How does the nurse define the term "neat"?

The section on *interaction between nurse and patient* is carefully examined to ascertain the extent to which the nurse is able to develop valid inferences regarding the meaning of the patient's behavior and to use behavioral concepts. The nurse assesses the success with which she achieved the goals of the nurse-patient interaction. Communication difficulties are identified, as are other emerging nursing problems. It is helpful to identify *who* seems to have the problem—the nurse, the patient, or both. A nursing problem may be just that, a problem of the nurse and not necessarily a problem perceived by the patient. The nurse consults the literature and resource persons for help in resolving any difficulties.

In the section *thoughts and feelings following the interaction* the nurse ponders the degree to which she was able to identify thoughts and feelings in relation to the patient. It is not sufficient simply to identify a problem. In analysis the nurse makes concrete plans to overcome or surmount whatever difficulty was encountered.

The section on *length of time spent with the patient* is studied. The nurse checks to see if she has identified the rationale underlying the length of time spent with the patient.

Reaction of others to the interaction is the next item examined. The nurse reviews this section to see if she has noted the reactions of patients and others to the nurse-patient interaction.

The section on *evaluation of nursing intervention* is carefully examined and the extent to which objectives were met is noted.

Plans for future interaction will be discussed in the section titled "Synthesis."

The section on *identification of customary patterns of reacting* is reviewed and the practitioner determines the extent to which she is able to audit her behavior. If the nurse is unable to identify her customary pattern of reacting she is encouraged to try to find the reasons for this difficulty.

SYNTHESIS OF DATA

Following analysis the nurse begins to synthesize the data; synthesis always follows analysis. *Plans for future interactions* are developed. The practitioner has collected and interpreted data, applied concepts and analyzed data and is ready to plan future interactions based on the insights and knowledge gained as a result of interpretation and analysis. She constructs goals for the next nurse-patient interaction and begins anew the process of writing and validating objectives. Following synthesis, the practitioner discusses the data in conference with the supervisor or in group reconstruction session.

GENERAL COMMENTS

Process recording is time-consuming and difficult to use. The collection of data is easy; the analysis and synthesis are difficult. Despite its many limitations, process recording is a most valuable teaching-learning device. With the increased use of videotape, it is probable that at some future time the written process record will be outmoded. Analysis and synthesis of data, however, will still be necessary. The ability to analyze and synthesize is prerequisite to the ability to plan, structure and evaluate nursing intervention.

The instructor or supervisor may modify the number of items to be included in process records after the learner has had several interactions with the patient and has developed some degree of skill in observation and interpretation. A short-form process record is outlined in Part V.

PART V—OUTLINE OF A SHORT-FORM PROCESS RECORD

After the nurse has secured background information about the ill person, knows the plan of therapy, and has adequately described the patient and the setting, it is no longer necessary to include these items in each process record. Information about these areas is revised as the need arises.

The short-form process record as outlined below is recommended for use when nurses have gained some skill in observation and interpretation and have satisfactorily written at least three "long-form" process records. Items to be included in the short-form process record are:

I. *Thoughts and Feelings of the Nurse Prior to Interacting*

II. *Objectives in Interacting*
Construct and validate objectives
N.B. Students in collegiate and graduate programs should operationally define the behavior and the area of life in which the behavior operates.

III. *Interaction* (include all communication which took place)
Interpretations. Validation of interpretations
Concepts explaining behavior
Principles and concepts underlying intervention

IV. *Length of Contact with Patient*
Rationale

V. *Evaluation of Nursing Intervention*

VI. *Plans for Future Interaction*
Rationale

Chapter VIII

THE NURSE-PATIENT RELATIONSHIP

The one-to-one relationship is a goal to be achieved, the end result of a series of planned purposeful interactions between a nurse and a patient. It is also a learning experience for both participants—an experience, or series of experiences, during which both participants change and develop increased interpersonal competencies. The nurse-patient relationship is an experience entered into and shared by two unique human beings. Each individual is involved in the experience although the degree, extent and kind of involvement may vary. Each is affected by, and affects the thoughts, feelings and behavior of, the other person. Each is affected by what is said or left unsaid during the encounter. The nurse-patient interaction occurs during a particular time in the lives of both and hence cannot be duplicated or replicated. *A characteristic of the nurse-patient interaction is that each encounter is unique and original.* A past encounter may resemble a present one and similarities between experiences may occur, but each encounter is singular. An experience once undergone is irrevocably in the past and hence cannot be repeated. Each encounter is final yet, in another sense, represents a beginning or a new starting point for subsequent interactions.

Although each encounter is unique, it is postulated that all nurse-patient interactions proceed through several general phases. These phases are not discrete entities; one phase often overlaps with another. Many factors determine the progress of nurse and patient through the various phases. These include the nurse's knowledge and her ability to use it, the ill person's willingness or capacity to respond to the nurse's effort, and the kind of problem experienced by the ill person.

The phases leading to the establishment of a relationship include the preinteraction phase, the introductory or orientation phase, the phase of emerging identities, and termination. Each will be discussed below.

PART I—THE PREINTERACTION PHASE

The first phase in establishing a nurse-patient relationship is that of preinteraction. This is the *only* phase during which the patient is excluded as an active and equal participant. The preinteraction phase begins when the nurse selects or is assigned to initiate a nurse-patient relationship and includes all that the nurse thinks, feels or does immediately prior to the first interaction with the patient. Actually the preinteraction phase does not end after the first interaction but in a sense precedes every contact the nurse has with the ill person. What the nurse thinks, feels or does during this phase may profoundly affect each subsequent interaction.

What the nurse thinks or feels about a patient prior to interacting may depend, in part, on the information she possesses about the ill human being. During this phase the nurse relies primarily on secondary sources for knowledge about the patient; these include the patient's chart, resource persons, co-workers or others who have interacted with the patient. As stated previously, some nurses choose not to read the patient's chart lest the information bias them in the interaction. Other nurses believe the more information they possess the more able they will be to initiate and maintain a helpful relationship. There is no *one* best way; there are many methods. Rigid adherence to one's own method as being the best way to help others should, at all costs, be avoided. Whether or not the nurse reads the chart, it is recommended that she ascertain if the patient is receiving psychopharmacologic drugs or somatic therapies; the patient's behavior may be modified as a result of such therapies. For example, a nurse may infer a patient is withdrawn because of something the nurse did or said when actually he is responding to the effects or side effects of the medication he is receiving. Nurses should also know if the patient is, or has been, receiving electric shock treatments.

Some nurses, before interacting, focus on the patient's diagnosis. For example, if the patient is diagnosed as paranoid schizophrenic the nurse reads articles relating to the dynamics of the development of the disorder or to the nursing care of patients so diagnosed. A danger inherent in this preplanning is the tendency to believe that knowledge about a behavioral syndrome is of assistance in establishing relatedness with the patient. This may or may not be true. In psychiatric nursing the diagnosis does not necessarily suggest the nursing care the patient may require. *As discussed earlier, the typical "schizophrenic" or "depressed" patient does not exist.* Knowledge of the dynamics of the development of the illness may, of course, help to explain the patient's behavior and may offer some clues to nursing intervention *provided* the nurse understands that knowledge *about* a behavioral syndrome is not to be equated with knowledge *of* the particular patient.

Some nurses ignore the diagnosis and focus instead on problems that emerge during the interaction. These are discussed in supervisory conference or during group reconstruction, and the nurse also consults the literature for clarification and assistance.

The nurse has *two* major tasks to complete prior to the first interaction with the patient. The first is to develop an awareness of her thoughts and feelings, and the second to conceptualize what she wishes to accomplish during the interaction.

AWARENESS OF THOUGHTS AND FEELINGS PRIOR TO INTERACTING

It is important for the nurse to become aware of her thoughts and feelings prior to interacting with the patient because these thoughts and feelings will have an effect on the nurse-patient interaction. *A major assumption is that most nurses experience anxiety of varying intensity during the preinteraction phase.*

The Problem of Anxiety

The degree of anxiety experienced by the nurse may not be incapacitating but it will be present. The nurse needs to become aware of *what* is being experienced, identify the threat, and decide what, if anything, needs to be done about it. It is particularly important that beginners in psychiatric nursing be helped to identify the habitual methods they use to reduce anxiety. Beginners who habitually react to anxiety by withdrawing from a situation may have great difficulty in establishing relatedness with a patient. Beginning students require the support of the psychiatric nurse supervisor in coping with their feelings of anxiety and incompetence.

Anxiety is manifested in many different ways. Some examples follow. A nurse is late for the initial interaction, "loses" the key to the ward, or spends an inordinate amount of time in the nursing station reading, and rereading, the patient's chart. Some beginners exhibit their anxiety through concern over "saying the wrong thing to the patient." When questioned the learner usually cannot state what she might possibly say that would "set the patient back." It is probable that the learner is really more concerned about displaying her inadequacies than she is in harming the patient. A student exposed to lectures on what and what not to say to patients may overlearn these directives. The learner needs to understand that she is not really so powerful as she imagines. One statement uttered by a nurse is not likely to harm a patient. The learner is probably more afraid of what the patient will say to her than she is of what she will say to the patient. She often fears physical or verbal attack by the patient. Some fear humiliation, i.e., "being made fun of," or rejection by the patient more than they fear assault. It is probable that most beginners are afraid of displaying their inadequacies to others. Beginners who have previously avoided closeness with patients by concentrating on treatments and techniques are particularly vulnerable to preinteraction anxiety.

Some learners experiencing preinteraction anxiety may be assisted by role-playing the anticipated interaction or by "rehearsing" what it is they are going to say or do when they enter the patient's room for the first time. As an actor memorizes the lines of a script and undergoes a dress rehearsal prior to a performance, so some nurses are assisted to cope with or lower their anxiety level. One disadvantage of the rehearsal technique is that the nurse may approach the patient in a stilted, wooden, artificial manner. Rehearsal may lessen the nurse's ability to be spontaneous, receptive and open during the initial interview. However, the alternative, an increased anxiety level, also produces the same effect. A hoped-for outcome of rehearsal is that the nurse, once the interaction has begun, will become more comfortable and less anxious.

Anxiety experienced during the preinteraction phase to some extent resembles "stage fright." The nurse in fantasy imagines everything that could possibly go wrong during the interaction. Anxiety, like stage fright, usually subsides once the nurse begins interacting with the patient. It is suggested that she interact with the patient as soon as possible after arriving on the unit. It is hypothesized that the longer the nurse remains away from the patient the more likely it is that the nurse's anxiety level will increase rather than decrease.

Not only the beginner experiences anxiety prior to interacting with a patient. Fear of the unknown may affect practitioners skilled in establishing relationships with patients. Usually, however, the experienced practitioner has learned how to reduce her anxiety level so that the patient is not unduly affected by the nurse's fear; anxiety is contagious, and a patient already burdened with anxiety should not be made more anxious by the nurse. The nurse must identify the cause of her anxiety as the first step in devising ways to cope with, and reduce, its effect. Anxiety, of course, may not be the only feeling the nurse will experience during the preinteraction phase but it is the most common. The nurse may also feel boredom, anger, indifference, depression. As with anxiety, the cause of the feeling must be identified.

Knowledge or awareness of one's feeling does not necessarily cause the feeling to subside. For example, knowledge that one is mildly depressed does not, in and of itself, cause abatement of the depression. Knowledge of one's depression can, however, assist one to control the outward expression of the feeling state. What one is thinking and feeling may be expressed behaviorally; on the other hand, the expression of these thoughts and feelings may be controlled so that the casual observer is not aware of them. Some individuals are more adept than others at controlling expression of their feelings.

While thoughts and feelings determine one's behavior, it is equally true that actions or behavior may change one's thoughts and feelings. Acting *as if* one is not mildly depressed may change the inner feeling state. In some instances this technique is highly effective.

CONCEPTUALIZATION OF GOALS TO BE ACCOMPLISHED

The second major task of the nurse is to conceptualize what she wishes to accomplish during the nurse-patient interaction. It is recommended that she identify in writing objectives or goals for the initial interaction and decide the methods to be used in achieving the goals.

Objectives are goals as well as guides. As goals, the nurse evaluates the extent to which she has achieved them. As guides, she conceptualizes, tentatively, what it is she wishes to accomplish. Knowing what one wishes to achieve usually suggests appropriate methodology, i.e., if one knows the *why* the *how* becomes apparent.

Objectives for the first interaction may include encouraging the patient to verbalize as a step toward assisting him to communicate and socialize with others. Making a pact or working agreement with the patient is also an objective for the first interaction (see Part II, "The Pact"). During this meeting, too, the nurse wishes to gain knowledge *of* as opposed to knowledge *about* the patient. The nurse tries to see the patient as a human being *before* identifying nursing problems. She may also attempt to assess the patient's anxiety level as well as her own.

Objectives conceptualized prior to an interaction serve as guides and goals, but because they are developed before the interaction they may have to be changed during the interaction if circumstances warrant. Knowledge of what the nurse wishes to accomplish *is* necessary in order to assist the practitioner to focus.

It is helpful to keep in mind the relationship between objectives and methods. An objective (goal) may be compared to a destination (city) one wishes to visit. The individual decides how (the method) he will travel, i.e., via automobile, bus, plane, etc. However, in order to reach his destination he may, because of conditions unforeseen, have to detour. During the trip he may decide his plan is not practical and therefore go to another city or return home. He may know in advance where he wishes to go and how he will get there, but has no real way of knowing if his plans are feasible, practical or sound until he begins the journey. When difficulties are encountered he decides what to do to overcome them. The same is true in regard to methodology. It is important to preplan, i.e., to construct objectives and conceptualize one's method of achieving these objectives. One does this with the realization that both objectives and methods may need revision.

What has been discussed thus far has relevance for the nurse who is constructing objectives for the first interaction. One must also consider the patient's probable needs and goals. While these cannot be conceptualized in advance, the nurse can speculate as to their nature. It is assumed that all human beings have a need for cognitive clarity. That is, the patient needs to know to whom he is speaking and the reason for the nurse-patient interaction. He also needs to be accepted as a unique human being, not as a "typical schizophrenic" or typical anything else. Generally speaking, the ill person wishes to feel comfortable with the person with whom he is interacting; hopefully, his anxiety level will be decreased during the nurse-patient interaction. However, any unknown person or new experience will usually engender anxiety. (A few patients need to have their anxiety levels increased, not decreased, so that the lowering of the patient's anxiety level cannot always be accepted as a goal.)

The human being who is the patient has a need for closeness with others. This may not be apparent in the behavior of some patients who seem deliberately to push others away and to give every indication that they do not desire companionship. Closeness, while it may be desired, is often feared. To be close to another human being, to experience the warmth of relatedness, is also to become vulnerable to hurt or disappointment. An individual who has been hurt often may attempt to solve his problem by withdrawing from others, thus not exposing himself to further disappointment. This does not produce the desired result of freedom from anxiety; what is produced in the individual who withdraws, or alienates others, is loneliness, estrangement and fear. One goal is achieved: the individual is not hurt by others; neither is he helped by others. After a time he finds he cannot reach out to others even when he needs the friendship and warmth of human companionship.

The nurse-patient relationship offers to the patient the closeness and warmth of relatedness and demands nothing from the patient in return. There are "no strings" attached, no conditions which must be met; the person is accepted *not* as a patient but as a human being whose problems in living have hampered him from enjoying his humanness. In relatedness gratitude is not sought as a return for interest, concern and caring. Hopefully, through the experience of relating, the ill person will be able to gain the courage needed to reach out to human beings. The eventual aim of the nurse patient relationship is to eliminate the necessity for the relationship.

Prior to the first interaction with the patient, it is also suggested that the nurse conceptualize how much time will be spent with the patient both during the initial encounter and in subsequent interactions. She may wish to spend a relatively short period of time with the patient during the first interaction and then slowly increase the time spent with him.

Other factors the nurse must consider during the preinteraction phase have already been discussed in Chapter VI, "The Selection of Patients." For purposes of review they are outlined as follows:

1. The nurse needs to become consciously aware of the reasons for selecting a particular patient.

2. The nurse develops an awareness of her thoughts and feelings regarding being assigned to a particular patient.

3. The nurse conceptualizes in advance the objectives to be achieved during the initial interaction.

4. A decision is made regarding the method to be used in collecting data, i.e., process recording, tape recording, videotape, etc.

5. A decision is made as to the setting in which the nurse will interact with the patient.

6. A decision is made as to the apparel the nurse will wear, i.e., uniform, street clothes, lab coat over street clothes, etc.

7. The nurse ascertains whether any clearances or permissions are required prior to interacting with the patient.

8. The nurse ascertains the extent to which staff members have been oriented as to reasons for interacting with the patient. Does the staff know when the nurse will be on the unit? How long a period of time will be spent with the patient?

9. The nurse ascertains whether or not the patient will be available during the time she wishes to interact with him.

10. The nurse decides how she wishes to be introduced to the patient, whether the nurse intends to introduce self or to have a member of the staff introduce her.

Following the accomplishment of these tasks the nurse is ready to interact with the patient and thus enters the second phase of a nurse-patient relationship, namely, the introductory or orientation phase.

PART II—THE INTRODUCTORY OR ORIENTATION PHASE

The introductory or orientation phase begins when two human beings who are strangers meet for the first time and become acquaintances. This phase is characterized by the formation of a pact or agreement between nurse and patient to work together to help the ill person toward social recovery. It is also a phase of assessment during which both nurse and patient develop assumptions and inferences about each other. The introductory phase probably ends when nurse and patient begin to perceive each other as unique human beings. The orientation phase may be completed within minutes of the initial interaction; on the other hand, several interactions may take place before nurse and patient are ready to proceed to the working phase of emerging identities. What occurs during the first interaction may determine the length of time it will take for nurse and patient to proceed to the next phase. Because the initial encounter between nurse and patient is extremely important, it will be discussed separately.

THE INITIAL ENCOUNTER

Introduction to the Patient

It is suggested that the nurse be introduced to the patient by a member of the staff. There may be disadvantages to this; not all staff members are tactful in their methods of introduction. For example, a staff member walked into a crowded day room and yelled: "Hey, Miss . . . , there is somebody here to see you." A variation of this approach occurs when a staff member tells a patient he has a "visitor." The patient comes out of his room looking for a visitor, i.e., a friend or relative, and instead encounters a stranger. If the nurse has any reason to suspect that she may be introduced as described above, she should ask a staff member to point the patient out rather than to introduce her to the patient.

As the nurse approaches the patient she begins to notice him within the total context of his environment. She focuses on the whole as opposed to parts of the environment. The nurse usually develops first impressions or inferences about the patient, which may or may not be valid. It is suggested that nurses become aware of these impressions and inferences, yet hold them in abeyance in order to experience the uniqueness of the human being who is the patient. Thus, before the nurse speaks to the patient the observational process has begun. Observation is always the first step in the nursing process. The nurse collects raw sensory data and probably begins an interpretation process prior to the interaction itself.

The nurse may ask the patient where he would like to sit while they talk with each other. The reasons for asking are to ascertain whether or not the patient does have a preference and also to discern whether or not he can make a decision. If the patient cannot decide, the nurse chooses the setting for the initial interaction.

The Pact

The first task of the nurse in the initial encounter is to make a pact or agreement to work with the patient for the purpose of assisting him toward social recovery. The nurse begins by introducing herself to the patient—by telling him her name and status, the school or agency she represents, and when she will be interacting with him. The patient is also told the length of time of each interaction, the number of days a week the nurse will meet with him, and the period of time over which the interactions will extend. During the initial encounter the patient is thus prepared for the eventual termination of the relationship. The nurse tells the patient the reasons for the interaction and discusses with him their respective roles. *Role interpretation, however, is a continuous process* and is not completed during this particular phase. A nurse may have to reinterpret her role and functions many times during the subsequent interactions.

When talking with the patient the nurse uses his title and name. If the patient's name is John Jones the nurse addresses him as Mr. Jones, not as John. The use of the first name is *not* recommended unless the patient requests it. When the nurse introduces herself she uses her title and last name.

There is no one way in which the nurse can best accomplish the task of making a pact with a patient. It is suggested that she assess and proceed at the patient's level of comprehension. If she infers the patient is unclear as to *why* he was selected, this should be clarified immediately. The nurse gives the patient an opportunity to ask questions about anything discussed with him, and informs him of the confidential nature of the discussions. If the nurse shares data obtained during the interaction with a supervisor, teacher or classmates, the patient is informed of this fact.

The Matter of Choice

As discussed in Chapter VI, the patient may or may not be given a choice as to whether he wishes to participate in a one-to-one relationship. The factor of choice is important as it profoundly affects what the nurse says to the patient and how she says it.

THE PATIENT IS GIVEN A CHOICE. When the patient is given a choice, the nurse completes all of the tasks as stated in the section entitled "The Pact" and asks the patient if he is willing to participate in the relationship. The patient may accept or refuse. In the case of refusal the nurse tries to elicit reasons for the patient's refusal. Some reasons why patients refuse follow. The patient may not understand the nature of the assistance the nurse can offer; he may not comprehend how the nurse can help by "talking with him." The patient whose concept of nurse is that of an individual who "gives shots and pills" and "carries out doctor's orders" may not be able to conceive of the nurse in any other capacity. A patient may refuse because he believes he will have to remain in the hospital to talk to the nurse.

There may be other more idiosyncratic reasons for a patient's refusal. For example, fear of closeness with another human being or the belief that he (the patient) "must be very sick" for a nurse to spend time with him may deter him. Whatever the reason, the nurse attempts to ascertain it and, if possible, clarifies any misconceptions the patient may have regarding the relationship. If the patient still refuses and the nurse cannot win his cooperation, she then selects another patient and goes through the same request process.

The patient may choose to participate in the relationship. Again, patients may agree for many different reasons. It may not occur to them to disagree with an authority figure; they may believe the physician "ordered" the nurse to talk with them. A patient may also believe the nurse will persuade the physician to "let him go home," to transfer him to another unit, to stop electric shock treatments, etc.

Some patients agree to participate because they are lonely and wish to talk about their problems. This is especially true in those units where the role of the nurse in the one-to-one relationship is well known to patients via the everpresent grapevine. They understand the type of assistance the nurse can offer and enjoy the attention. A patient may agree to participate because, as one patient stated: "To have a nurse of your own means you're important and special." Being asked to participate, for this patient, was almost a status symbol. There may be many other more idiosyncratic reasons why patients agree to participate in a one-to-one relationship; the desire to improve and "get well" may or may not be the prime reason.

THE PATIENT IS NOT GIVEN A CHOICE. When a patient is not given the choice of whether he wishes to participate in the interaction, the nurse completes all of the tasks as stated in the section "The Pact." The ill person, in effect, is told he *is* to participate. As stated, a patient may become frightened or overwhelmed by this approach but the structure of the approach and the fact that he has no choice can be helpful and comforting. Because of his illness a withdrawn, depressed or confused individual may not be able to arrive at a decision. The nurse who makes the decision for the patient communicates, in essence, that she cares about the patient and will help him whether or not he wants help. It should be recognized that the nurse is communicating to the patient that he is not capable, at this time, of making a choice. The nurse assumes the *entire* responsibility for initiating the relationship and bears the burden of earning and maintaining the patient's cooperation throughout the interaction cycle. From the nurse's viewpoint, there is actually little difference in regard to the tasks which must be completed; whether the patient is given a choice or not she *still* assumes the entire responsibility. She also still must cope with the problem of resistance. Patients who agree to participate may exhibit less resistance than those who have no choice; however, this is by no means always true.

Viewing the matter of choice from the patient's perspective, it would seem that some patients appreciate being asked (as opposed to being told) what to do. Being asked connotes to the patient that he is a person who is responsible, a person who is free to decide. On the other hand, being told (if ever so gently) that he (the patient) *is* to participate and is denied choice may indicate to him that he is a sick person who is incapable of making a decision.

Lest not giving a patient a choice sounds too arbitrary, it should be remembered that nurses, at times, must in conscience make decisions for the good of the ill person. For example, a nurse will not let a patient starve himself; she will intervene. Despite the fact that a person may *choose* to die by suicide the nurse does not, because of respect for his wishes, allow him to commit this act; she intervenes. It is much the same with patients who are unable by virtue of their illness to give consent. The nurse must decide for the patient who is unable or incapable of choosing.

During the introductory process and thereafter the nurse begins to focus on the patient as a whole in the total context of his immediate environment, then on more specific details. The details of observation are summarized in the section on "Physical Description of the Setting" and "Description of the Patient" in Chapter VII, Part III. The nurse collects raw data about the patient and begins to develop tentative interpretations. The patient, meanwhile, is also gathering data and developing inferences about the nurse. Thus a circular reciprocal process is constantly taking place in every nurse-patient interaction.

Talking With the Patient

Beginners frequently have difficulty knowing "what to say" to patients during the initial encounter. What one says and how one says it are determined by purpose. What are the goals of the nurse during the initial encounter? What does the nurse wish to accomplish?

If the nurse's only goal during the initial encounter is to form a pact with the patient, then this is done and the interaction is terminated. The nurse may have other goals (see Chapter IV, "The Nurse's Goals"). She may wish to assist the patient to communicate and may say to the patient: "Tell me why you are in the hospital (or agency)." The statements made by the patient may assist the nurse to see how he perceives his problems, and at the same time assist the patient to communicate. The nurse thus begins to achieve the goals of the nurse-patient relationship during the initial encounter. By use of the communication skills she begins to assist the patient to conceptualize problems and, eventually, to perceive his participation in life experiences.

THE SPIEL. Some patients who have been interviewed many times by members of, and learners in, the other health disciplines (psychologists, psychiatrists, medical students, social work trainees, etc.) may present a prepared "spiel" to the nurse when she asks: "Why are you in the hospital?" One gets the impression the patient is rattling off a statement that has been repeated ad infinitum. Following the spiel the patient may say: "I don't have anything else to say. Now you know all about me." It takes experience to recognize a spiel. One characteristic is that the patient says little if anything definitive about himself. He usually employs vague generalizations and one gets the impression he is talking about someone else—not himself.

When recognized, the spiel is sometimes interrupted by the nurse who seeks clarification regarding the generalizations made. On the other hand, she may choose to listen to the entire spiel and then give her impression of it to the patient; this may help the patient recognize it for what it is—a statement prepared to meet the expectations of health workers. The practitioner may do this by stating: "I get the impression you have had to tell many different nurses and doctors why you are in the hospital. You must get pretty tired of this." Most patients who rely on spiels are relieved when at least *one* health worker recognizes what they have had to do to meet health workers' expectations.

Patients who use spiels do so because they believe health workers are not really interested in them as human beings, and are talking with them merely to extract information for a case history or a progress report. A patient under this impression will react in the same manner toward a nurse attempting to establish relatedness. The patient has no way of knowing the nurse is *not* merely extracting information to write on a chart.

It may be necessary for the nurse to reinterpret her role and the nature of the assistance she has to offer the patient. She does this by taking the blame for failing to communicate. The nurse may say: "I probably didn't make it clear. I am here to talk with you about anything you want to talk about. I am not here just to get information from you. This is not my purpose." She then gives the patient an opportunity to ask questions or to correct misconceptions.

It should be emphasized that the main purpose of the nurse-patient relationship is not to gather information. The nurse does not interact to obtain information *about* the ill person but to get to *know* the ill person. There is a vast difference between these two purposes.

Toward the end of the first interaction the nurse reminds the patient of the time of the next meeting. The interactions should begin and end on time. This point is very important. *The nurse is to abide by the time limits set.* For example, if a nurse tells a patient she will talk with him from 8:00 a.m. to 8:50 a.m. she must begin the interaction at 8:00 a.m. and terminate it at 8:50 a.m. Why? It is necessary that the patient view her as a reliable, dependable person who means what she says; if the nurse says one thing and does another the patient can hardly develop trust in her as a model of reliability, whose behavior is consistent and whose statements are truthful. Exceptions to this rule may occur: a nurse obviously will not leave a patient who is in panic or actively contemplating suicide. Exceptions, however, are just that—exceptions. In general, it is strongly suggested that nurses adhere to the time limits set and that they inform patients when the interview is drawing to a close. For example the nurse says: "I will be leaving in five minutes." This gives the patient an opportunity to tell her anything he may be "saving till the last minute."

Following the initial encounter, unless the nurse has used verbatim recording, it is recommended that she immediately write an account of the interaction. She assesses the extent to which objectives were achieved and begins to conceptualize goals for subsequent interactions. It is on the basis of interpretations made from data obtained during the initial encounter that she plans for the next interaction.

BARRIERS TO ACCOMPLISHMENT OF TASKS

Some beginners may believe that not knowing what to say to patients is *the* major barrier encountered during the introductory phase. Others may think that forming the pact is *the* major problem. However, *the major barrier encountered during the introductory phase is related to the manner in which nurse and patient perceive each other.* Each participant in the interaction may view the other as a stereotype rather than as a unique human being. It is also possible that one person will see the other as a replication of a significant person from his past; this also hinders the perception of uniqueness. *In order to proceed beyond the introductory phase it is essential that the nurse understand how she is perceiving the patient as well as how the patient is perceiving her.* Factors which may influence this include age, status, social class and anxiety level of both participants. These factors—which interfere with the ability of each participant to see the other as unique—are discussed in greater detail below.

A nurse may react to a patient, not in terms of his uniqueness, but in terms of the nurse's stereotyped view of "psychiatric patient," or she may, because of her theoretical background (or lack of it), react in terms of diagnostic categories. For example, she may relate to depressed patients in one stereotyped way and to schizophrenic patients in another. Since interaction is a reciprocal process, the patient also perceives the nurse in his own idiosyncratic manner. He may react to a nurse, not as a unique human being, but in terms of his stereotyped view of nurses in general or of "psychiatric nurses" in particular.

The social class of either participant may be a barrier. The classic study of Hollingshead and Redlich seems to indicate that psychiatrists from the highest social classes have difficulty talking with patients from the lowest social classes.[1] The same may be true of psychiatric nurses. There are few research studies in the literature which support this assumption or explore the effects of social class differences between nurses and patients. It can be postulated, however, that some nurses do have difficulty talking with patients from different social classes. A nurse from one of the lowest social classes, as defined by Hollingshead and Redlich, may find it hard to establish relatedness with a patient from a higher social class. This may be especially true if the nurse has strong feelings or prejudices about individuals in these social classes; one nurse commented on the behavior of a very ill patient from one of the highest socioeconomic categories by saying: "There's really nothing wrong with him. He is just one of the idle rich." The nurse, of course, may also have strong feelings about individuals from the lower socioeconomic groups. These feelings may be expressed in generalizations such as: "Well, what can you expect from them? They don't want to work for a living or improve themselves. All they want is a welfare check and a handout." A nurse who has been able to move from a low socioeconomic group to a higher one may believe other members of the low socioeconomic group should be able to do the same, and she may communicate these feelings to her patients.

Another barrier is related to the status (real or supposed) of the participants in the interactive process. For example, some nurses —particularly beginners—have difficulty appreciating the uniqueness of a patient who happens to be a physician, a lawyer, a member of the clergy or religious order, a nurse or a member of some other health discipline. One learner who was to interact with a physician stated: "How can I possibly help him? He knows a lot more than I do!" Beginners need assistance in comprehending that status, position and social class need not affect the nurse's ability to assist patients *provided* she recognizes and takes into account the effect of these factors on her perception of the patient and understands the nature of the assistance she can offer him. The physician, in the example above, may "know medicine" but his knowledge of medicine does not negate the fact that he is an ill human being in need of the assistance the psychiatric nurse can offer.

---

[1] Hollingshead, August B., and Redlich, Frederick C.: Social Class and Mental Illness. John Wiley & Sons, New York, 1958.

Another possible barrier involves the anxiety level of both participants in the interaction. A nurse having difficulty in coping with her own anxiety can hardly focus on the patient. A very anxious nurse is focused on self and on her own feelings, and obviously cannot "get beyond self" to the human being who is the patient. Unless such a nurse can find ways to resolve her own feelings she cannot assist the ill human being. The patient, of course, may also have difficulty relating with the nurse because of *his* high anxiety level.

Another barrier which is more difficult to recognize occurs when either nurse or patient views the other participant as if the other were a replication of a significant individual from the past. For example, a male nurse may perceive and relate to an older male patient as if the patient were his (the nurse's) father. The nurse may then displace to the patient the feelings he has for his father. This phenomenon is roughly equivalent to the concept of countertransference as described in psychoanalytic literature. A similar process occurs when the patient perceives and relates to the nurse as if the nurse were his son (or his daughter) and displaces to the nurse the feelings he has about his child. This is somewhat equivalent to the psychoanalytic concept of transference. The process is basically one of distortion. The individual is not perceived as he is—as a unique being—but as a figure from the past. Physical similarity to a significant individual from one's past may trigger the process but this is not necessarily the case, although it is probable that similarity of some kind initiates the distorting phenomenon. The similarity may be that of age, attitude, general behavior, interest, etc. A nurse or patient may perceive and relate to the other in terms of any significant figure from their past lives. This may be a friend, acquaintance, co-worker, aunt, uncle or some other relative. A patient who is within the nurse's age group (or younger) may be related to as if he were the nurse's sibling.

It is probable that a certain amount of distortion operates in most human relationships. It is the nurse's task to become consciously aware of the nature of the barriers which hinder her from experiencing the uniqueness of the human being who is the patient. What can be done to overcome these barriers?

SUGGESTIONS

The supervisory conference and group reconstruction sessions are, at the present time, two of the best media through which the nurse can be assisted to identify and overcome the barriers which prevent her from perceiving the patient as he is. The nurse must be willing to relate honestly her perceptions, thoughts and feelings and to share the data collected during the nurse-patient interaction. This presupposes a willingness to expose oneself—what one has thought, said and done during an interaction—to supervisors and peers. This is no easy task for some nurses. The supervisor must provide an atmosphere in which the nurse feels free to reveal self without fear of censure.

Supervisors and group members can usually tell when nurses are reacting to patients in rigid stereotyped manners—in terms of diagnostic categories, social classes, or positions. It may be sufficient to bring this tendency to the conscious attention of the practitioner. However, as it takes time to develop a stereotyped view so it will take time to change it. Gradually, with assistance, nurses can begin to audit their behavior and then to change it. This behavioral change takes place over a period of time if the nurse begins to recognize that the patient does not, in fact, fit the stereotype. If the patient does "fit the stereotype" the supervisor assists the practitioner to understand that her value judgments are interfering with her ability to perceive the patient as he is. He is himself—a one-time-being on this earth—alike yet utterly unlike any individual who has ever lived or will ever live.

It is difficult to assist a nurse who perceives a patient as if he were someone from her past life. Is it possible for the nurse to develop insight into the fact that she is relating to the patient in this way? She is usually not aware of so doing since most (if not all) of this behavior is unconsciously determined. An astute supervisor can usually, during conference or in group session, detect that the nurse is distorting the patient by viewing him as someone else. It may be necessary to bring the problem to the nurse's attention so that she can examine her behavior.

There is no substitute for a capable, prepared supervisor. Such a person can assist nurses to identify and overcome the barriers which prevent them from being of assistance to ill human beings, and to grow both professionally and personally.

PART III—THE PHASE OF EMERGING IDENTITIES

The phase of emerging identities probably begins when the barriers to the tasks inherent in the introductory phase have (in part) been overcome. This phase ends when relatedness has been established and when termination of the one-to-one relationship becomes necessary.

A characteristic of the phase is that nurse and patient become increasingly acquainted with each other. At the beginning of the phase neither nurse nor patient really knows or understands the motives of the other. As a result both assess and test the other in a variety of ways. It is during this phase that the patient is likely to test the nurse's ability to set limits and to abide by them. It is therefore essential that the practitioner engage in behavior that causes the patient to develop trust and reliance. For example, if a nurse is ill and must cancel an interaction it is her responsibility to notify the patient of the cancellation and the reason for it.

During the phase of emerging identities both nurse and patient begin to perceive the other as a unique human being. Each may distort or fail to perceive the other as he is, but a beginning is made. If some degree of distortion occurs the problem is not so serious as initially. During this phase the nurse is usually less anxious when talking with the patient, probably because fear of the unknown has decreased; she now knows the patient better. Also, the nurse may be more comfortable with the patient because of the assistance received from the supervisor in identifying and coping with the anxiety engendered in developing closeness with the ill person. Because anxiety is reduced the nurse may be able to "get beyond and outside of self" to focus on the ill human being and his difficulties.

TASKS OF THE NURSE

The nurse strives to increase her ability to observe and to interpret her observations on a suppositional or hypothesis level. As she collects data and interprets and validates the meaning of the data with the patient, she tries to experience the patient as a human being —i.e., as a presence—rather than an object of study or source of information.

The nurse separates data from interpretation when conversing with the patient, with the view of helping him to overcome difficulties in communicating and relating. The nurse attempts to develop her ability to apply theoretical concepts to explain or predict the patient's behavior while conveying to him the warmth of sincere interest. In many instances the goals of nurse and patient are identical. For example, the nurse strives to assist the patient to identify problems while trying to accomplish the same thing herself. The nurse helps the patient to realize he is an active agent—a participant in life experiences—at the same time she is trying to perceive her own participation in life experiences with an increased sense of immediacy.

She assists the patient to face emerging problems realistically while striving to accomplish this same goal in her own personal and professional life. She helps the patient to test new patterns of behavior while at the same time auditing and attempting to change her own behavior.

The nurse assists the patient to communicate and socialize with others while also trying to improve her own ability to communicate effectively.

Helping the patient to find meaning in illness is another major task of the nurse during the phase of emerging identities; she also works toward accomplishing this goal herself. Unless the nurse is able to find meaning in suffering (whether this suffering be predominantly mental, physical, or spiritual in origin), she will hardly be able to assist the patient to do so.

There are many other tasks to be accomplished during this phase. The nurse prepares the patient for the eventual termination of the relationship by reminding him, at various times during the interactive cycle, of the number of interviews remaining. During this phase she assists the patient to differentiate between problems he (the patient) can resolve and problems which will not be changed as a result of the nurse-patient interaction. Both the ill human being and the nurse must accept that which cannot be changed. Beginners in psychiatric nursing are quite likely to be discouraged by the fact that a mentally ill person often must return to the environment and the individuals which may have helped to precipitate the patient's illness. One does hope, however, that as a result of the relationship the ill person may be strengthened to endure that which cannot, at least at the present time, be changed.

During the phase of emerging identities the nurse also assists the patient to recognize the effect of his behavior on those with whom he comes in daily contact. She also has the similar task of identifying the effect of her behavior on others.

There are numerous other tasks. For example, the nurse is committed to improve her clinical competence. This involves auditing her behavior and changing it as the need arises, sharing analyzed data obtained during the interview with the supervisor and others, and study. Clinical competence is improved by a *continuous* pursuit of knowledge through the literature or resource persons in order to study, clarify, and get assistance with particular problems or to enhance understanding of emerging difficulties. Clinical competence does not "just happen"—it is developed by a nurse committed to the pursuit of excellence. Competence is achieved by a nurse who dedicates herself to the monotonous, exciting, exacting, tiresome, exhilarating and always satisfying task of assisting ill persons to improve, and who perseveres when problems and difficulties seem insurmountable. It is probable that clinical competency of a high degree in psychiatric nursing is developed by self-disciplined individuals who enjoy change and challenge and dislike routines, directives and set ways of accomplishing tasks. Such persons are adventurous, intellectually curious, and willing to commit themselves without reservation to increasing their ability to help others.

As the phase of emerging identities draws to a close the nurse will have been able to achieve some (if not most) of the goals inherent in this phase. She will have been able, to some extent, to help the patient identify and cope with present (here-and-now) problems, conceptualize problems, test new patterns of behavior, communicate and socialize with others, and find meaning in illness. The practitioner has, through use of communication techniques and the impact of her own personality, been able to assist the ill person to verbalize, focus, identify cause and effect, and perceive his participation in an experience. During the phase of emerging identities both nurse and patient establish relatedness, and each is able to see the other as a unique human being.

RELATEDNESS

The establishment of relatedness is the culmination of the phase of emerging identities. One major prerequisite for relatedness is that each person develop the ability to perceive the other as a unique human being. In actuality, this is a most difficult task to accomplish. The barriers of position, role and status must be transcended. It is less stressful for nurses to view ill persons as "patients" than as human beings who happen to be in the role of patients. The terms *nurse, patient,* and *nurse-patient relationship* may connote stereotypes and thus become barriers to relatedness. Unless ill persons perceive nurses as helpful human beings it is hardly likely that relatedness will be established. It is therefore important that the stereotyped roles of patient and nurse be transcended by both persons in the interaction if relatedness is to be achieved. A nurse and a patient do not develop a relationship. Relationships are established only by human beings who are able to transcend the barriers of role, status and position. The terms nurse, patient, and nurse-patient relationship are used in this text only for purposes of communicative economy.

What are some outcomes of relatedness? The ill person will have been given an opportunity to engage in meaningful interaction with a warm, sensitive, concerned, knowledgeable individual who is not afraid to exhibit humanness or interest and who does not blame, condone, or express value judgments about him or his behavior. He will have been spared false reassurance, useless advice, and pep talks.

The practitioner is a human being who can and will make mistakes—who may, for example, inadvertently hurt the feelings of the patient. If such an incident occurs, the nurse apologizes for the behavior and discusses what occurred with the ill person. Thus she is revealed to the patient as a fallible human being. There are some who will disagree with this, believing that nurses should invariably present a "front of expertise" and should not admit errors in judgment since this will diminish the ill person's respect for them. However, ill persons are not gullible; they know when a nurse has made a mistake or angered them or made some error in judgment. A nurse can hardly serve as the model of a healthy mature human being if she cannot admit that she too is human, makes mistakes, and does not possess all of the world's wisdom. The mantle of infallibility is a heavy burden to bear. If the nurse is not permitted to reveal her humanity by admitting errors, she may resort to behavior such as becoming angry with, or defensive toward, the ill person who "caused" the behavior. Her inability to admit error or lack of knowledge may destroy any vestige of a relationship developed with the patient.

Perhaps most important of all, as a result of the experiences encountered during the phase of emerging identities the ill person will have been given the opportunity to experience acceptance from an individual who neither demands nor expects gratitude, gifts, or praise in return for services. Some ill persons, in the past, have been "accepted" by significant individuals only when they have fulfilled certain requirements. When such persons are offered unconditional acceptance, during the one-to-one relationship, they show marked growth as human beings.

BARRIERS TO ACCOMPLISHMENT OF TASKS

In this section only commonly encountered barriers to goal accomplishment will be discussed. (For detailed discussion of specific problems and suggested solutions see Chapter IX, "Problems in the One-to-One Relationship.")

As stated, a characteristic of the phase of emerging identities is that the patient engages in a process of testing the nurse. If the nurse is unable to withstand the anxiety aroused by the ill person's testing it is unlikely that she will be able to accomplish her goals. The patient may test the nurse for a number of reasons. He may wish to check her ability to set limits and abide by them or to discover if the nurse is reliable and truthful. An ill person with problems related to aggression may deliberately attempt to provoke the nurse to determine whether or not she will become punitive. A patient may try to get the nurse to talk about herself; if she does, this may be taken as proof that the nurse is more interested in self than in him. Testing is inevitable during the phase of emerging identities, and is considered a normal component of this phase. One might well wonder what is wrong if testing does not occur rather than become annoyed or anxious when it does. Knowledge that testing will occur, recognition of the testing behavior, and ability to withstand the anxiety involved in being tested are most helpful. It is recommended that the nurse discuss with the supervisor the testing behavior that is occurring, her thoughts and feelings about the testing, and her plans for coping with it.

Another barrier to task accomplishment is the nurse's unrealistic assumption as to the progress the patient "should" be making. It is not uncommon for the patient to show desirable changes in behavior after several interactions. Following these improvements, the patient seemingly retrogresses or remains "fixed," neither progressing nor regressing. A nurse may therefore be enthusiastic about the patient's improvement, only to become discouraged when the patient does not progress at a steady rate. It is easy to forget that lasting behavior changes are effected, or become relatively stable, only after a fairly long period of time. Improvement is never demonstrated by continuous uphill progression. It is expected, during the one-to-one relationship, that a patient will take three steps forward during one interaction and five steps backward during the next. Eventually the ill person may be able to stabilize the behavior change, but it is unrealistic to assume that this will invariably be the outcome. For example, a patient who has been ill for twenty years will not have his behavior permanently altered as a result of two to three hours of contact with a nurse, no matter how competent or experienced she may be.

A further barrier to task accomplishment is the nurse's unwillingness to engage in the tedious task of improving her ability to collect and interpret data, to apply concepts to the data, and to share her findings with others. If the nurse does not invest the time and energy required, it will not matter how well intended she may be, how many kind thoughts she has about the patient, or how much she desires the patient to recover—her actions will inevitably be ineffective. Kind thoughts without purposeful action do not effect behavior changes in anyone.

The nurse's fear of closeness may be another barrier. If the nurse cannot "forget self," or fears to reveal self, it is obvious that she cannot serve as a model for the human being who is the patient. If the helping person resorts to "ostrich techniques" she can hardly expect patients to engage in the anxiety-laden process of testing new patterns of behavior. If the nurse cannot communicate or socialize she can hardly serve as a model for a patient whose major difficulty may be in these areas.

If the nurse can find no meaning in illness and resorts to the use of blame objects ("It's always the fault of the mother") to explain discomfort she cannot expect anything else from the patient. A nurse who has difficulty in coping with her own life problems—who rebels against fate and circumstances of life—is hardly in a position to help a patient gain the courage required to return to a situation which may have precipitated his mental illness.

SUGGESTIONS

The supervisory conference and group reconstruction sessions are, at the present time, the media through which the nurse can best be assisted to see and overcome the barriers encountered during the phase of emerging identities. It is during this phase that the supervisor helps the learner to increase her ability to collect and interpret data, apply concepts, and synthesize the data obtained.

The practitioner has much to learn during this phase and the very number of the goals to be accomplished may, at times, be discouraging. It is the task of the supervisor to encourage the practitioner to persevere. As patients reach plateaus, so do nurses arrive at impasses. There will probably be times, in a nurse-patient interaction, when (according to the nurse's perception) "everything went wrong." There will be times when the nurse believes she is making little or no progress either in helping the patient or in gaining knowledge. It is at such times that encouragement and emotional support are needed. A statement by the supervisor that impasses are inevitable during the one-to-one relationship is sometimes helpful. Nurses who have unrealistic ideas about the progress a patient "should" be making often benefit from a frank discussion of these ideas. The goals of the nurse may not be unrealistic; however, she may have unrealistic expectations regarding her ability to achieve these goals. The nurse may not be expecting too much of the patient but rather expecting too much of herself. Again, a frank discussion with the supervisor may be helpful.

At one time or another during the phase of emerging identities most practitioners will exhibit a reluctance to write and analyze process records or to engage in a discussion with the supervisor about content of the records. There may, of course, be many reasons for this behavior. The supervisor may have said or done something which affected the practitioner adversely. Fatigue, boredom, discouragement or an apparent impasse in interacting with a patient may cause the reluctance. A discussion of the meaning of the behavior and of ways to overcome it is essential. Such a difficulty cannot be ignored on the premise that it will "go away." Practitioners are not allowed to remain indefinitely at an impasse, either in learning to assist patients or in increasing their knowledge.

It is suggested that supervisors check to see that recommendations are carried out. If, for example, a supervisor requests a learner to read a certain article which in the supervisor's opinion will assist her to render improved patient care, the supervisor should determine if the learner has read the article and whether or not plans have been made to implement the suggestions in the article. In short, the supervisor asks for both a critique of the article and the student's plans for using the information.

Throughout the phase of emerging identities the supervisor helps the practitioner increase her theoretical understanding, i.e., knowledge of the concepts and principles applicable in nurse-patient situations and of how to use these concepts and principles to predict or explain behavior. Opportunities for increased insight into the nurse's own behavior and increased sensitivity to other human beings are inherent in the one-to-one relationship, the supervisory conference and group reconstruction sessions. (Supervisory conferences and group reconstruction will be discussed in detail in Chapter X.)

If the nurse is able to accomplish the tasks essential to the phase of emerging identities then both participants—nurse and patient—are ready to proceed to the fourth and last phase, namely, termination of the relationship.

PART IV—TERMINATION

As stated in the section on "The Pact," one of the tasks of the nurse during the initial encounter is to tell the patient the number of days a week she will interact with him and over how long a period of time. Thus the fact that the interactions will be terminated within a particular time is established. During the phase of emerging identities the patient is also reminded of the time remaining for the nurse-patient interactions.

CAUSES OF TERMINATION

A relationship may be terminated for a number of reasons and under a variety of circumstances. The ill person may be discharged without the nurse's knowledge; hence she is not given an opportunity to assist him to work through the difficulties involved in termination. It is recommended that, if at all possible, a nurse working with a patient on a one-to-one basis be informed by a nurse on the unit (or in the agency), or by the patient's physician, that discharge is contemplated. Of course, the practitioner should attempt to ascertain when the patient will be discharged before initiating the one-to-one relationship.

A patient may discharge himself, i.e., he may go out on pass and not return, or may leave against medical advice. A nurse who is working with a patient who does this may fear that perhaps something she did or said may have caused the patient to act in this manner. The nurse's reasoning may or may not be valid.

The nurse may terminate the one-to-one relationship. There are several reasons why the nurse may choose to do so. A student, for example, may complete a psychiatric nursing course and have to end the relationship for this reason. A practitioner may decide that, in her judgment, the patient no longer needs the intensive experience of the one-to-one relationship; he may have reached a state of being able to function effectively without the support of the relationship.

PREPARATION OF THE PATIENT FOR TERMINATION

If the nurse terminates the relationship, it is recommended that specific plans be made to prepare the patient for this experience. The patient has the right to know the reasons for the termination, whatever they may be. Vagueness is to be avoided; the patient should be given clear unequivocal reasons for termination. All persons need cognitive clarity, and the ill person is no exception. If the patient does not understand why the relationship is being discontinued he will supply in fantasy reasons for termination—reasons which may or may not be valid. The patient should be allowed and encouraged to express his thoughts and feelings regarding termination.

Termination When the Patient is to Remain in the Hospital

A nurse may begin to prepare a patient for termination by assisting him to interact with other patients on the unit (or in the agency). She encourages him gradually to become involved with other patients on the unit and to participate in group projects. Some nurses help patients prepare for termination by intentionally, slowly, and with great tact and timing introducing other patients as participants in the interaction, so that the one-to-one relationship becomes a group relationship. The nurse then gradually withdraws from the group situation.

Patients differ in their reactions to nurses' attempts to prepare them for termination. The practitioner does not really know what the ill person thinks or feels about termination unless he (the patient) communicates these thoughts and feelings to the nurse. An ill person who has experienced trust, support, and the warmth of caring may be reluctant to discontinue the nurse-patient contact. Some patients experience termination as desertion. This feeling may persist even though the patient intellectually may comprehend the necessity of, or reasons for, concluding the relationship. The ill person may demonstrate angry behavior. Some patients attempt to "punish" the nurse for this desertion by not talking during the last few interactions or by ignoring termination completely, i.e., talking about everything *but* the fact that the relationship between nurse and patient is coming to an end; they act as if nothing has changed and that the nurse-patient interviews will go on as before. Other ill persons react to the threatened loss by becoming depressed or assuming an attitude of "not caring." Some patients, when questioned as to whether or not anger is related to termination, can express their anger openly; others cannot. Those who cannot seem to need to make the nurse feel uncomfortable for leaving them. If the nurse is able to understand what is occurring and to withstand the patient's provocative behavior without retaliating, usually the behavior will change. Angry feelings dissipate and the crisis of abandonment gradually diminishes. The nurse can assist some patients by openly eliciting their thoughts and feelings about termination. Patients who do not respond to such cues should not be pushed to respond. With time and patience many such individuals are finally able to discuss the meaning of termination to them.

Termination When the Patient Is Discharged

Patients who are being discharged do not feel "deserted" by the nurse since they (the patients) are the ones leaving the situation—

not the nurse. However, even under these circumstances some patients may display a reluctance to terminate the interaction. The problem, however, may be reluctance not to conclude a relationship but to cope with problems in the home situation. Not all patients are "glad to be going home" or happy at the prospect of discharge. Many ill persons experience ambivalent feelings about their ability to "make it" outside of the hospital. As one patient stated:

> The doctor says I'm ready to go home but he (the doctor) told Helen (another patient) the same thing. She was only able to stay outside a week and now she's back in again. I want to make sure that when I go home I'll be able to stay there. I never want to see this place again.

The hospital, its personnel and routines are known to the patient. Problems to be faced in the community are unknown and sometimes frightening.

It is recommended that the nurse assist the patient to discuss frankly his thoughts and feelings about discharge and to identify *specifically* what he is afraid of, i.e., what *specific* problems or people engender feelings of anxiety, inadequacy or incompetency. In the example given above, one might ponder what the patient actually does fear. Is she doubting the physician's ability to determine whether she is ready for discharge? In she generalizing from Helen's experience to her own? If so, on what basis? She and Helen are not the same human beings; they have not had identical life problems or attempted to cope with these in the same manner. Is there some reason why the patient does not feel ready for discharge other than the reason given the nurse? The nurse may discover the patient's fears simply by asking. The problem is identified and validated with the patient before appropriate nursing action is taken. Individual patients express their fears regarding discharge from the hospital in many ways. The following excerpts from process records exemplify some of these fears:

> "I don't know if I will be able to face my friends and relatives. . ."
> "I don't know if I can handle the children . . . they make me so nervous. I love them but they get me so tensed up. . . ."
> "I'm not sure I can do my housework . . . it wears me out so."
> "I don't know if I'll be able to get my old job back."
> "I live in a small town and everyone knows I've been in (a large state mental hospital). I don't know how my relatives and friends will accept me."
> "If I apply for a job should I tell them I've been in a mental hospital for two years?"

There are no standard methods or techniques one can use to help a patient resolve fears other than that of giving the patient an opportunity to discuss his thoughts and feelings. As stated, it is helpful if the nurse is able to assist the patient to identify the problem most feared. Following identification of the problem area, she then helps the patient make plans to deal with it. For example, how would a nurse assist the patient who said: "I don't know if I will be able to face my friends and relatives?" The nurse might ask the patient to explain in greater detail what she fears. What does she mean by "face my friends and relatives?" To whom is the patient referring? Is there a specific friend or relative the patient has in mind? Depending on the nurse's clinical judgment, she may suggest a role-playing session in which the patient plays herself and the nurse assumes the part of the "friend or relative." Roles are then switched and the role-playing is discussed. Emphasis is placed on developing specific approaches to the problem presented. Not all patients are willing, or feel comfortable enough, to role-play; neither do all nurses. In such instances the nurse, after obtaining specific data from the patient about the nature of the problem, begins to help the patient to design ways of coping it.

In some settings, psychiatric social workers are available for consultation as resource persons throughout the one-to-one relationship. Prior to termination by discharge, the nurse may wish to consult the social worker about problems the patient may expect to encounter upon returning to the community. Psychiatric social workers can assist patients with problems of employment and housing, and with possible family problems resulting from the patient's discharge from the hospital. Social workers can refer patients with limited incomes to agencies which will assist them to purchase drugs. Many patients discharged from hospitals (or clinics) are given prescriptions by their physicians for psychopharmacological drugs and may have to take them for a period of months to years. These drugs are expensive; a patient with barely enough income to buy food or pay rent is not likely to buy expensive medications, no matter how important, without some assistance.

The patient to be discharged should, if possible, be referred to a public health agency to receive regular home visits from a public health nurse. The public health nurse is in the enviable position of being able to see the patient in his natural milieu, identify problem areas as they emerge and initiate appropriate intervention. In some few instances discharged patients are "followed" by a psychiatric nurse who makes home visits.

The discussion thus far presupposes the availability of psychiatric social workers and public health nurses who are prepared to assist the discharged mentally ill patient. It also presupposes the existence of such facilities as comprehensive mental health centers, including in-patient and out-patient services, neighborhood service centers, half-way houses, "walk-in" psychiatric clinics and ex-patient clubs. In actuality most areas in our country, at the present time, do *not* have either prepared personnel or the facilities listed above. What can the nurse do under such circumstances? She does what she can to assist the patient to identify problems and to envisage and test alternative ways of resolving them. She also must know the resources available in the community and how to utilize these when necessary.

As stated, most patients about to be discharged from the hospital are able to express, to some extent, the difficulties they expect to encounter. A few ill persons may be unable or unwilling to talk about such matters, for many reasons. For example, an ill person may realize that he will indeed face difficulties at home, but may be unwilling to admit this for fear he will not be discharged. Another patient may deny possible future difficulties because he truly believes that once discharged all his problems will automatically cease; this person acts as if his problems can be tied into a neat bundle and left at the hospital, while he emerges unencumbered by problems. The hospital, in the patient's mind, is the *cause of* as well as the potential depository for his troubles. If the individual admits to having experienced difficulties he may blame the hospital for "causing" his problem; he thus exonerates himself from any personal responsibility. In fairness it cannot be denied that hospitalization—depending on the quality of care rendered—can indeed increase problems for a patient, but the original source of the patient's difficulties in living cannot be blamed on the hospital per se. Individuals with such problems may be identified fairly early in the initial interaction if the nurse is astute enough to pick up certain cues. For example, such individuals have a tendency to solve complex problems by resorting to extremely simplistic solutions. They tend to utilize the "if only" mechanism—"If only I had a job all of my problems would be over" or "If only my wife (or husband) would treat me better I wouldn't be in the hospital," etc. A nurse attempting to structure a one-to-one relationship with such a patient is at a marked disadvantage if he is to be discharged before she has had an opportunity to assist him to relinquish such ineffective tactics. How can she help him? One might argue that it is better to ignore the problem, to let the patient have his little illusions since they serve a purpose and make him feel comfortable and competent. Also, one might feel that since the patient will invariably encounter problems once he is home it is best to "leave well enough alone." What is the nurse's responsibility? It is believed the nurse, in good conscience, cannot ignore the situation and react on the same level as the patient, i.e., by ignoring the possibility of future problems. Whether or not the nurse can change the patient's behavior at this stage is problematic, but she must at least try to help the patient become more realistic about the problems he may encounter. How does the nurse accomplish this? She may begin by casting doubts on the patient's assumption that "everything will be fine once I get home." This maneuver may or may not be successful. One method which helps some patients is asking them to describe specifically what they will do when they arrive at home. For example, the nurse asks: "What will you do first?" "*Then* what will you do?" The purpose of the inquiry is to assist the patient to discover possible problem areas. Again, this method may or may not be helpful, but the nurse can try to prepare the person psychologically for termination and discharge. As can be anticipated, patients who truly believe that all of their problems will automatically and magically cease once they are discharged are soon disillusioned upon returning home. Often these individuals cannot maintain themselves outside of the hospital setting and are soon readmitted.

Thus far the necessity of psychologically preparing the ill person for termination has been stressed. However, the nurse who has worked to establish relatedness with the patient also needs psychological preparation.

PREPARATION OF THE NURSE FOR TERMINATION

Nurses must be prepared for all kinds of terminations. Patients may be discharged, run away, or leave the hospital against medical advice. Nurses must also be prepared for termination when patients no longer require the services they can render during the one-to-one relationship. As with a patient, the human being who is the nurse may experience varied and conflicting feelings about termination.

Termination Without the Nurse's Knowledge

A nurse may arrive for the scheduled interaction to discover that the patient has been discharged by the psychiatrist, has left the hospital against medical advice, or has not returned from a weekend pass. A nurse may react to a discharge without her knowledge by becoming angry at personnel or the psychiatrist for not having informed her, or at the patient for having deserted her. This anger may be turned inward, resulting in a mild transient depression, or may be expressed openly or covertly to personnel and others. The nurse may believe that her efforts were not appreciated by the psychiatrist or by the patient himself.

If she has established a working relationship with the psychiatrist, it is probable that the nurse will be told when the patient is to be discharged. This assists her in preparing the patient for his eventual release from the hospital. However, in actuality there are many reasons why nurses may not be informed. Relatives may exert pressure on the psychiatrist to release the patient, or psychiatrists may be rotated from one service to another and may not know that a nurse is interacting on a one-to-one basis with a particular patient. Personnel on the nursing unit may "forget" to notify the nurse. There may be a number of reasons to explain why personnel "forget" other than the usual "We were so busy." If the nurse receives the "too busy" explanation it is recommended that she attempt to increase her ability to communicate with and establish improved relationships with personnel.

The nurse who has been attempting to establish a one-to-one relationship with a patient who leaves against medical advice, deserts, or does not return from a pass may experience guilt feelings. She may believe that something she did or said caused the patient to react in this manner. It is hardly likely, however, that the nurse is quite so powerful.

Termination by the Nurse

The nurse terminates the relationship when the patient no longer requires the services she can offer in the one-to-one relationship. The nurse who terminates a relationship for this reason when the patient is not discharged has three major responsibilities: she prepares the patient for termination of the relationship, prepares herself psychologically for withdrawing from the patient, and initiates and implements plans for the ill person to become more involved in group activities.

A nurse who has invested time, energy and effort in establishing and maintaining a relationship may experience mixed feelings about withdrawing from the patient even though she may realize, on an intellectual level, that withdrawal is necessary to help the patient progress more rapidly toward social recovery. The nurse has achieved the purpose of the one-to-one relationship—the patient no longer requires intensive counseling. However successful the nurse may feel, there may be a reluctance to "let the patient go." It is well recognized that a patient can become dependent on a nurse for support, comfort or decision making. A nurse can also become dependent on a patient in the sense of developing a feeling of possessiveness about "releasing" him to others.

It is recommended that the nurse attempt to identify her thoughts and feelings about the impending termination. She may experience depression or anxiety as a result of the imminent loss. These feelings may be related to beginning a relationship with a new and unknown patient. It is helpful if the nurse can explore and express with the supervisor her feelings in regard to termination. It is also recommended that, once the nurse terminates the relationship, i.e., interacts with the patient for the last time, she no longer attempt to see him, revive the relationship, or in any way make contact with him. If possible, the nurse should be assigned to, or select, a patient on another nursing unit, i.e., not the unit where she has interacted previously. If she does encounter her "old" patient in the hall or in any other part of the building the nurse, of course, speaks with him, but does not attempt to reestablish the terminated relationship.

The nurse who must terminate a relationship with a patient because he is soon to be discharged should attempt to identify her thoughts and feelings in relation to the patient's discharge. The nurse may not have been able to achieve her goals in working with the patient, or may have achieved them only partially, and hence experiences a sense of frustration and incompleteness. She may believe the patient is "not ready for discharge" (whether this is true or false) and may "blame" the psychiatrist for sending the patient home too soon. There are, of course, exceptions to this; the nurse may believe the patient *is* ready to go home. However, she may still have mixed feelings about discharge; while pleased that the patient is going home she may still experience sadness at the departure of an individual in whom she has invested considerable feeling, interest, effort and time.

A nurse who must terminate a relationship, whether through her own choice or because the patient is being discharged, invariably arrives at the last nurse-patient interaction. How can this interaction be used as a profitable learning experience for both nurse and patient?

THE LAST NURSE-PATIENT INTERACTION

What the nurse and patient say or do during the final nurse-patient interaction is determined by many factors: the thoughts and feelings of both participants regarding the final interaction, the extent to which both persons are prepared psychologically for termination, and the way in which each participant perceives the separation from the other. There are no specific methods to be used which will insure that participants in the interaction feel comfortable with termination. What has been initiated must now be concluded; termination is an ending. Yet in another sense it is a beginning, in that both participants will go on to other life experiences. Hopefully they will have been enriched by the experiences they have shared with each other.

Certain problems may emerge during the last nurse-patient interaction. For example, the patient may ask the nurse to write to him or to "come back and see him." He may ask the nurse for her address or phone number so he may "keep in touch." There can be many reasons for such behavior. The patient may not wish to conclude a satisfying relationship; he may not wish to say good-bye. The patient may test the nurse to ascertain how reliable she is. If she has said: "Today is the last interview," the patient may try to see whether she means what she says. Beginners in psychiatric nursing tend to have difficulties in resolving these problems. It is believed that termination should be *final,* that nurses should not write to patients or give patients their phone numbers or addresses. It is recommended that beginners in psychiatric nursing conceptualize in advance the method they will use to deal with these situations. Beginners who do give patients their phone numbers or addresses, or promise to write, many times do so because the patient's request has "caught them off guard," or because they don't "want to hurt the patient's feelings." Another reason often given is: "I didn't want the patient to think I wasn't interested in his progress." It is probable that such nurses are motivated not by their desire not to upset the patient but by their inability to say "no" and mean it.

Termination can be a learning experience for both nurse and patient. Most human relationships eventually must terminate; except for relatives or close friends, very few last over a prolonged period of time. For the most part one meets, interacts with, and eventually parts from another individual. This is reality. The human being who is the patient has undergone partings in the past; so has the nurse. Termination can be a learning experience for the ill person if he is helped to understand the necessity of parting and the finality of good-byes. With some patients, the loss experienced may trigger remembrances of past separations and losses. It is not always easy to help an ill person comprehend that the present termination is not a replication of an earlier loss. It is only by the nurse's continuous attempt to prepare the patient psychologically for termination, by eliciting from the patient his thoughts and feelings regarding termination, that she can sense this possible problem area and institute appropriate intervention. The final nurse-patient interaction is *not* the time to *begin* such intervention. It is much too late.

Another problem which may emerge during the last nurse-patient interaction is that of gift giving. A patient, during the last interaction, may wish to give the nurse a gift. The policies of the institution or agency in which the nurse practices may prohibit the receiving of gifts. Some agencies have no stated policy; however, there may be unwritten rules about accepting gifts from patients. For example, it may be acceptable in some settings for attendants to accept "going-away presents" but not for professional nurses to do so. Nurses tend to have mixed feelings about accepting gifts from patients which usually stem from nursing school teachings. Such nurses believe it is "unprofessional" for a nurse ever to accept a gift from a patient.

The nurse needs to conceptualize her thoughts and feelings about accepting gifts from patients and decide *before* the final interaction with the patient whether or not to accept a gift if offered. It is also recommended that a nurse who has strong feelings about accepting a gift from any patient plan in advance how she will refuse the offered gift without offending the patient. Should a nurse *ever* accept a gift from a patient? A simple answer cannot be given. If the nurse feels strongly against accepting gifts, she should refuse them. Some people will not agree with this statement on the basis that the patient's feelings may be hurt by the nurse's refusal. This, however, is not invariably true. A case in point follows:

> During the final nurse-patient interaction the patient handed the nurse a wallet he had made in occupational therapy and told the nurse he wanted her to have something to remember him by. The nurse, who did not want to accept the wallet, said very gently: "Thank you, Mr. X, but I do not need a wallet to remember you by. I shall not forget you." The nurse then suggested the patient give the wallet to his son.

If the nurse is tactful and gentle, it is quite possible to refuse a gift without hurting the patient's feelings.

There are times when it may be appropriate to accept a gift from a patient. Much depends on how the nurse perceives gift giving and, equally important, her inference as to the patient's reason for offering the gift. Nurses do not accept money or gifts of any sizable monetary value. Sometimes, however, the individual who can least afford to give a gift seems to have the greatest need to give something tangible to the nurse. An example follows:

> The nurse had established a one-to-one relationship with an elderly bed-ridden lady. The patient had a great pride in her ability to embroider and crochet, and received pleasure from compliments from patients, relatives and others regarding her very obvious skill. Her financial resources (and those of her family) were limited; however, members of the patient's church organization supplied her with embroidery materials. It was the patient's great pleasure in life (and one of the very few pleasures she actually had)

to give her completed work to others. During the last nurse-patient interaction the patient gave the nurse an embroidered dish towel and told the
nurse she (the patient) wanted the nurse to have it because the nurse had
"done so much for her." The nurse, sensing that refusal might be interpreted by the patient as a negation of her ability to embroider, accepted the
gift and thanked the patient for her thoughtfulness.

In summary, no clear-cut directives can be given to enable the
nurse to decide automatically whether or not to accept a gift from
a patient. The nurse should make certain of her thoughts and feelings
regarding gift giving and receiving and, if possible, validate with the
patient her inferences as to the patient's reason for offering the gift.

When the time comes for conclusion of the final nurse-patient
interaction, the nurse says good-bye to the patient and wishes him
well. She may shake hands with the patient in the event he extends his
hand. The nurse then leaves the patient and the one-to-one relationship is terminated.

BARRIERS TO ACCOMPLISHMENT OF TASKS

The major tasks of the nurse during the phase of termination
are to prepare the patient psychologically for conclusion of the relationship and to implement plans to assist the ill person (if he is to
remain in the hospital) to become involved in group activities. The
nurse helps the patient who is to be discharged to anticipate problems
he may encounter upon his return to the community. Another task of
the nurse is to prepare herself psychologically for termination.

Many of the barriers to accomplishment of these tasks have already been discussed. For example, it is not possible to prepare the
patient for termination if the patient is discharged without the nurse's
knowledge, runs off from the hospital or does not return to the hospital from a weekend pass. These are factors over which the nurse
has no control. When the nurse *does* have the opportunity to terminate the one-to-one relationship, the barriers to goal accomplishment
seem to be related to the nurse's inability or unwillingness to make
specific plans and implement these. Plans for termination are essential, and nurses need to conceptualize these plans in advance. A nurse
who does not discuss frankly the reasons for termination or elicit from
the patient his thoughts and feelings about the impending experience
obviously cannot help prepare a patient psychologically. A nurse who
cannot or will not explore her own thoughts and feelings about separation from the patient also is unable to accomplish the goals related
to termination.

SUGGESTIONS

The supervisory conference and group reconstruction session are, at the present time, the best media through which the nurse is assisted to identify and overcome the barriers to task accomplishment during the phase of termination. The supervisor assists the practitioner consciously to focus on preparing self and patient for the eventual conclusion of the relationship. During the phase of termination the supervisor may notice that the nurse is showing less interest in the patient than previously, and may be disengaging self from the patient several weeks *before* the final nurse-patient interaction. Such behavior should be brought to the attention of the practitioner in order to identify possible causes. Some nurses resort to "early withdrawal" almost as a psychological defense mechanism, and by doing so reduce or deny the anxiety they are experiencing as a result of the impending termination of the relationship.

Some nurses, especially beginners in psychiatric nursing, demonstrate a decreased interest in the patient once they learn the patient is to be discharged. This disinterest may be exemplified by reluctance to write and analyze process records or to engage in meaningful discussion with the supervisor about the content in the record. The quality of the student's written work may decline, and during group reconstruction sessions she may make only superficial comments regarding the nurse-patient interaction. The task of the supervisor, when working with beginners, is to discuss frankly with the student the meaning of the behavior. Does the student perceive the patient's discharge from the hospital as a sign that the patient is "well," and hence feel she does not need to strive so intensively to help him, or is discharge perceived as desertion? Once clear as to possible reasons for such behavior, the supervisor initiates action to assist the learner to persevere. The psychiatric nurse practitioner does not "give up" once it is learned the patient is to be discharged. Quite the contrary—the nurse intensifies her efforts to prepare both self and patient for his eventual release from the agency. The patient is as needful of the services the nurse can offer during this phase of the relationship as he was during the preceding ones.

If the practitioner is to be assisted, however, it is essential that she feel free to reveal her thoughts and feelings and to discuss them frankly with the supervisor. The nurse's inability to discuss the problems which are the inevitable result of establishing, maintaining and terminating a one-to-one relationship make it impossible for the supervisor to help. The nurse's inability to discuss problems results in her failure to accomplish the major goals of the one-to-one relationship. She is therefore unable to be of real assistance to the human being who is the patient.

If a nurse given the opportunity to help an ill person chooses not to do so, what is the effect of this decision on the patient? A nurse who could have helped but didn't may change the course of a patient's life. Bluntly, the nurse's decision not to help may cause a patient to spend months and years in a mental hospital or to develop a chronic mental illness. Eventually the patient may reach the point of no return in terms of social recovery. Granted, it is not *always* or *just* the nurse's refusal which is the *sole* determinant of whether or not a patient will recover. However, it cannot be denied that a nurse who has been given an opportunity to help a patient and fails to do so— through negligence, incompetency, or other reasons—actively contributes to the maintenance of the patient's illness and cannot hope to be exonerated from this responsibility. It is probable that acts of omission in nursing care cause more needless suffering than do acts of commission. Further, it is easier to hide incompetent nursing care given psychiatric patients than poor care given patients with medical or surgical problems. There seems to be a belief held by some nurses that "mistakes" made when caring for psychiatric patients are not so important as mistakes made when caring for medical or surgical patients. For example, an instructor on a medical unit said: "If one of our students makes a mistake the patient may die. This is not true in psychiatric nursing." There may be some small degree of validity to the instructor's statement. However, it is often overlooked that, although the psychiatric patient may not die, he may be condemned to a lifetime of psychological dying. One does not die of mental illness, but mental illness can become a kind of dying even though one "lives."

In addition to the patient's progress, the nurse's decision not to become involved also affects the nurse. She may be successful in concealing her noninvolvement decision from supervisors, peers and others. The nurse, however, knows of her decision, and must live with this knowledge. A process of character erosion begins, and this process continues with each act of self-betrayal. Nurses who choose noninvolvement lack the courage to commit themselves to others, and courage is prerequisite to rendering the highest quality of care. "Heroic plodders" are needed—conscientious nurses who commit themselves to accomplish each day's tasks to the best of their ability, no matter how tedious these tasks may seem. It is probable that the greatest assets the psychiatric nurse practitioner can possess include commitment to accomplish the tasks willingly accepted, active pursuit of excellence in practice, and ability to endure and persevere in spite of the many barriers to accomplishment of goals.

Chapter IX

PROBLEMATIC AREAS OF THE
NURSE-PATIENT RELATIONSHIP

Many general problems related to establishing, maintaining and terminating the one-to-one relationship have been discussed in Chapter VIII, "The Nurse-Patient Relationship." There are, however, many other problems which may be encountered. Those to be discussed in this chapter are divided into four major categories: problems related to habitual behavioral patterns of individual patients, specific problems of individual nurse practitioners, problems encountered in working with personnel, and problems encountered in trying to work collaboratively with members of other health disciplines. There is much overlap among these groups. For example, problems encountered in working with individual patients are not only "patient problems" but also problems of the practitioner trying to establish relatedness.

Suggestions and recommendations to resolve difficulties discussed in this chapter are *not* to be considered as *the* sole means of coping with particular problems. Each nurse-patient, nurse-personnel or nurse-health worker interaction is unique. The suggested approaches are *not* panaceas or easy methods to problem resolution, and should not be considered as such. They are simply recommendations which may or may not be effective.

PART I—SPECIFIC PATIENT PROBLEMS

One of the major obstacles to be surmounted in establishing relatedness is the barrier of noninvolvement (or uninvolvement) on the part of one or both participants. For example, if the nurse does not desire to become involved with the human being who is the patient relatedness cannot be achieved.

A major assumption in this work is that mentally ill individuals are unable to establish satisfactory interpersonal relationships with other persons and to derive satisfaction or enjoyment from these relationships. Mentally ill people are unable to become emotionally involved, on a mature level, with other human beings. Noninvolvement is characterized by the inability of a person to perceive himself as an active participant in life experiences. Such a person tends to view life as observer or passive agent, acted upon by experiences but not actively engaged in these experiences. Uninvolvement is probably a defense against anxiety. As a behavioral response uninvolvement may be viewed as a continuum ranging from the unconcern or indifference about others exhibited by "normal individuals" to the profound withdrawal into fantasy of the intensely preoccupied hallucinating individual. There are many variations of behavior between these bipolar manifestations.

Uninvolvement is characterized by an inability to develop meaningful relationships with other human beings and implies a fear of, but not necessarily a lack of desire for, emotional closeness with others. The uninvolved individual may display his inability to become emotionally committed by use of maneuvers expressly designed to keep others at a distance. In this chapter detachment (or withdrawal), dejection (or depression), superficiality, manipulatory behavior, suspiciousness, anxiousness, and other such methods will be discussed. Approaches will be suggested which may assist the nurse in coping with, or helping the ill person to resolve, the problem presented.

DETACHMENT

Establishing an emotional bond with a detached, withdrawn patient presents a challenge to the novice as well as to the experienced practitioner. Communication (verbal and nonverbal) is the medium used to reach toward the detached person. His speech behavior (or lack of it) may present a definite problem. The use of speech by the detached person may range from responding by the use of monosyllables or short phrases to complete muteness.

When talking with a detached person one may get the impression that he is "uninhabited." The individual, as a unique person, seems to disappear for a period of time and the nurse may feel she is talking with a shell, not a living human being. It may be difficult to perceive any kind of emotional or feeling response. The nurse may conclude that the ill person lacks affect—that she may as well "talk to the wall." Not all detached individuals are devoid of affect to this extent but many demonstrate either lack of affect or inappropriate affect.

Schizophrenia is the most common diagnostic label given the individual whose habitual behavioral response is detachment. The label *schizophrenia* is not important in terms of nursing intervention. The activities of the nurse, regardless of the diagnosis, include carefully assessing the individual's behavior and making plans to assist him to resolve some of the problems related to detachment.

The label schizophrenia is, as has been stated, relatively unimportant in terms of nursing intervention. However, practitioners should have an understanding of the theories regarding the etiology of the schizophrenic syndrome. These abound in the literature (see Bibliography, Appendix I, Chapter IX). However, at the present time there is no one generally accepted theory. Whether schizophrenia is caused by some undetermined genetic factor or is primarily a result of early exposure to anxiety-laden life experiences is not definitely known at this time.

The nurse who works with the detached person is presented with the problem of breaking through the facade of unconcern and establishing an emotional bond. This can be very difficult. The detached person tends to fear closeness with others, and therefore the one-to-one relationship presents a definite threat to him. In the past closeness with others may have brought only mental anguish, and there is a natural protective reluctance, on the part of the ill person, to expose himself to unnecessary pain. An ill person has no way of knowing in advance if the nurse will help him or hurt him or whether she is a person who can be trusted. The nurse's attempt to establish relatedness may be viewed by the patient as an attempt to deprive him of the only protective means at his disposal, noninvolvement by detachment from others.

It cannot automatically be assumed that an ill person's reluctance to engage in an interaction is *always* motivated by a fear of closeness. The nurse-patient encounter is resisted for a variety of reasons. The most common is that the ill person does not understand the nature of the interaction or of the assistance the nurse can offer. The practitioner through adroit inquiry can detect whether or not the ill person understands the purpose of the interaction. As stated, role interpretation is a continuous process and not a "one-shot" affair.

Detached individuals may resort to various maneuvers to keep the nurse away. Some of these include: refusing to talk with the nurse, answering only when asked a direct question, running away or hiding when the time for the nurse-patient interaction approaches, "forgetting" appointments, remaining in a group situation to avoid talking with the nurse, or attempting to engage the nurse in a card game to avoid any meaningful dialogue. Only the most common maneuvers will be discussed here. There are, of course, many other tactics the ill person can use to avoid the interaction.

What can the nurse do to assist the individual whose predominant behavioral response is detachment? It is suggested that she first assess the extent of the individual's capacity to relate with others and identify the particular maneuvers he uses to avoid relating. It may be assumed that maneuvers to avoid closeness will be utilized by the ill person until he realizes there is no need for them. It is therefore one of the tasks of the nurse to help him gradually to relinquish the need for such behavior. (The problem of breaking through the facade of detachment is compounded when the nurse is assigned to work with an ill person who has not been given a choice as to whether or not he wishes to participate in the relationship.)

It must be emphasized that there are no easy methods by which the nurse can assist all ill persons. There are several approaches the practitioner can try; however, there is no guarantee that any of the suggested approaches will work with all detached individuals. Creativity and ingenuity are required to establish relatedness with the individual who strives to block the nurse in her attempt to do so.

The Individual Who Remains in a Group or Plays Games

As stated, the nurse tries to get the ill person to relinquish the maneuvers used to avoid closeness. To do this the nurse, after identifying the particular ploy and what it represents in the life of the patient, may, for the time being, have to go along with the maneuver. For example, if the patient will not talk to the nurse except in a group setting then she joins the group and interacts with the person within the group. The nurse may engage in card games or checkers with the patient if this is the only way to interact with him. The nurse's purpose in so doing is to demonstrate to the patient that she is a non-threatening, adaptable individual. Hopefully, the ill person eventually may be able to trust the nurse as an individual who will not rush him into a relationship for which he is not prepared. Gradually the ill person may be able to relinquish his defensive maneuvers and converse with the nurse without the need of a group for support or a game to keep her at a distance. It should be emphasized that the nurse's focus, whether in a group situation or in a card game, is on the individual patient—not on other group members or on the game. The group or the game is used by the nurse as a way of reaching the ill person and establishing emotional contact with him.

The Individual Who Hides From the Nurse

Some ill persons literally run away and hide when the time arrives for the nurse-patient interaction. Others emerge from their hiding places when there are only minutes remaining for the interaction. If the patient is not present on the unit when the nurse arrives, she ascertains where he is. If the patient is in the bathroom the nurse may ask a member of the staff to tell him she is waiting for him; she then sits and waits. Some patients emerge from the bathroom five minutes before the scheduled end of the interview. Ill persons may give "logical" reasons for not being on time such as "I forgot" or "I was taking a bath when you came." Others give no explanation and wait for the nurse's response to their failure to be on time. The ill person's behavior may be an attempt to test the limits of the relationship or to provoke the nurse into a punitive response, or it may exemplify his fear of developing an emotional attachment to the nurse.

If the individual gives "I forgot" as a reason for lateness, and it *is* the first time he has been late, the nurse may decide to accept the explanation at face value. Before leaving, she reminds the patient of the date and time of the next interview. If the lateness persists or if the patient has to be sought for each interview the nurse uses more appropriate approaches. She may confront the person with his behavior: "Why have you been late for our last three appointments?" The nurse should, when confronting the ill person, convey an attitude of sincerely desiring to understand the meaning of the behavior. Her demeanor is not that of condemnation, recrimination or blame. The attitude she wishes to communicate is: "I don't understand; help me to understand." Such advice is easy to give but difficult to practice. The nurse, as human being, has feelings; she may well experience anger at having "wasted time" or at having been "stood up" for an appointment. Such behavior on the patient's part is not always easy to accept. Understanding and acceptance unfortunately are not synonymous.

If the ill person has not been given a choice regarding interaction, additional difficulties become apparent. For example, a patient may say that he did not choose to talk with the nurse, he doesn't have anything to say, and he wishes the nurse would select someone else. One patient stated: "There are other patients here who would be glad to talk with you; why don't you pick someone else?" The nurse can handle this rebuff in a number of ways—by remaining silent and indicating nonverbally that the patient tell more about his refusal to participate; by questioning the individual regarding his refusal; or by attempting to convince the person of the benefits he will derive through the nurse-patient interaction. The latter is not recommended as a way of resolving the problem; neither is a precipitous decision to stop seeing the ill person and to select another patient for the relationship.

It is recommended that, in instances where an ill person is not given a choice and indicates rather consistently to the nurse that he does not wish to interact, she confront him directly in an attempt for both to understand the reasons for the behavior. An excerpt from a process record is an example of such a confrontation.

> The ill person had not been given a choice as to whether she wished to inter-act with the nurse. The patient had been thirty minutes late for the second interaction. Her explanation was that she forgot the nurse was coming and overslept. The present interaction is the third and the patient is fifteen minutes late. The nurse searches for the patient and finds her in the bathroom. The patient states: "I'll be right with you." The nurse sits and waits. Ten minutes later the patient emerges from the bathroom and says: "I'll be there in just a minute. I have to hang up my towel and comb my hair." Ten minutes later the patient returns, sits down, gets up to get a drink of water and then sits down again.
>
> Nurse: You are late this morning . . .
> Patient: I have so much to do in the morning.
> Nurse: Oh?
> Patient: Well, I have to bathe, comb my hair, make up my bed and fix my face.
> Nurse: Is that why you are late for our meetings?
> Patient: Yes.
> Nurse: Would another time be better for you?
> Patient: No, not really . . .
> Nurse: I don't understand. What do you mean?
> Patient: I don't really have anything to say to you. (The patient's hands begin to shake.)
> Nurse: Is this why you have been late for our meetings?
> Patient: Yes. (She begins to twirl a button on her dress.)
> Nurse: You say you have nothing to say to me yet we're talking now . . .
> Patient: I mean I don't know what I am *supposed* to say. You're not a doctor and I don't have to tell you anything.
> Nurse: No, I am not a doctor. And I wonder if I have made clear to you my reasons for wanting to talk with you.
> (The nurse reinterprets her role and explains to the patient that she is there to talk about problems on the ward or any other problems the patient wishes to discuss with her.)
> Patient: Tell me why you picked me to talk to. There are plenty of other patients here . . .
> Nurse: I wanted to talk with you.
> Patient: Why?

Nurse: You seem to place a great deal of importance as to why I selected you rather than someone else. Why?

Patient: I thought maybe it was because I was the sickest patient here.

Nurse: No, I didn't believe you were the sickest person then and I don't now.

Patient: Oh! (pause of approximately ten seconds) Nurse, you can come and talk to me. I don't mind. I'll be here.

In the above example the patient initially stated she was late for the appointment because she "had so much to do." When confronted with another possible appointment time the patient *was* able to say that the time factor was really not important. She then explained: "I don't know what I am supposed to say" and indicated that, since the nurse was not a doctor, she "didn't have to tell her anything." The nurse's assumption, at this point, was that the patient did not comprehend her role. The nurse then reinterpreted her role and explained why she wished to speak with the patient. The nurse's role, however, was not the ill person's primary concern. She was afraid the nurse had selected her because she was "the sickest patient on the ward." The nurse stated she did not believe the patient was the sickest patient on the unit. (The nurse, in this instance, honestly did not believe the patient was the sickest patient on the unit. If she had, she obviously would not indicate this to the patient.) The nurse's frank expression of opinion seemed to assist the patient. What may have occurred, although there is no way of validating this, is that the patient believed that the nurse recognized the obvious areas of wellness in her; perhaps she experienced hope. The patient was on time for appointments with the nurse for the remaining seven interactions prior to her discharge and seemed to benefit from the interactions. Perhaps one of the most important aspects of the nurse's reaction to the ill person's hiding was that she waited for the patient; she did not berate her, blame her or endeavor to make her feel guilty.

The Relatively Mute Individual

The ill person whose habitual behavioral response is that of muteness presents a challenge. Psychopharmacological agents have proved effective in the treatment of such patients; however, they are still encountered by nurses in receiving units of hospitals and in back wards of large mental institutions.

Why does an individual choose muteness rather than hiding or some other maneuver to avoid closeness? At the risk of sounding simplistic, one can only surmise that such behavior has worked for the person in the past and continues to work for him. Muteness is a passive-aggressive method of keeping others at a distance by refusing to respond. Complete muteness is an extreme deviation from behavior encountered in "normal" individuals who, under stress of provocation (whether real or imagined), stop speaking to certain people. Some may do this temporarily—for two to three days—and then resume conversation. In the meantime they manage to make those around them feel guilty and generally miserable. Some individuals hold out longer than two to three days, or may speak only when spoken to and then respond in monosyllables while displaying an attitude of sullenness. Resumption of conversation may only occur after the individual to whom the person has stopped talking apologizes or in some other way makes amends; the person who makes amends may be subjected to angry comments or "forgiven" under certain conditions laid down by the "offended" person. If not speaking has worked for an individual, such behavior may well become an habitual rather than a temporary method of controlling the behavior of others. Not speaking serves various purposes. It forces others to make efforts to engage the silent person in conversation. It also can be used to punish others. Frequently the person subjected to the silence may tire of trying to engage the nonverbal person in conversation. A one-sided conversation is tedious for most people. The person who is silent as an habitual mode of behavior is therefore thrown back on his inner resources and may, in compensation, become increasingly preoccupied with fantasy.

During the first encounter with the relatively mute individual it is recommended that the nurse sit a few feet away from him. Clinical observations seem to indicate that many such persons seem to fear physical closeness. It has also been repeatedly noted that such patients tend to avoid direct eye contact with the nurse.

As discussed in Chapter VIII, "The Nurse-Patient Relationship," Part II, the first task of the nurse is to form a pact with the ill person. How can she form a pact with an individual who does not or will not respond? Granted, the nurse's comments may elicit no discernible response in the person; nevertheless, she engages in the activities inherent in forming a pact. She introduces herself to the patient, tells him that she is a nurse, and states the name of the school or agency represented. She tells the patient the date and time of the next interaction, the length of each interaction, the number of days a week she will meet with him and the period of time over which the interactions will take place. The nurse is thus in effect forming a pact with the ill person even though he may not respond verbally to anything she says.

It is recommended that the nurse speak quietly and allow time for the ill person to comprehend what has been said. The nurse pauses after one statement, waits, and then resumes. She speaks slowly, distinctly and purposely uses the ill person's name whenever appropriate during the course of the one-sided conversation. The nurse asks the patient if he has any questions. If he does not respond, this in no way can be construed as indicating that he did not hear or understand what the nurse said. Many mute persons, when they begin to recover, are often able to report statements made by the nurse during interactions held some weeks previously.

During the second interaction it is suggested that the nurse re-introduce herself to the patient. What does the nurse say or do, when confronted with remaining with a mute person for fifty minutes? Does she talk to him or merely sit by him in silence? There are differences of opinion about ways to helping the nonverbal person. Some clinicians advocate sitting in silence with the ill person without speaking directly to him while conveying an attitude of belief that he can improve. Not all nurses, however, are able to sit in silence for fifty minutes and concentrate on the ill person; the mind wanders and attention may be distracted. Further, not all mute persons are helped by sitting silently with a nurse who does not speak during a fifty-minute period. It is recommended that the nurse speak to the ill person with the attitude that she realizes he will respond when he is ready. The nurse greets the patient and waits for a response. If none is received she may comment on something in the immediate environment. The comment should be such that the ill person is invited to respond but is under no pressure to do so. For example, the nurse might say, "It is warm today . . ." She pauses and waits for a response. If one is not forthcoming, she may comment on something else in the environment—the growth of a potted plant—and the process is repeated. The nurse consistently strives to elicit a response from the patient by providing conversational openings. Over a period of time she may begin to receive nonverbal responses, i.e., the patient may glance briefly at her and turn away, may have fleeting eye contact with her, or may stare at her when he believes she is not looking. Such responses are encouraging.

As the interactions proceed the nurse may try more direct approaches. Instead of sitting a few feet from the patient she may sit nearer while still maintaining a physical distance; she then ascertains the effect on the ill person of changing the distance between them. The nurse discovers, from the patient's relatives, friends or other resource persons, the patient's particular interest area prior to hospitalization. For example, one nurse working with a mute individual discovered the patient had been interested in sailing and in repairing boats. In the course of an interaction she mentioned to the patient that she heard he was interested in sailing. There was fleeting eye contact, then the patient stared again at the floor. The nurse said: "I will bring a magazine on sailing when I come to see you Wednesday at 10:00 a.m. Perhaps we can look at the magazine together." The nurse brought the magazine and sat by the patient, and together they looked at the pictures. At one point the patient pointed to a picture of a boat. The nurse said: "The picture reminds you of a particular boat, doesn't it?" and the patient agreed. The nurse left the magazine with the patient at the conclusion of the interaction and suggested to him that, when she returned to see him, perhaps he would tell her about the boat. As the interactions proceeded the ill person began to verbalize more and to take increased interest in his personal appearance. What caused this patient to respond as he did? The nurse's sincere desire to help and her consistent attempts to reach the patient were important and cannot be underestimated. The nurse, however, went one step further. She displayed to the ill person that she cared enough to find out his interests. She gave him tangible evidence of her caring—a magazine. A magazine is something to keep, to hold onto; it is a tangible reminder that someone *does* care. Magazines do not help ill persons recover, but caring can and does. The use of magazines and pictures can be helpful in working with the nonverbal individual and may be the means through which the person begins to respond.

Some nonverbal patients do not sit alone. They pace the floor or walk up and down the corridor. It is recommended that the nurse walk with the patient, talk with him, and try to elicit a response by providing conversational openings. Nonverbal persons tend to react more to a nurse's nonverbal actions than to her words. It is therefore suggested that the nurse audit her habitual nonverbal behavior. For example, a nurse had a habit of looking at her watch while trying to converse with a mute patient. The patient interpreted the nurse's behavior as meaning she did not wish to talk with him. The patient was correct; the nurse stated during group reconstruction session that she "could not reach" the patient and wished she were not assigned to interact with him.

The Individual Who Hallucinates

Working with an individual who hallucinates may be a disturbing and somewhat threatening experience for the novice in psychiatric nursing. Beginners are apt to be concerned by admonitions concerning hallucinations. There are many "do"s and "don't"s in the literature about ways in which nurses should act when working with an hallucinating individual. For example, the nurse is *not* to agree that she believes a patient's hallucination is reality-based; neither should she deny that the ill person's hallucination is very real to him. In actuality ill persons seldom ask nurses to verify the validity of their hallucinations. It *is* important that the nurse remember that hallucinations are symptoms of a mental disturbance and, in functional disorders, will tend to disappear as she achieves relatedness with the ill person. As the warmth of human relatedness is experienced by the ill person, his need to hallucinate unreal individuals, objects or voices hopefully will dissipate and eventually disappear. A problem area may develop if a nurse becomes so interested in the content of the hallucination that she reinforces hallucinatory behavior by focusing on the hallucination rather than on the developing relationship.

The Individual Who Responds with Monosyllables or Short Phrases

While it may be difficult and frustrating at times to work with the mute patient, it is equally difficult to achieve relatedness with a person whose habitual response to comments and questions is a monosyllable or short phrase. The following excerpt from a process record is an example of a nurse's efforts with a patient who habitually responds in this manner.

The patient is a fifty-four year old female who has been hospitalized in a large state hospital for six months. The patient has been diagnosed "Schizophrenia—Undifferentiated." The following interaction took place during the nurse's second contact with the patient.

Nurse: Good morning, Mrs. X. How are you?
Patient: O.K.
Nurse: You went out on pass last weekend. Tell me about it.
Patient: It was O.K.
Nurse: What do you mean by O.K.?
Patient: Oh, it was all right.
Nurse: What did you do at home?
Patient: Nothing much.
　　　　(Silence)
　　　　I watched T.V.
Nurse: Tell me about one program you saw.
Patient: I don't remember.
Nurse: What else did you do?
Patient: Not much.
　　　　(Silence)

The nurse, during group reconstruction, reported frustration in trying to get the patient to "open up" and stated she felt she wanted to "push the patient in order to force a response." Gradually the nurse began to realize that the patient was responding on the only level possible for her at the time. The nurse's approach eventually was to try to elicit a response by providing conversational openings. Patience, perseverance and the ability to wait in silence are necessary to initiate a relationship with individuals who use monosyllables or short phrase responses. Such persons do not respond to prodding, probing, rushing or hurrying. An excerpt from the tenth interaction with the patient quoted above indicates the extent to which the nurse was able to establish a degree of relatedness.

> The patient was standing by the window staring. I came into the room. She turned around. I could see she was crying.
>
> Nurse: What's wrong?
> Patient: I am so lonesome. (She began to cry. I led her over to a chair. She sat on the edge of the chair and cried. She wrung her hands. I noticed her fingernails were bitten and the skin around her nails was macerated. She kept pulling at bits of skin around her nails.)
> Nurse: You went home this weekend?
> Patient: I just came back this morning.
> Nurse: It was difficult to come back?
> Patient: It gets harder every time. My husband is going to talk to the doctor and see if I can go home for good. I want to go home and stay. I am going to talk to the doctor myself.
> (Silence)
> Patient (smiling). My husband was so glad to have me home.
> Nurse: His being glad made you feel good.
> Patient: I never had many friends in my life and I've never been any place. I lived out on a farm and never saw many people. These other people in here might not need someone but I do. I know it now.
> Nurse: It *is* important to know that someone cares about you.
> Patient: Yes, I know that . . . it took me a long time to learn.

The patient was discharged three days after the above interaction and remained at home for approximately four months. Upon readmission she was almost completely mute. A clinical nurse specialist began to interact with the patient and at last report she was beginning to respond in monosyllables and short phrases. Whether or not Mrs. X. will be able to maintain herself outside of the hospital setting is not known. Mrs. X. may, because she has had the experience of relatedness with a nurse, be able to move rapidly toward social recovery and eventually to maintain herself outside of a mental institution. There is no way, however, to say definitely that this will be the case.

DEJECTION

Establishing closeness with a dejected (depressed) individual presents as much of a challenge as does developing a relationship with a detached person. The dejected person also may respond to comments or questions by monosyllables or short phrases, or may be mute. The approaches suggested in establishing relatedness with the detached person are also utilized in developing closeness with the dejected person.

While similarities in behavior exist there are also differences. Whereas the nurse may feel that some detached persons are "uninhabited," she perceives the "thereness" of the dejected person. The feeling tone or mood emitted by the dejected patient is one of sadness (in varying degrees of intensity and depth), despondency, gloominess, pessimism and hopelessness.

Why does an individual develop dejection as an habitual manner of avoiding relatedness with others? It is hypothesized that the dejected person, through his childhood experiences, is especially sensitized to loss of love (or self-esteem). Loss of love may be perceived as rejection and can arouse feelings of anger; anger may be turned inward, resulting in depression. The dejected person is usually an angry person—an individual who blames either himself or others for loss of self-esteem. Dejection is also a manipulatory tactic, in that the dejected person may attempt to make those about him feel guilty by overtly displaying his misery. Depression thus may be both a cry for help and attention and a way to punish others.

The individual whose habitual behavioral response is dejection is usually diagnosed as having a depressive reaction. The term *depressive reaction* may include the following: manic-depressive reaction—depressed, psychotic (or neurotic) reactive depression, or involutional depressive reaction. Again, the label is not important in terms of nursing intervention. It *is* important that the nurse assess the individual's ability to relate with others and then design and test approaches to assist him to break the bond of dejection.

Dejection as an experience is probably more readily comprehended by the nurse than is detachment, since all human beings, at one time or another, feel some degree of depression in response to real (or imagined) losses. The "normal" individual usually knows the cause of his unhappiness and has at his disposal various ways of dealing with it. For example, some individuals relieve feelings of depression by expressing anger overtly, breaking objects, cleaning house, taking a walk, eating, or going on a shopping spree. The person who habitually responds to loss by intense depression may find that he is unable to relieve his feelings; he gradually sinks into a more-or-less persistent state of depression.

What can the nurse do to assist the individual whose predominant behavioral response is that of dejection? The practitioner specifically endeavors to structure the interaction to encourage the patient to respond to her as a unique human being. The desired goal is for the ill person to perceive the nurse as knowledgeable, helpful, concerned human being instead of as "nurse." This point is stressed because it is believed that only if the dejected individual experiences human warmth can he break through the miasma of despondency which envelops him. Granted, many depressed individuals, in time, respond without therapy or nursing care. It is believed, however, that such individuals will respond more rapidly when given the opportunity to relate with a concerned knowledgeable person who cares for and about them. If communication is a problem the nurse uses the approaches suggested in the section in this chapter titled "Detachment."

The Problem of Suicide

Many problems will confront the nurse working with a dejected person. The safety of the person, his sheer physical survival, may well depend on her ability to establish relatedness with him. There is always the possibility that a dejected person may envisage suicide as "the only way out" of his dilemma. Clinical observations seem to support the belief that the dejected person is most likely to attempt suicide when his depressed mood lifts. Sudden improvement is an ominous, not an auspicious, sign. The nurse needs to be cognizant of the danger of suicide when working with any mentally ill person but particularly when working with a depressed individual. The dejected person most likely to attempt or commit suicide is one who makes demands on personnel, complains, and is generally dissatisfied. Such persons seem to want closeness, yet use tactics which will drive others away. There are some indications in the literature to support the assumption that persons contemplating suicide will communicate their intentions to one other person at least. Such intentions may be disguised, i.e., the patient may not state overtly: "Nurse I am going to kill myself." However, at the end of an interaction a patient may say "Good-bye" in a way which indicates the patient never expects to see her again. If the nurse suspects the patient is contemplating suicide, immediate intervention is necessary. "Intuitive" warnings are *never* to be dismissed lightly. Under such circumstances the nurse returns to the patient and shares with him her impression that he said "good-bye" in a way that made her believe he would not see her again. She asks for an explanation, but does not challenge the ill person. The attitude conveyed is: "I didn't understand what you meant when you said good-bye—tell me about it." The patient may tell the nurse he *is* in fact contemplating suicide or he may deny his "good-bye" meant anything at all.

There is probably nothing so frightening, to the most experienced practitioner in psychiatric nursing, as listening to a human being speak of his desire for death and his intent to kill himself. Mere words in a book cannot convey the impact of this experience. Such an experience may never happen, but, if it does, the nurse has but one task—to save the life of the ill person. The practitioner listens and gently tells the patient he will not be allowed to kill himself. This is not said in a challenging manner, as if to dare him to commit the act, but in a way which conveys to the person: "I care about you and will not let you harm yourself." The nurse immediately alerts *all* personnel. The psychiatrist is notified. Even though the nurse may have promised the patient, during the pact, to keep all conversation between them confidential, this is one time when she must, in conscience, break this promise. Hopefully, this situation may be prevented if the nurse or another health worker is able to establish communication with the ill human being. If, however, the nurse at any time believes, or feels, that a patient is contemplating suicide—even though he does not state this intention—she must report her feeling, however vague and nebulous it may seem, to other personnel on the unit. It is better to err on the side of overprecaution than to wish one had.

Suicide has been discussed at some length because it is an ever-present possibility when working with the depressed person. For further readings regarding this problem see Bibliography, Appendix I, Chapter IX.

Other Problem Areas

Many other problems encountered by the nurse working with a dejected patient are directly related to the maneuvers used by the dejected person to avoid closeness. For example, some depressed patients talk continuously of their physical complaints. Their conversations include a litany of complaints, i.e., constipation, anorexia, insomnia, nausea, reiterated again and again. If distraction or diversion does not lead the person to focus on anything else the nurse has no recourse but to discuss with the patient the problems as perceived by him. If, for example, the problem is insomnia, the nurse inquires about the patient's prior sleeping habits as compared to present ones, in order to have a baseline for comparison. She asks what the patient thinks about or does when he is unable to sleep and attempts to help him discover a pattern preceding the insomnia, i.e., what tends to make sleeping difficult, what seems to help him sleep, etc. What does he think causes him to be unable to sleep? Eventually the ill person may be able to discuss his feelings of sadness and hopelessness without stressing physical complaints. It is important to convey the attitude that the patient *will* improve. Clinical observations reveal that dejected persons are *not* helped by "cheery" attitudes on the part of nurses or other health workers. It is suggested that, when a depressed person begins to show signs of improvement, the nurse *not* comment on the apparent improvement. Such comments may have a paradoxical effect, i.e., they may cause some ill persons to revert to their previous level of despondency.

The dejected person is not an easy individual with whom to work. The nurse well may be affected by his mood of unhappiness and sadness. It is not unusual for a nurse working with a dejected person to experience a transient state of depression following an interaction with the person. If the nurse does not experience depression she may, and usually does, feel "drained" emotionally or exhausted physically.

There are no set phrases one can utter which will restore hope to the hopeless, optimism to the pessimist or enjoyment to the pleasureless. There is only the day-by-day interaction whereby, with knowledge, perseverance and a true desire to help, the nurse can assist the ill person.

SUPERFICIALITY

Superficiality as an habitual behavioral response is characterized by the individual's inability (or unwillingness) to engage in meaningful dialogue with others. The purpose of this behavior is to avoid closeness, to avoid thinking, to impress others, or for more idiosyncratic reasons. Why choose superficiality as a maneuver to avoid closeness? Again, one can only surmise that such behavior has worked for the person in the past and continues to work for him. Superficiality as a habitual behavior response is encountered in "normal" individuals as well as in the mentally ill. A wide variety of behavior may be exhibited. Some individuals give the impression of being flighty and, in conversation, flit from topic to topic. This conversation tends to revolve around the obvious, the apparent and the trivial. One gets the impression that such persons are striving, at all costs, to avoid thinking. If they do talk about themselves their conversation tends to be limited to their preferences, tastes, likes and dislikes.

Some individuals engage in monologues and pour forth a torrent of words. One gets the impression that they use words as weapons with which to bombard others and keep them at a distance. The monologist frequently talks about himself and gives "his" opinion on topics, but one feels that he is not giving "his" opinion at all—he does not have an opinion and is merely repeating someone else's as his own. As is the flighty person, the monologist is striving to avoid thinking. Both "flitters" and monologists are able, through their behavior, to avoid involvement with others. Such persons are invariably boring, their conversations are tedious and they seldom *listen*. They may be tolerated by others but are not sought out as companions or friends.

Another tactic often used by the individual who uses superficiality as an habitual behavioral response is "pseudocommunication." A person who engages in pseudocommunication seems to be verbal, open and free in his expression and, when conversing with him, the listener often, at the time, thinks she understands the content of the conversation. However, after the conversation, the listener is unable to state *what* the speaker said or *meant*. Why? An examination of the content of the conversation of the individual who pseudocommunicates usually reveals his proclivity for abstruse words and phrases, generalities, and abstract constructs. He may also rely heavily on the use of jargon, such as psychoanalytic terminology. The listener may be impressed by the speaker's erudition but usually does not understand what he is trying to say.

What can the nurse do to assist ill individuals who remain on a superficial verbal level during the nurse-patient interview? When talking with a person who flits from topic to topic, she assists him to remain on *one* topic—to explore it in some degree of depth. When necessary the nurse interrupts the patient, asks for more information regarding the topic, or in some other way helps him to remain on the subject. If the patient goes on to another topic the nurse gently brings him back to the point under discussion. The nurse's intervention is based on the assumption that the patient is helped if he focuses his attention, in depth, on one topic. By developing this habit, he is gradually able to identify problems, discern cause and effect, perceive his participation in life experiences, envisage alternatives, test new patterns of behavior, and audit and change his behavior. An improved ability to relate more meaningfully with others will result in an improved ability to socialize.

Intervention with the individual who engages in monologues is similar to that with the flighty person. The nurse may have to cut into the conversation or interrupt frequently. She may choose, depending on her relatedness with the individual, to be directive and confronting. For example, the nurse reminds the patient engaging in a monologue that he is monopolizing the conversation. She strives to help him to develop interpersonal skills such as listening, and to learn the give and take of conversation.

Assisting the pseudocommunicator is probably a more difficult task than is assisting the flighty person or the individual who uses monologues to avoid closeness. A major difficulty which may be encountered by the novice nurse is a tendency to become fascinated by the patient's ability to engage in "profound" discussion. The following excerpt from a process record is an example.

Nurse: How are you, Mr. Z.?

Patient: I'm fine. I've been sitting here thinking about life. What *is* its ultimate purpose? And how do we as individuals fit into the general scheme of things? Have you ever really given it much thought?

Nurse (hesitantly) : No.

Patient: You should. I was thinking about the difference between Cogito, Ergo Sum and Bierce's statement Cogito Cogito, Ergo Cogito Sum. My conclusions are that it is simply a matter of semantics. Korzybski, Hayakawa and Carnap were essentially correct although I cannot agree with all of their concepts. Perhaps the problem is one of a life design or how a life is patterned. What do you think?

Nurse: I don't understand what you are saying.

In this example it is apparent that the nurse encouraged the patient to continue his pattern of pseudocommunication by not intervening after his initial comment. Instead of answering his question, the student might have effectively asked the patient to relate his comment about "life's ultimate purpose" to *himself* and his own life experiences. She might also have focused on the patient's question ". . . how do we as individuals fit into the general scheme of things?" by asking him to explain what this statement meant *specifically* in terms of *his* life experiences. In this case, the nurse's fascination with the patient's erudite conversation was a major barrier in assisting him to communicate intelligibly with others. One of the nurse's tasks with the pseudocommunicator is to help him practice the ability to communicate intelligibly with others. Such a process is a gradual one, requiring patience, perseverance and diligence on the part of the nurse practitioner. Every time the patient engages in pseudocommunication she interrupts him and assists him to relate what he has said to his personal life, to become less vague and more specific. The nurse does not encourage the patient to use generalities or abstract constructs; instead, she challenges him whenever he engages in such maneuvers.

A similar problem is presented by the patient who uses psychiatric jargon. One patient said to a nurse: "The last analyst I had said my problems were caused by my inability to control my id impulses and resolve my Oedipal difficulties." A novice may be intrigued by the patient's "insight" into his condition. However, it soon becomes apparent that the ill person is engaged in pseudocommunication. However profound his statements may seem, he is operating on a very superficial basis. When the pseudocommunicator realizes he is not impressing the nurse with his profundity, and begins to develop a feeling of trust in her, he may be able to engage in genuine meaningful dialogue with other human beings. If the patient can experience the warmth of relatedness and engage, if only for minutes, in meaningful dialogue with another human being, he may be able gradually to become a more authentic person who is able to audit and eventually to change his habitual behavior pattern. Such behavioral changes take time, but they *can* and *do* occur.

MANIPULATORY AND PROVOCATIVE BEHAVIOR

Manipulation broadly defined is a means of influencing the behavior of others by covert or overt methods. For example, teaching may be considered a form of manipulation since teachers attempt to effect behavioral changes in students. Manipulation may be constructive or destructive. As defined in this work, manipulation is an attempt deliberately to control the behavior of others in order to meet one's own needs or goals. The wants, wishes, or desires of the manipulated person are disregarded or are not considered important. Other human beings are reduced to objects whose purpose is to fulfill the needs of the manipulator.

Because human beings are social creatures, all persons engage in some form of manipulatory behavior to meet their needs. However, the "normal" individual does not deliberately, consciously, and consistently try to coerce or control the behavior of others; neither does he disregard their innate rights. The manipulator has no such scruples. Any human being who can be forced to meet his needs is "fair game."

Why does an individual develop destructive manipulatory behavior? The dynamics of the development of this pattern are not clearly defined and many factors undoubtedly are involved. At the risk of sounding simplistic, one can speculate that an individual frustrated by parental figures in achieving need satisfaction discovered a way in which he could meet his needs, namely, by influencing and coercing others. A child who has been controlled by his parents and who lacks corrective emotional experiences with nonmanipulatory persons soon learns the tactics of manipulation. He can hardly avoid it; he has been given lessons by good teachers. The individual subjected to such childhood experiences may know right from wrong; conscience, per se, may not be entirely lacking. However, the person's sense of what is right or wrong may be relatively inoperative in his interpersonal contacts with others. He may know he is not supposed to lie or steal but, if lying and stealing meet his needs, he may resort to these behaviors. Individuals who habitually engage in destructive forms of manipulation may be diagnosed as having sociopathic personality disturbance or Main's syndrome. Destructive manipulatory behavior is also exhibited by individuals having other diagnostic labels.

In the hospital situation various maneuvers used by the destructive manipulator may become apparent. Some of the most common tactics include: "playing up" to the physician or nurse to secure special privileges, pitting personnel or patients against each other, eliciting secrets from patients and personnel and then informing others regarding them, breaking rules and regulations, making deliberate attempts to anger or provoke patients and personnel, and causing quarrels between patients. The manipulator, for example, may tell one patient in secret that another patient made disparaging or insulting remarks about him. The manipulator then sits back and enjoys the uproar created. He is often an expert in the art of provoking others.

The ill person who is habitually manipulative and provocative presents definite problems to the nurse striving to establish a relationship. Her first task is to identify the individual's habitual way of responding and interacting. The nurse recognizes that, sooner or later, the patient will attempt to manipulate her, by any one of a number of strategies. Some of these have already been discussed—for example, asking for special privileges. The ill person may use flattery, telling the nurse she is the *only* person with whom he can *really* communicate; she is the best nurse on the unit and no one but she really understands him. This ploy is usually followed by an appeal for assistance in obtaining some special concession. When such strategies fail the patient may resort to other methods, such as trying to provoke, embarrass, or anger the nurse. Provocative tactics may be overt or covert, obvious or subtle. The patient may deliberately try to destroy the nurse's composure by insulting or embarrassing her. For example, the patient may focus on the nurse's physical characteristics and make comments such as "Gee, you're ugly. You have a face that would stop a clock" or "Hello, fatso, when are you going on a diet?" Another patient may use flirting as a manipulatory maneuver and make comments such as "You're cute. How about going out with me?" When the nurse inquires as to the reasons for such mechanisms he may say he was "just teasing" and wonders why the nurse "can't take a joke." The nurse is placed on the defensive—one of the purposes of the patient's behavior.

Some manipulators tell dirty jokes or make obscene comments to embarrass the nurse. Other patients may attempt to discuss in detail their sexual lives, habits and preferences with the intention of embarrassing the nurse or arousing her sexually. Novices in psychiatric nursing seem to be particularly selected by some patients as recipients of conversations focused on sex.

Other patients are not as overt in trying to control the nurse's behavior but may engage in sabotaging her attempt to establish relatedness. For example, a patient may relate in detail an experience that did not occur. The nurse may focus on an in-depth discussion of the experience only to discover that it did not take place. She then must inquire as to why the patient has the need to make up stories and must explore this particular aspect of the patient's life problem.

In order to assist the individual, the nurse first must recognize that his habitual behavioral response is that of manipulation and must understand that manipulation is, for the most part, unconsciously motivated. The nurse needs to know, and to recognize, the tactics frequently used by the manipulating individual. Intervention is based on the asumption that, if the patient learns the nurse will not be controlled by manipulatory maneuvers, he may use them less consistently, and will become aware that other human beings are not objects whose sole purpose is to gratify his needs and desires. Specifically how does the nurse establish a working relationship? As mentioned, the nurse needs to *recognize* the manipulatory tactics used by the individual. She does not permit the patient to use manipulatory maneuvers on her, nor does she encourage his use of such tactics by approving of them. An excerpt from a process record exemplifies one aspect of the nurse's intervention.

Patient: You look cute today. How was your weekend? Did you have an exciting date?

Nurse: Let's talk about you.

Patient: He must have given you a rough time.

Nurse: What did *you* do over the weekend?

Patient (leans back in chair and smiles) : I had a ball. You know Dr. X. Well, he came to see D. (another patient) but he's my doctor too, so I cut D. out of the picture. He just sat there like a dum-dum. I made Dr. X. talk to me instead. He never got a chance to talk with D. (laughs)

Nurse: Oh?

Patient: You don't think it is funny? I had a ball. Dr. X. didn't want to talk to me but before I let him go I had his head swimming. He didn't know if he was coming or going.

Nurse: And what did you accomplish by this behavior?

Patient (startled) : What do you mean?

Nurse: Just what I said. What did you accomplish by this behavior? (Silence)

Patient: I don't know. I just didn't think about it at the time. Like I said— I was just having a ball.

Nurse: Now that you've thought about it, what do you think about your behavior?
Patient: I don't know. No, I really don't. I don't know what made me do it. I guess I was just bored.
Nurse: Was that really the reason?
Patient (laughs): No, I am just saying that. I guess I wanted to get a rise out of Dr. X.
Nurse: Did you?
Patient (pauses): I'm not really sure. He listened to me but didn't really say anything.
Nurse: So what did you accomplish?
Patient: I'm not sure now. You think I should have let Dr. X. talk with D.?
Nurse: What do you think?
Patient (not certain): I guess so. I'll try to do better in the future and that's a promise. No, I won't make that a definite promise because I don't know if I'll be able to keep it. But I will give it a try. Will that make you happy?
Nurse: It's not my happiness we're talking about—it's your behavior.
Patient (glumly): Yes, you're right.

In the above interaction the nurse did not respond to the patient's attempt to discuss the nurse's weekend nor did she share his amusement regarding his manipulatory exploits. The patient was, according to the nurse, attempting to elicit a favorable comment about his behavior. The nurse did not respond to this obvious maneuver. Her focus was on what the patient accomplished by his behavior. The nurse's rationale was as follows: the manipulatory patient wishes to control the behavior of others; if his maneuvers are not successful he may abandon such tactics and substitute socially approved behavior, provided by use of such behavior he is able to secure need gratification. The nurse did not allow the patient to use boredom as the reason for his actions but helped him to admit, intellectually, that he was indeed attempting to provoke Dr. X. The patient was able to admit his uncertainty as to whether or not his maneuvering was successful. The nurse did not "rise to the bait" when the patient promised "to do better in the future." She did not permit the patient's comment "Will that make you happy?" to go unchallenged but directed his attention back to his behavior instead of her happiness.

The nurse worked with the patient for four months. At the conclusion of the relationship the patient still tried to use manipulation in his interactions with the nurse but less frequently. He was able, at times, to control his manipulative impulses, but was by no means cured.

Trying to establish a relationship with a manipulatory person is a difficult but not an impossible task. Probably not all nurses should attempt it. From unvalidated clinical observations it appears that those nurses who are most successful are persons able to endure the constant testing without becoming unduly threatened or offended. They are sensitive but not gullible, and are not easily flustered or shocked by startling revelations, sexual disclosures or tall tales. They are interested in the patient but are not impressed by the patient's superficial charm, verbal abilities or flattery. They do not respond to insults by engaging in punitive actions. These nurses understand and accept, intellectually and emotionally, the patient's need to indulge in manipulatory behavior and are able to set limits when necessary. Such nurses are kind, concerned human beings but at the same time can present themselves to patients as firm authority figures. Social recovery may not be a realistic goal in working with a manipulatory person. The nurse may, however, be able to assist the patient to delay immediate need gratification or lessen his proclivity to manipulate other human beings.

SUSPICIOUSNESS

Suspiciousness, as an habitual behavioral response, is defined as a more-or-less persistent tendency to mistrust or doubt the sincerity, truthfulness or honesty of others.

Why does an individual become suspicious? No one is born suspicious; therefore, it is assumed that such behavior is learned. If a child's parents persistently doubt or mistrust others, the child may learn that "others" are not to be trusted. A child who is not loved or trusted himself will hardly be able to love or trust others.

The childhood background of suspicious individuals often reveals parental neglect or coldness. Parents may also be overly ambitious. A child told by parents that he must get the highest grades in his class may blame the teacher or other pupils if he fails. Parents may also inculcate a general attitude that others are to blame for one's misfortunes. As an individual grows older he tends to keep using denial and projection if these mechanisms have helped him circumvent anxiety. Suspicious persons are unable to perceive any viewpoint other than their own can be correct. Rigidity becomes pronounced unless the person receives therapy or is changed by corrective life experiences.

The suspicious person may believe others do not like him and, indeed, this belief may have an actual basis in fact. Generally not liked are the inability to admit a mistake in judgment and the tendency to misinterpret the innocent comments of others as being personally directed. The suspicious person cannot admit an error because to do so would expose his inadequacy and vulnerability. Further, he lacks the ability to compromise or cooperate in a work relationship.

Many mildly suspicious persons are able to maintain themselves in the community and hence are not admitted to a mental hospital. Their behavior is, often, not recognized as pathological. Categorizations are, at best, risky, but the ranks of the mildly suspicious may include the malicious gossiper, the injustice collector, the ostentatious martyr, the killjoy, the crusader, and the pathologically envious person.

The Delusional Individual

The suspicious person is an individual who lives in a hostile jungle waiting for an attack. He may be able to work and live in the community provided he is not subjected unduly to anxiety or competition. However, if such a person encounters a situation which intensifies his anxiety or his basic underlying hostility, the use of projection may no longer diminish the anxiety. The individual because of his need for cognitive clarity seeks an explanation for what is happening around him. Why was he not promoted? He may be puzzled and, as his anxiety level increases, he searches for reasons. Since he does not make mistakes and is by far the best employee in the office, therefore it must be that he was not promoted because of a plot to thwart him. Although the suspicious person may be given logical reasons for his situation, it is difficult, if not impossible, for him to believe them. In an atmosphere of increased anxiety the person needs to discover someone or something to blame. It is not he; therefore, someone else caused the failure. He looks for signs to confirm his suspicions and soon finds them, and concludes that he was not promoted because of a plot against him. The conclusion, based on erroneous assumptions, is delusional in nature. Delusions may be of a persecutory, grandiose, or other nature. (See Bibliography in Appendix I, Chapter IX for references regarding delusion formation.)

Suspiciousness may range on a continuum from the transient doubt or mistrust seen in the "normal" person to the delusions of the highly suspicious individual encountered in the mental hospital or clinic. The latter are usually diagnosed as being paranoid schizophrenics, having paranoid tendencies, or being in a paranoid state.

One of the first tasks of the nurse is to identify the patient's habitual mode of responding—the maneuvers he uses to avoid closeness. The attitude, posture and facial expression of the suspicious person do not invite conversation with others; such an individual often assumes a superior, condescending attitude which conveys the message: "I am important and not to be treated as an ordinary person."

A major objective in working with the highly suspicious person is to help him learn to trust. How? It is recommended that the nurse pay strict attention to interpreting her role to the highly distrustful person, because of the general tendency of such persons to misinterpret the remarks and behavior of others. Trust, once developed, is fragile and must be carefully nurtured; it can be easily destroyed. The suspicious individual does not make allowance for human error.

> The nurse was trying to develop a working relationship with a highly suspicious person. She was entering the patient's room when she saw a psychiatrist whom she had not seen for some time. She excused herself and chatted for a few minutes with the psychiatrist. When she returned to talk with the patient, the patient refused to respond and accused the nurse of "sneaking off and telling the doctor everything I say." The nurse listened, apologized, and told the patient she didn't blame her for being angry. The nurse explained to the patient who the psychiatrist was, and in general what the nurse and psychiatrist discussed. The patient did not believe the nurse and it took many weeks before the nurse and patient were able to reestablish the working relationship.

It is recommended that nurses be scrupulously honest and consistent in their interactions with the suspicious person. Deviations are suspect and are not conducive to the development of trust.

Working with individuals who are delusional may be disturbing for the novice in psychiatric nursing. The beginner is quite apt to be concerned with various admonitions about reinforcing delusions. There are many "do"s and "don't"s in the literature concerning behavior when working with a delusional individual. For example, the nurse is supposed to be neutral, i.e., neither agreeing nor disagreeing with the content of the patient's delusions. If she follows such advice, what does this do *for* or *to* the ill person? *What message is conveyed?* The patient may believe his thinking is correct, since the nurse does not discuss the content of the delusion with him. The point may be academic since few suspicious individuals ever ask nurses to verify the validity of their delusions; they are usually not interested in the opinions of others. However, neutrality about the content of his delusions may not always be the most effective method of helping the ill person.

It is suggested that the nurse listen carefully to the patient's account of what he believes has happened to him, question him about any obscurities, and clarify what he seems to be experiencing. She may then begin *slowly* to create doubt in the patient's mind as to the validity of the belief. For example, the nurse might ask: "Is it possible that *everyone* in the office dislikes you?" She conveys the message that she finds the patient's statement difficult to believe and asks him to elaborate, give specific examples, and cite incidents which illustrate his point. The ill person eventually may be able to admit that not everyone dislikes him and to narrow the range to one or two persons in the work setting. Gradually the nurse helps the patient to perceive his participation. He is encouraged to cite specific incidents and to discuss what *he* said, did, thought, and felt prior to, during, and following the incidents.

The ill person is *not* reasoned out of a delusional state. He *is* given the opportunity to discuss his frightening experience with an interested, attentive and kind individual. As his anxiety lessens he may be able to tell the nurse of his fear, anger and puzzlement regarding what has happened to him. If necessary the nurse tells the patient she does not agree with him while, at the same time, telling him she *does* realize that he (the patient) believes his statements to be valid. Usually, however, such a confrontation is not necessary.

It is recommended that nurses avoid an "overly friendly" approach. A certain amount of interested detachment may be more comforting and less threatening to the highly suspicious person than oversolicitude.

There are other barriers to establishing relatedness with the suspicious individual, such as the superior or condescending attitude mentioned previously. One psychiatric nurse stated when discussing her initial interaction with such a patient: "She acted like a queen. I felt like a subject graciously being granted an audience with Her Highness. I almost felt like bowing when I left her." It is important that the nurse truly understand the ill person's desperate need for, and fear of, closeness with others and that she not permit the patient's distance maneuvers to keep her from interacting with him.

ANXIOUSNESS

A basic assumption of this work is that all human beings experience anxiety of varying degrees of intensity throughout their lives. Basic anxiety is intrinsic to the human condition and hence is not learned. However, the techniques developed to cope with or circumvent anxiety are learned. Basic anxiety may be intensified in response to real or imagined threats to basic need fulfillment. It may also be increased when an individual faces the unknown, the new, the different, the unfamiliar, or is confronted with a loss or crisis situation. Change, however exciting the prospect may be, increases anxiety in most human beings, and the opportunity or freedom to choose may have similar results.

Anxiety is defined broadly as a subjective experience characterized by tension, restlessness, and apprehension prompted by real or imagined threats to need gratification. Since anxiety is not pleasurable, the individual develops various ways of reducing or coping with it. However, in periods of great or prolonged stress, the coping mechanisms may not serve their purpose and the individual may be flooded with anxiety or experience a chronically high anxiety level over a prolonged period of time.

The energy generated by anxiety is discharged into overt or covert behavior. Behavioral manifestations are dependent upon the degree of anxiety experienced by the individual as well as upon the efficacy of the coping mechanisms used to circumvent its effects. A certain degree of anxiety may be useful. However, as a person's anxiety level increases, and if he is unable to counteract its effect, his personality may become completely disorganized by progressively mounting anxiety. Such personality disorganization results in a psychotic condition.

The overt and covert manifestations of anxiety are legion and may include: tachycardia, dilated pupils, sweating, rigid shallow respiration, tremors, anorexia, nausea, insomnia, polyuria, vertigo, fatigue, headache, "tunnel vision," increased motor activity, exaggerated responses to petty annoyances, inability to concentrate, and irritability. All individuals are anxious, but the mentally ill person's ability to cope with anxiety is markedly diminished. This latter statement needs qualification, since many mentally ill persons cope with anxiety by developing symptoms which may relieve it to some extent. Generally speaking, the inability to cope with anxiety is a primary causative factor in the creation of pathological behavior.

In establishing a one-to-one relationship with any ill person the nurse attempts to assess the patient's anxiety level. This feat is easier to suggest than to accomplish. This is especially true when the ill person has been heavily tranquilized, or in the jargon has been "snowed under" with drugs. The nurse observes the patient's overt behavior for signs of anxiety, develops inferences as to the level of anxiety and attempts, if possible, to validate these inferences with the patient. She is alert to the topics of conversation which tend to increase the patient's discomfort.

What does the practitioner do when the patient is becoming increasingly anxious during an interaction? She begins a process of inquiry to validate, if possible, the inference that the patient is becoming increasingly anxious. For example, the nurse may say: "You seem anxious" or may focus on the patient's overt behavior by saying: "Your hands are shaking." The ill person may deny that he is anxious, or may admit that he is anxious yet be unable to explain why. The nurse may notice that whenever a certain topic of conversation is discussed the patient's anxiety level seems to increase. She may bring this to the patient's attention and gradually, over a period of time, help the patient to express why the discussion of the topic creates discomfort. She is attempting to assist the ill person to perceive cause and effect.

The ability to verbalize one's thoughts and feelings and to relate one's frightening experiences to another human being, in and of itself, may be helpful to some mentally ill persons. The nurse's interaction, however, is more than mere listening. She helps the ill person gradually to understand what he does that adds to his discomfort, alienates those about him, and prevents his seeking the warmth of human contact and companionship. The nurse serves as a model of emotional health as well as a teacher in assisting the ill person to learn to identify his present problems, to set realistic goals and, if possible, to achieve these goals. What is a realistic goal for one patient may not be for another. For one individual the ability to communicate freely with a human being other than the nurse may be a realistic goal. For another it may be developing the ability to feed himself, or to comb his hair. Even small gains are evidence of realistic goal setting and accomplishment.

MISCELLANEOUS PROBLEMS

In addition to the problems related to habitual behavioral responses of particular patients, the nurse may encounter other difficulties. For example, the nurse may have started to establish a one-to-one relationship with a patient who is discharged following the first interaction. She selects another patient and begins interacting with him when the "discharged" patient is readmitted. The nurse, in such a situation, may experience divided loyalties and wish to interact with her "old" patient as well as with the newly selected patient. She actually has no alternative, once a pact has been established, but to continue to interact with the new patient. This is not to say that she is not to speak to her old patient; it does imply that the nurse's time and attention must be devoted to the newly selected patient.

A nurse may discover that an old friend or acquaintance has been admitted to the unit where she is interacting with a patient. The friend may or may not choose to recognize the nurse's presence on the unit; he may ignore the nurse completely or may seek her out and elicit help. Discussion of this problem with the supervisor is recommended because of the many variables operating in the situation.

The nurse may also have problems which interfere with her ability to establish and maintain a relationship. These are discussed below.

PART II—SPECIFIC PROBLEMS OF NURSE PRACTITIONERS

The human being who is the practitioner brings to the one-to-one relationship the uniqueness of her individuality, her strengths as well as her personality problems and deficits. Both the patient and the practitioner have been molded by life experiences. Both have attempted to cope with problems in the ways least threatening to them. The practitioner, as human being, may have encountered problems in living which have *not* been satisfactorily resolved and which may emerge as obstacles to establishing relatedness with patients. For example, a nurse who has experienced marked difficulties in her relationship with a parent may be unable to work effectively with a patient who represents a parental figure.

Some nurses are seemingly unable to establish relatedness with patients displaying particular kinds of behavior. For example, a practitioner will not elect to work with a dejected individual and instead will prefer to interact with a detached person. Why? One assumption is that the dejected patient's problems too closely resemble the unresolved problems of the practitioner; the practitioner may be too threatened by the patient's difficulty to be of any assistance to him. Often the nurse is unable to state the reasons why she is unwilling to work with a specific patient. This raises an interesting question: Should a practitioner who feels unable to work with a certain patient be forced to work with him? The answer is an unequivocal no, unless the nurse voluntarily undergoes therapy or wishes to work with the patient, under the guidance of the supervisor, to identify what is blocking her ability to help the ill person. There are some clinicians who do not agree with this, and maintain that nurses "should be able to work effectively with all patients." It is believed that this position is unrealistic. What kind of relatedness will be developed by a practitioner who finds it impossible to interact with a patient? What does "forced interaction" do to the patient?

As patients utilize various maneuvers to avoid closeness, so do many nurses. Such maneuvers, on the part of nurses, include keeping conversation on a superficial level to avoid problem areas, focusing on trivial subjects rather than on the patient's problems. Some nurses, because of their problems, may need to be praised and appreciated, and may attempt to extract praise and gratitude from patients; they are often not aware that they habitually act in this manner. In such instances, the nurse seeks to meet her needs at the expense of the patient's. The astute supervisor can usually detect the situation and can intervene directly if this be necessary.

Another common maneuver used by some nurses is to terminate an interaction as soon as the patient begins to show increased signs of anxiety, rather than to assist the ill person to identify its cause. The nurse may excuse her behavior on the basis that she did not wish to increase the patient's anxiety. There may be many reasons for such withdrawal. An obvious one is lack of knowledge of how to intervene. Another, less recognized, reason well may be that the nurse has never been able to cope with her anxiety and hence cannot be truly helpful to the anxiety-laden patient. When she withdraws from an interaction under such circumstances, it is not to protect the patient but to protect self.

A nurse may attempt to bribe the ill person into liking her by bringing gifts to the patient. Either she lacks knowledge of the role of the nurse in the one-to-one relationship or this behavior represents an habitual manner she has developed to please others and to win their approval.

Another problem—frequently not identified by supervisors, much less discussed—is presented when the nurse experiences a strong physical attraction for the patient, or is sexually stimulated by the patient's comments or behavior. Some nurses, because of their own problems, may pry into the patient's sexual life and spend a disproportionate period of time discussing his "sexual problems." Some mentally ill individuals *do* have sexual problems, and these should be discussed when introduced by the patient during the interview. The ill person's sexual problems, however, are but symptoms of disorganization in other aspects of living. Some nurses discuss patients' sexual problems to experience vicarious pleasure, not to assist the patients.

Nurses may behave in the nurse-patient situation as they do socially toward members of the opposite sex. That is, the nurse may unconsciously flirt with the patient and may not realize that her behavior is provocative or seductive. If the supervisor suspects the practitioner is engaging in "unconscious flirtation" it is recommended that she observe the interaction to ascertain whether or not this is indeed the case. Relationships between members of opposite sex may well arouse sexual feelings of one kind or another. This is normal. The problem arises when an ill person receives a double-bind communication from the nurse, one verbal message conveying "This is a professional relationship" and another, contradictory, impression that "I want to be more than a friend to you."

A nurse who is a member of a religious order and wears her habit may encounter unique problems. The ill person may wish to relate to the nurse as a religious, not as a nurse. He may not wish to discuss certain problems with the "nun" because he fears censure or does not wish to shock her. The nurse who is also a nun may not help the situation if she shows interest *only* in the ill person's religious habits. This is *not* to suggest that religious matters should not be discussed; they can and should, provided the patient introduces these topics into the conversation. It *is* suggested that the nurse who is also a religious endeavor to assist the patient to perceive her less as a stereotyped "nun" and more as a helpful human being with whom he can share his problems without fear of blame, censure or lectures on proper behavior. This is *not* meant to suggest that nurses who are nuns invariably engage in blaming or censuring. It means that ill persons may have stereotypes of nuns which may affect their ability to communicate and establish relatedness. It is the nurse's task to assist the patient to shatter the stereotype and to perceive her as a human being.

Nurses who experience some of the problems discussed in this section may not recognize their nature or may, in fact, be unaware that problems exist. The practitioner may "know" something is wrong, i.e., something is interfering with her ability to establish relatedness, but is usually unable to identify the difficulty. The tasks of the supervisor and instructor are to identify the problem behavior displayed by the nurse, explore with her its possible meanings, and assist her to audit and, if possible, change her behavior. It should be emphasized, however, that a practitioner may understand a specific problem which interferes with establishing relatedness and yet be unable to change her behavior, because the behavior is usually unconsciously motivated. The supervisor, therefore, helps the nurse to develop the ability to identify the problem and to cope with it. These problems do not disappear even with intellectual insight. However, the relationship between the supervisor and practitioner can be the means through which the practitioner is enabled to audit and gradually to change her behavior even though she may never, without therapy, understand the genesis of her problem.

PART III—PROBLEMS WITH PERSONNEL

The nurse trying to establish a one-to-one relationship interacts with the patient in a particular setting, i.e., a nursing unit, clinic or other agency. Some of the problems practitioners encounter in working with personnel in the setting are a direct result of lack of knowledge and understanding on the part of personnel as to the role of the practitioner. This is especially true in settings where establishing such relationships is not a function of the nurses working in the setting. It is strongly recommended that all personnel working in the setting—other nurses, aides, attendants—be oriented as to the role and function of the nurse in the one-to-one relationship.

As stated in Chapter VI, "The Selection of Patients," Part II, some personnel may misinterpret the nurse's functions and believe she is on the unit to "check up" on them or on the quality of care given. *The nurse cannot assume that personnel in an agency understand the nature of the one-to-one relationship unless the practitioner interprets and reinterprets her role and functions to them.* Knowledge of the nurse's role, however, is *not* sufficient. The practitioner is encouraged to elicit the opinions of personnel and to share with them data about the patient, provided such sharing does not violate the confidential nature of the one-to-one relationship. If the nurse working with an individual patient does not write observations on his chart, it is recommended that she report to, or share with, the head nurse on the unit her data regarding the patient's progress. If the nurse shares information about the patient with members of the staff, it is recommended that she so inform the patient.

It is the nurse's task to establish relationships with co-workers. Unless she does so, and exhibits respect for them as unique human beings, she may be subjected to attempts to undermine her efforts to establish the one-to-one relationship. Sabotaging, on the part of personnel, is suspected when the patient is never "on the unit" when the nurse arrives for the interview. The nurse has informed personnel verbally and has supplied a written statement of times and dates for each interaction. If the patient is not on the unit when the nurse arrives, she inquires as to why. Staff members may say that the patient was sent on an errand or that they "forgot" the nurse was coming. If such behavior on the part of staff members is habitual, the nurse has a problem to solve. She is advised to examine the extent to which she has tried to develop a working relationship with personnel. She must repair a damaged relationship before attempting to elicit the staff's cooperation. Blaming and complaining are *not* ways to resolve such difficulties; neither is going "over the heads" of staff members to complain to higher authorities. The nurse must resolve the problem with the individuals concerned rather than with their superiors.

Attitudes of staff members reflect their opinions of the practitioner's role and are invariably conveyed to the practitioner. While such attitudes may not be translated into sabotage, the practitioner may be subjected to comments regarding the desirability of the one-to-one relationship. Some personnel disapprove of the one-to-one relationship as being valueless. The nurse is not bound to change the beliefs of others regarding its value; she *is* obligated to interpret to others what she wishes to accomplish in the relationship. She does not defend the relationship, and it is not desirable that she try to do so. She can best help staff members to change their beliefs about the value of the one-to-one relationship by example—not through persuasion. The practitioner is a role model for both patients and personnel.

Some staff members attempt to provoke the practitioner by such comments as: "You have an easy job—you only have one patient to care for. We have sixty" or "I wish all I had to do was talk to one patient." It is recommended that a practitioner subjected to such comments state her appreciation that personnel *do* indeed have a difficult job and that it is *not* easy to care for sixty patients. Again, she does not defend the one-to-one relationship or attempt to convert personnel to her way of thinking.

Everyone—nurses, patients and personnel—benefits when a collaborative working relationship is developed. In addition, however, the practitioner must establish working relationships with members of other health disciplines—social workers, psychologists, psychiatrists, occupational and recreational therapists, etc.

PART IV—PROBLEMS IN WORKING WITH MEMBERS OF OTHER HEALTH DISCIPLINES

It is the nurse's responsibility to understand the role and functions of other health workers. It cannot, however, be assumed automatically that other health workers understand the nurse's role or functions—the possible exception being her *one* dependent function, namely, "following the doctor's orders." That nurses even have independent functions does not occur to many health workers, probably because it is easier to observe nurses "carrying out doctor's orders" than engaging in health teaching, counseling or other activities. Further, nurses are not vocal regarding the independent functions of nursing practice, and do not interpret their roles to other health workers.

Problems in establishing and maintaining a one-to-one relationship may arise when nurses do not clearly interpret their functions to psychiatrists and other health workers. For example, a nurse attempting to establish a relationship was interrupted twice during one week by the patient's psychiatrist who wished to talk with the patient. The nurse could not prevent the psychiatrist from talking with the patient; she *did* discuss with the psychiatrist the problem of conflicting time arrangements. The psychiatrist, who knew the time of the nurse's interaction, agreed to see the patient at another time and apologized for interrupting the interaction. Some psychiatrists will interrupt an interview because they do not comprehend what the nurse is trying to accomplish. One psychiatrist told a nurse: "I thought you were just chatting with the patient."

There are still a few psychiatrists who are definitely opposed to the one-to-one relationship on the basis that the nurse is trying to become "a junior psychiatrist." Such physicians believe that the nurse "should stick to doctor's orders and do as she is told." The practitioner who encounters such a physician attempts to explain the changing role and functions of the psychiatric nurse—to educate the physician without alienating him. Such advice is easy to give but difficult to apply in actual situations, when a nurse is confronted by a psychiatrist who states bluntly: "You're not nursing, you're doctoring." At the risk of sounding condescending it is suggested that nurses remember such views are derived from the past when the "handmaiden to the physician" was the *only* role assumed by most practitioners. That the role and functions of the nurse have changed over the years is not understood by some psychiatrists or by some nurses. It is through interpreting and reinterpreting the functions of nursing, as well as by providing opportunities for psychiatrists to observe professional nurses performing independent functions, that such physicians may gradually change their views.

It is suggested that nurses attending interdisciplinary patient care conferences become vocal in expressing their opinions and in giving suggestions. Too often nurses sit and listen while members of other health disciplines discuss the care—sometimes the nursing care—of the patient. It has been noted that, in such conferences, psychiatrists make the largest number of contributions followed by psychiatric social workers, psychologists, occupational and recreational therapists and nursing personnel in that order. *Only nurses can speak for nursing.* Failure to communicate with members of other health disciplines has often been construed, sometimes correctly, to indicate that nurses know nothing because they contribute so little to inter-disciplinary conferences.

As stated, nurses need to understand the functions of other health workers. For example, many nurses have circumscribed ideas as to the nature of the assistance which can be given the patient, and the nurse, by the psychiatric social worker. Social workers are not "ladies bountiful" any more than nurses are "handmaidens to the physician." The psychiatric social worker can be of invaluable aid to the nurse who wishes to develop a deeper understanding of the patient's family, his environment, the community from which he came, and the community resources which he can utilize upon discharge from the hospital.

Some of the more common problems found by nurses in establishing one-to-one relationships have been discussed in this chapter. Many others, of course, may be encountered. While problems will, and do, occur they are not insurmountable. Through the medium of the supervisory conference or group reconstruction sessions the ingenious practitioner is assisted to identify obstacles and to devise methods to resolve the difficulties.

Chapter X

SUPERVISION OF THE PRACTITIONER: THE SUPERVISORY PROCESS

Nurses engaged in establishing one-to-one relationships, specifically beginning practitioners and students enrolled in psychiatric nursing courses, require the guidance and direction of qualified psychiatric nurse supervisors. A qualified psychiatric nurse supervisor is an individual who possesses a master's degree in psychiatric-mental health nursing and has demonstrated, under supervision, a high degree of clinical competency in establishing and maintaining one-to-one relationships. Nurses with baccalaureate preparation and broad experience *can* and *do* serve in supervisory capacities. However, it is believed that individuals with graduate preparation not only will possess a high degree of clinical competency but will have developed a greater in-depth understanding of the concepts underlying nursing intervention.

The psychiatric nurse supervisor is employed by hospitals, clinics, schools of nursing, and other agencies for the *express* purpose of assisting nurses to develop, or increase, their competency in group work or in establishing one-to-one relationships. The tasks and functions inherent in supervision are of such diversity, magnitude and complexity as to necessitate full-time employment.

The supervisor is primarily a teacher, *not* a practitioner. The two roles are not mutually exclusive; however, the understandings and skills required for supervision differ in some respects from those required for clinical competency. Not all competent practitioners have the capacity, or the desire, to become supervisors.

What are the qualifications needed to supervise others? The supervisor understands the nature of the supervisory process, is able to identify learning problems, and possesses the ability to assist the supervisee in solving problems in learning. She understands the concepts and principles underlying nursing practice and is herself a skilled practitioner. She is aware of and can cope with the common problems inherent in supervision, namely, those related to authority and dependency. The supervisor is a professionally mature individual, a scholar committed to continuous study and improvement of her skills; she is not content with the status quo. The supervisor keeps abreast of current changing trends in the field of psychiatric-mental health nursing through the literature and by attending professional meetings, workshops and institutes. She possesses a knowledge of source materials and knows how to seek and find information regarding problems in nursing. The supervisor also knows *what* resources are available within the community, i.e., those agencies and organizations to which patients may be referred upon discharge from the hospital or clinic.

Supervision requires other, more intangible, attributes—a commitment to the work undertaken, humility, courage and perseverance, the ability to inspire confidence in others. Personal charisma is also desirable, *provided* it is combined with knowledge and commitment. Not every supervisor will possess personal charm. All supervisors, however, can be knowledgeable, committed, dedicated individuals; indeed, they must be if they are to persevere in the difficult, but stimulating, task of supervising others.

Over how long a period of time should the individual practitioner be supervised? It is believed that nurse practitioners whose primary function is that of establishing one-to-one relationships require supervision for at least one year. The suggested one-year period, however, is not to be considered an arbitrary rule; some practitioners may require less supervision and others more. Too long a period of supervision may engender dependency on the part of the practitioner and impede, rather than help, her achievement of professional maturity. Following approximately a year of supervision, it is recommended that the practitioner assume responsibility for her own actions and have recourse to the supervisor's assistance only when encountering problems which cannot be resolved. Ideally, practitioners who have undergone a period of supervision hold regularly scheduled meetings at which time they can discuss problems of mutual interest and concern. It is believed that students enrolled in psychiatric nursing courses require supervision throughout their courses.

Who supervises the supervisor? It is recommended that supervisors meet with their peers, i.e., other supervisors, to discuss common problems and seek assistance in finding ways of resolving them. This presupposes that there is more than *one* qualified supervisor in the hospital or agency. In some areas, however, there may be only three or four qualified psychiatric nurse supervisors in the state. It is recommended, under such circumstances, that the qualified supervisors hold regularly scheduled meetings to discuss problems and to recruit other qualified psychiatric nurses into the state. This point is stressed. Because of the shortage of prepared psychiatric nurse supervisors there may be a tendency to request members of other health professions to serve as supervisors to nurses engaged in establishing one-to-one relationships. *It is believed that only nurses should supervise practitioners of nursing.* Members of other health professions, i.e., social workers, psychologists or psychiatrists, are not qualified by education or experience to supervise the activities of nurses.

PART I—NATURE OF THE SUPERVISORY PROCESS

Supervision is a way of assisting practitioners to develop or improve clinical competence. The supervisor's major concern is the identification of the practitioner's learning problems and needs. The ultimate aim of supervision is the improvement of nursing practice by assisting the practitioner to solve learning problems. The ill person is helped because the practitioner is enabled to bring increased understanding and skills to the nurse-patient situation.

The role of the supervisor is that of teacher to learner, *not* psychotherapist to "supervisee-patient." This point is stressed. The purpose of supervision is defeated if the supervisor focuses on the personal problems of the practitioner. If the practitioner's personal problems are such that she cannot benefit through supervision, then the supervisor may have no recourse but to suggest she seek therapy.

Not all practitioners benefit from supervision to the same degree; this is determined by many factors. Probably one of the most important is the ability of both supervisor and practitioner to establish a working relationship with the other. This, however, does not occur automatically; it is achieved gradually and over a period of time. To establish a working relationship the supervisor attempts to relate to the practitioner as a unique human being rather than as "a learning problem," and to grant her the freedom to grow, develop and make use of her particular talents in interacting with others. A danger inherent in supervision is the tendency to "mold" the practitioner, i.e., to impose upon the learner the supervisor's own style of interacting or theoretical bias. This is not to suggest that the practitioner should be encouraged to intervene in any manner she chooses. It does suggest that the supervisor allow the practitioner the freedom to deviate, *provided* she bases her intervention on a sound theoretical framework.

Establishing the working relationship is a shared responsibility; the practitioner also has obligations. What is required of the practitioner? A willingness to share problems and expose one's vulnerabilities, errors and successes to the supervisor is essential. If a working relationship is not established then it is probable that learning will be minimal or nonexistent. When the maturity and interest level of the practitioner are such that she *can* become actively involved, the vicissitudes of the supervisory relationship are attenuated.

Some of the problems encountered in the supervisory relationship seem to stem from the fact that some nurses, especially students in schools of nursing, are not given the choice of whether or not they wish to be supervised. The nature of supervision offered in psychiatric nursing may differ from supervision previously experienced by the student in other clinical nursing courses. The student is asked to reveal herself as a person, to discuss her thoughts and feelings, and to analyze her habitual manner of interacting with others. Self-scrutiny is encouraged, as is the ability to change one's behavior. Some students have a natural reluctance to reveal themselves and thus may initially resist supervision; this is also true of graduate nurse practitioners. However, in time, the supervisor can usually help the student to understand and accept the nature of the assistance offered.

What are the characteristics of a working relationship? A working relationship is characterized by the ability of both supervisor and practitioner to share and speak freely about the data of the nurse-patient interaction. Each is able to discuss with the other the problems which emerge as a direct result of the supervisory relationship. As there are phases leading to the development of a nurse-patient relationship, so there are phases leading to the establishment of a supervisor-practitioner relationship. Some of the problems encountered in establishing a nurse-patient relationship may also be encountered in developing a working supervisor-practitioner relationship. Problematic areas which may be encountered include parataxic distortion, stereotyping and the inability to perceive the other as a unique human being. Both practitioner and supervisor have thoughts and feelings about the other. Either may experience varying degrees of anxiety, stress, anger or frustration during the supervisory relationship. Tranquility and contentment are *not* necessarily the hallmarks of a working relationship; rather, the habitual existence of these states may indicate that learning is not occurring. Learning requires a change in behavior and, thus, almost inevitably engenders some anxiety and stress as the practitioner begins to examine her motivation and to test new knowledge in the clinical situation. The anxiety experienced, however, is motivating—not incapacitating. One outcome of the working relationship is that both supervisor and practitioner learn as a result of their interaction. It is the supervisor's responsibility to guide the learning experiences of the practitioner; however, in reality, both individuals teach and learn from each other.

TASKS AND ACTIVITIES OF THE SUPERVISOR

The supervisor is the resource person with whom the practitioner shares data regarding the one-to-one relationship during regularly scheduled conferences or group reconstruction sessions. The supervisor attempts to create a psychological climate which enables the practitioner to feel free to discuss the problems inherent in the one-to-one relationship as they emerge from the discussion of the analyzed data in the practitioner's process record.

Major tasks of the supervisor include assisting the practitioner to achieve relatedness with the ill individual, to recognize barriers to goal accomplishment, to identify the genesis of problems, and to devise ways of solving the problems encountered. More specifically, the supervisor guides the practitioner to develop an increased ability to collect and interpret data, to apply concepts to data, and to analyze and synthesize collected data. Other supervisory tasks include helping the practitioner to become aware of her habitual patterns of communicating and interacting with others and to assess the effects of these habitual patterns on the ill person and others. The supervisor assists the practitioner to identify and clarify problems and determine needed action—as opposed to "telling the practitioner what to do." This does not mean that supervisors are never to suggest possible approaches to problems. It *does* imply that the practitioner is encouraged to think through problematic areas for herself rather than to depend on the supervisor for "the answer." The supervisor assists and motivates the practitioner to persevere in the difficult task of trying to achieve relatedness with the ill person, and encourages her to focus on the ill person's potential for growth as well as on his pathology.

Some practitioners become overwhelmed by the multiplicity of problems presented by patients and by the harsh realities of the setting in which they practice the one-to-one relationship. They may question whether or not they can accomplish anything of value. In such instances the supervisor's task is to assist them to accept the reality of the situation and yet to persevere in effecting changes.

METHODS OF SUPERVISION

There are three major methods used to supervise practitioners— direct "on-the-spot" supervision, supervisory conference and group reconstruction. Each of these methods will be discussed.

Direct On-The-Spot Supervision

Some supervisors are available on the nursing unit, or in the agency, where the practitioner is engaged in the one-to-one relationship, for "on-the-spot" counseling and guidance. The supervisor serves as a resource person, or consultant, to the practitioner, and discusses problems as these are encountered and reported by the practitioner. The availability of the supervisor for guidance not only assists the practitioner to resolve problems but offers a means of providing support to her. Occasionally a supervisor engages in an interaction with a patient, to provide a role model for the practitioner. However advantageous this practice may be, its major drawback is that the supervisor is not available for on-the-spot conferences with the practitioner. It is recommended that the supervisor be available for conferences as needed. The supervisor does not interfere in the interaction between practitioner and patient. That is, unless an emergency situation occurs, the supervisor does not attempt to intrude self into the practitioner's interaction with the patient. This does not mean that supervisors should not talk with the patient. It *does* imply the supervisor does not interrupt the conversation between practitioner and patient. Neither does the supervisor interact with a patient assigned to a practitioner for the purpose of "checking" on the practitioner or to develop inferences regarding the degree to which practitioner and patient are achieving relatedness.

The Supervisory Conference

The supervisory conference is a regularly scheduled meeting of supervisor and practitioner for the express purpose of discussing the practitioner's analyzed process record; it is usually held once a week. The conference may be the sole means of supervising the practitioner or it may be combined with direct on-the-spot supervision or group reconstruction. The conference may last from one to two hours, with one hour the preferred time. The number of practitioners an individual can supervise through the conference method is obviously limited. Ideally, the supervisor should hold only five scheduled conferences a week. Eight conferences are recommended as the maximum load.

The practitioner brings to the supervisory conference analyzed process records for discussion. However, it is obvious that some system must be devised to allow the supervisor time to read the records and make suggestions. If a nurse interacts with a patient one hour a day, five days a week, five process records will have been written during that period. Obviously the nurse cannot wait for the weekly supervisory conference to discuss problems. Direct on-the-spot supervision *does allow* some opportunity for the practitioner to seek guidance. However, more time is usually required than can be provided by this means. Many nurses are not aware that problems exist until they begin to discuss their interaction with the supervisor. To assist the practitioner in the day-to-day interaction with the patient, the supervisor may request her to hand in a daily process record. The supervisor reads the record, writes comments and suggestions to help the practitioner intervene more appropriately, and returns the record to the practitioner prior to the next scheduled interaction with the patient. The practitioner needs this assistance in order to avoid error, solve problems, and devise alternative methods of intervening prior to the interaction. During the weekly conference the practitioner discusses the process records written during the week or, in detail, the most recent process record.

Process records are invaluable as a learning tool; their use, however, is time-consuming for both practitioner and supervisor. Unless the supervisor has the time to read and critically study the analyzed process records, she cannot expect such records.

Group Reconstruction Method

The group reconstruction method is based on the assumption that members in a group influence and are influenced by each other, teach and are taught by each other. Group members, i.e., practitioners and supervisors, are in the roles of both teachers and learners. *Another major assumption is that practitioners are responsible for their own learning as well as the learning of others in their peer group.* Each nurse is considered a resource person, teacher as well as learner, and is expected actively to assist other members of the group to learn. The group reconstruction method offers an opportunity for members to learn from the experiences of others, and to test and validate the usefulness of knowledge and its application in practice. The sharing process allows members to discuss ways of resolving the problems encountered in interacting with patients. Practitioners both give and gain support as a result of this sharing.

The ability to lead a group reconstruction successfully, i.e., so that learning occurs, may seem to be a relatively easy task. However, the group reconstruction method is one of the *most* difficult teaching tools to master. Different understandings, skills and abilities are required of the supervisor in a group reconstruction session than are required in conference.

The sessions are relatively unstructured, i.e., the supervisor does not always know in advance the problems that will be presented. The successful conduct of the session therefore requires that the supervisor be an individual who is comfortable in unstructured situations. The supervisor who uses this method should possess an understanding of the group process, the ability to foster group cohesiveness, and the talent to motivate individuals within the group. She must also be able to relinquish the role of leader and assist group members to exercise leadership functions. Since the supervisor helps practitioners to utilize theory in practice she must possess an understanding of the theory underlying nursing practice and be able, without advance preparation, to assist practitioners *consciously* to apply theoretical concepts to the analyzed data. Other skills, abilities and understandings needed by the supervisor will be discussed in the sections which follow.

Before initiating the group reconstruction session it is recommended that the supervisor orient practitioners as to the purpose of the sessions, the assumptions underlying the use of group reconstruction, and the roles and responsibilities of the supervisor and practitioner. Expectations and objectives are clearly defined and discussed, as are methods of evaluating the practitioner's performance in the group. The behaviors the supervisor may wish the practitioner to demonstrate in group reconstruction may include:

Ability to communicate effectively in writing process records
    Uses correct format
    Uses correct spelling and grammar
    Writes intelligibly

Ability to participate and contribute in group reconstruction sessions
    Speaks clearly, concisely and to the point under discussion
    Shares analyzed data
    Describes and explores the meaning of one's thoughts and feelings with others
    Explores and analyzes ideas
    Validates ideas
    Raises pertinent questions
    Cooperates, collaborates and competes with others
    Listens attentively when others are speaking

Ability to apply theoretical concepts to analyzed data
> Uses theory to guide, structure and evaluate intervention
> Contributes pertinent theoretical concepts
> Applies past learning to present situation
> Applies research findings to clinical data

Ability to use the problem-solving approach
> Uses logical analysis
> Identifies problems
> Formulates working hypothesis
> Recalls and uses relevant theory
> Tests hypotheses
> Verifies or discards hypotheses

Ability to assume responsibility for own learning
> Seeks help when needed from supervisors, peers or resource persons
> Is relatively self-directing
> Uses the literature to study, clarify or help in solving problems

Ability to promote the learning of others
> Is supportive of peers
> Helps others to apply theory
> Encourages others to contribute, explore and actively participate
> Assumes responsibility for group discussion
> Shares knowledge with others
> Is able to criticize ideas held by others and to do this tactfully

Ability to assess self—limitations and assets
> Assesses own anxiety level
> Identifies blocks to learning
> Identifies ways of resolving learning difficulties
> Makes use of talents and capabilities

Ability to make use of supervision
> Accepts criticism, directions and suggestions
> Follows through on recommendations
> Questions unclear suggestions or directions

Ability to experiment in developing approaches to nursing intervention
> Explores rationale underlying innovations in nursing practice

METHODOLOGY. Group reconstruction sessions are scheduled after practitioners have interacted with patients and have had an opportunity to analyze their process records. Usually a period of one to two hours is required for writing and analyzing a process record. The supervisor meets with the group for a two- to four-hour session. The number of individuals in the group, exclusive of the supervisor, should not exceed eight. Depending on the content in the process record, one practitioner may need two hours in which to report the interaction in depth. As the practitioner presents the interaction the other members of the group are expected to ask questions, make comments and suggestions, assist the practitioner to communicate, and identify the theoretical basis for intervention used. Problems are identified and various approaches to problem resolution are discussed. Recommendations are made to prepare the practitioner for her next interaction with the patient.

Obviously only a few practitioners will have the opportunity to discuss in depth their interaction during the two- to four-hour period. To assist other members who may need advice on particular problems, the supervisor may allot a time during each session for practitioners to seek the help of the group. Practitioners who have not presented their interactions hand in their process records; the supervisor reads the records, writes comments and suggestions and returns the records to the practitioners *prior* to the next scheduled interaction.

Supervisors using the group reconstruction method for the first time may wish to design some criteria as a basis for deciding which practitioners will present their records during a particular session. Some supervisors request volunteers; the rationale is that practitioners who need the guidance of the group will volunteer. This, however, is not always true; sometimes the most verbal members of the group, and not necessarily the practitioners with problems, may volunteer. Another approach is to encourage the group to decide *who* will present her records. The disadvantage here is that the most verbal, or easily influenced, practitioner may be "chosen" by the group. Some supervisors "call on" a different practitioner each session in order to allow all members of the group the opportunity to present their interactions with patients in depth. Usually after the first few group reconstruction sessions, as members feel less threatened, problems related to "who will present" are no longer pronounced. As each group is different, no definite rule can be made. Beginners in psychiatric nursing, especially undergraduate students, may have to be "called on" until group members feel comfortable enough to make this decision on the basis of individual need to discuss problems.

What is the role of the supervisor in conducting the session? The supervisor encourages members to participate, raises questions, and assists members to relate theory to practice. The importance of the theoretical rationale underlying nursing practice is consciously stressed during each session, since one of the major purposes of group reconstruction is to provide practitioners with the opportunity to test the usefulness of theory and its application in practice. The supervisor helps practitioners to focus on the reasons underlying intervention—the *why* as contrasted to the *how*.

Some supervisors list the concepts explored by members during each session. Dearth of knowledge in particular areas is noted. The supervisor may provide the group with the knowledge needed to proceed with the presentation or may give individual or group assignments, for example pertinent reading references. It is recommended that supervisors do not make a habit of providing members with content materials, i.e., concepts, principles, etc.; rather, group members are encouraged to seek needed information themselves instead of depending on the supervisor. Group members are responsible for their own learning and are expected to come to the session *fully prepared* to contribute and participate.

The supervisor observes the behavior of group members and notes the quantity and quality of contributions made by individuals. Some supervisors take notes, during the session, of the number of times each member contributes and categorize the quality of the contributions made. For example, quality of contributions may be divided into: stating opinions, generalizing with sufficient (or insufficient) data, making relevant (or irrelevant) comments, asking clarifying questions, making valid (or invalid) inferences, giving information, giving support to others, etc. The supervisor informs the group that such notes are being taken. Some supervisors request either another supervisor or a group member to serve as an observer and to give a brief summary of observations at the conclusion of each session.

When a practitioner is presenting her record, the supervisor assists in identifying problems and attempts to learn from group members whether they have encountered similar problems. The supervisor may ask members how they solved their problems as contrasted to the way in which the practitioner resolved (or did not resolve) hers. The underlying theoretical rationale is also discussed. Members are asked to make recommendations to the practitioner. Problems commonly encountered in establishing relatedness with patients are emphasized, so that each group member can profit from the discussion. In the event some practitioners have not as yet encountered the problem under discussion, the supervisor stresses that they probably will do so in a future interaction. Practitioners are assisted to develop foresight and to discuss problems which *may* emerge, along with ways of dealing with them.

The supervisor also discusses her inferences regarding the group's productivity and participation. Any problem which seems to be interfering with the learning process is a subject for discussion. The problem is identified and discussed, and recommendations are elicited from the group as to ways of resolving the difficulty. If a supervisor decides to use this method, she should be prepared to accept the recommendation of the group and act upon it. If not, then the supervisor states to the group that she reserves the right to make the final decision regarding the group's recommendation. For example, a majority of group members may state they are "too tired" to proceed with the session and recommend adjournment. The supervisor who has said she will act on the group's recommendation has no recourse but to adjourn the session, whereas the supervisor who has reserved the right to make final decisions must decide whether or not to assent to the group's request and then must express her reasons for the decision.

It cannot be overly emphasized that group reconstruction is one of the most difficult teaching tools to master and use expertly. It is time-consuming and emotionally exhausting for supervisors and practitioners alike. The advantages of group reconstruction, however, outweigh the disadvantages and—until some other method is devised which achieves the same goals—group reconstruction is recommended as one of the best teaching methods in psychiatric nursing courses.

PROBLEMS IN SUPERVISING PRACTITIONERS

The genesis of some difficulties seems related to the character structure, personality, and maturity level of practitioners and supervisors. Supervision is an educational process. It is assumed that the practitioner will have varying degrees of ambivalence about the learning process, i.e., she will possess the desire to learn as well as some resistance to behavioral change. Learning problems and personality difficulties are identified by the supervisor through observing the practitioner's behavior in supervisory conference and group reconstruction, and can be inferred by reading the practitioner's process records.

It is difficult to generalize about learning problems in group sessions, since supervisors and groups of practitioners possess unique and individual characteristics which elude categorization. Common recurring learning problems exemplified in certain types of behavior, however, can be identified.

Supervisors, at one time or another, will encounter practitioners who have difficulty in participating in group sessions. Some practitioners are relatively silent but are attentive and "involved" on a nonverbal level. Other members are silent, inattentive and unresponsive even on a nonverbal level; such individuals give the impression of being "uninhabited" or simply "not there." Some practitioners are highly verbal, yet their contributions either are not pertinent to the discussion or reflect personal opinions and subjective judgments. Some nurses share thoughts and feelings but have difficulty accepting criticism, directions and suggestions from peers and supervisors, and hence have difficulty modifying their behavior; such individuals may be able to offer suggestions but cannot accept them. Others accept recommendations readily—too readily—and seldom question the validity of the recommendations; their attitude seems to be: "You tell me what to do and I will do it." Other nurses contribute, yet, when questioned as to the validity of their ideas, retreat and are unable to defend them.

Other common problems include the inability to apply theory to practice, to use the problem-solving approach, to assume responsibility for one's own learning, and to promote the learning of others. Some practitioners have difficulty in perceiving their participation in an experience, or in assessing their limitations and assets. Another problem is found in the inability to accept the fact that behavioral changes in self and others occur slowly and over a period of time. Some practitioners become discouraged when they reach an impasse in the development of the nurse-patient relationship. Nurses who lack confidence in their ability frequently experience a breakdown in motivation. A feeling of helplessness may be experienced when the practitioner is faced with the realities of the setting in which she practices or with problems relating to the patient's family situation, environment or socioeconomic status. As one nurse stated: "Why should I try to help (a patient)? He's going back to the same family situation. He'll be back here within a month."

What can be done to assist practitioners to recognize the existence of those problems, to confront them, and to find ways to resolve them?

The Noncontributing Practitioner

How may the supervisor help the practitioner who has difficulty in participating and contributing during group reconstruction sessions? It should first be recognized that encouraging practitioners to participate is a responsibility of the *group* and not solely of the supervisor. It cannot be overly emphasized that practitioners need a thorough orientation to the roles and responsibilities of the supervisor and practitioner. Expectations and objectives are clearly defined. The practitioner is given the opportunity to understand the behaviors she is expected to demonstrate during group reconstruction sessions. Participation and contribution in the group are expected behaviors.

As stated, practitioners are responsible for the learning of other group members as well as for their own. The nurse who does not contribute is not assuming this responsibility. The noncontributing practitioner is, in effect, depriving others of the opportunity to learn. It is recognized that each human being differs in ability to express and reveal thoughts and feelings to others. The ability to express oneself verbally and to engage in a sharing process is learned behavior. The individual who is hesitant, reluctant, or unable to express herself verbally often needs an "unlearning" process before she can share and disclose self to others. The supervisor can, to some extent, provide corrective experiential learning experiences for such an individual. Obviously if the noncontributory behavior is of long duration, i.e., is an habitual behavioral response developed over a period of years, the supervisor's attempts to assist the person may be to little or no avail. Generally, the supervisor tries to develop an atmosphere in which each participant feels free to share her thoughts and feelings with others. Such an atmosphere, however, may not assist the noncontributing practitioner. Individual conferences are recommended to provide the supervisor with the opportunity to assess probable reasons for noncontributory behavior. Statements usually given as "reasons" for not contributing during group reconstruction sessions are:

A. "I was thinking and by the time I had something to say the group was already talking about something else."

B. "I didn't believe I could add to the discussion so I kept quiet."

C. "I was going to contribute but Miss X. (another student) already said what I was going to say."

D. "I've always had this problem. You're the fourth teacher to tell me this. I never was able to talk much in a group."

E. "I had something to say but everyone was talking so fast I didn't get an opportunity . . . I didn't want to interrupt when they were talking."

F. "I learn more by listening to others."

G. "I didn't agree with Miss X. (a student) but I didn't want to hurt her feelings."

Reason A (". . . by the time I had something to say the group was talking about something else") may be given by practitioners who require a period of time to think through a topic before discussing it. The supervisor may recommend that the practitioner share his contributions even though members may then be talking about another topic. If the reason is not a valid one, the practitioner will be unable to implement the supervisor's recommendation.

Reason B ("I didn't believe I could add to the discussion . . .") may be given by practitioners who are afraid to disclose themselves to others. Such practitioners are often difficult to assist. The individual does not know whether or not she could have added to the discussion because she did not attempt to contribute. It is essential to help such persons to develop the courage to reveal themselves and permit others to decide whether or not their comments "added" to the discussion. This statement, however, is easier to make than it is to implement in practice. It is *not* recommended that individuals be subjected to lectures by the supervisor regarding their obligation to help other members; such exhortations are exercises in futility. The supervisor can only encourage. Ultimately the noncontributing practitioner must choose, and must bear the consequences of a decision freely made.

Reason C ("I was going to contribute but . . . another student . . . said what I was going to say") is often given by nurses who habitually defer to others. The individual who gives this reason is also stating that ignorance did not keep her from contributing ("I was going to contribute"); she was prevented only because another nurse "said what I was going to say." In individual conference the supervisor explores the reason with the practitioner. The supervisor's aim is to assist the practitioner to "look at her behavior" and to envisage alternatives available to her in the situation. Again, it is the practitioner's prerogative to decide whether or not to contribute.

Reason D ("I've always had this problem. . . .") is often given by nurses who are unable to change their behavior pattern. Such persons are very difficult to help. In talking with them, the supervisor may get the impression that they are astonished by her perception in detecting the difficulty. Some practitioners will request advice. One gets the impression that what is sought is a method for quickly resolving the problem. "You tell me what to do and I will do it" is a common verbal maneuver. The responsibility is shifted to the supervisor; if the advice does not assist the practitioner, the "blame" is attributed to the "faulty" advice given by the supervisor. It is recommended that the supervisor elicit from the practitioner what she intends to do about the difficulty. If the problem is of long-standing duration, and such difficulties usually are, intensive counseling or therapy may be recommended. The practitioner, however, must make the decision as to whether or not to undergo therapy.

Reason E ("I had something to say but everyone was talking so fast I didn't get an opportunity . . . and I didn't want to interrupt. . . .") is often given by practitioners who blame the group for their inability to contribute. The practitioner presents herself as an individual who does not wish to be impolite. Noncontributory behavior is thus presented as laudable. It is recommended that the supervisor assist the practitioner to "look at" her habitual noncontributory behavior and envisage alternatives to circumvent the difficulty.

Reason F ("I learn more by listening to others") is often given by practitioners who fear disclosing themselves to others. Such individuals really may learn more by listening. However, the effect of such behavior in group reconstruction is to deprive others of the opportunity to learn. The problem is discussed in conference and the practitioner is permitted to decide what (if anything) she intends to do about the problem.

Reason G ("I didn't agree with . . . another student but I didn't want to hurt her feelings") is often given by individuals who desire to present themselves as sensitive to the feelings of others. In conference it may become apparent that the practitioner is not so afraid of "hurting" others as she is of being "hurt" by the criticisms of members of the peer group. The supervisor explores with the practitioner the reason given for nonparticipation and asks: "What evidence do you have to support your conclusion?" If the practitioner provides evidence that Miss X.'s feelings are easily hurt by criticism, it may be that Miss X. has the problem and not the practitioner. In conference the supervisor assists the practitioner to explore in depth the causes of noncontributory behavior and to work through these difficulties.

The Highly Verbal Practitioner

Some practitioners are extremely verbal during group reconstruction sessions; however, the quality of their contributions leaves much to be desired. Typical responses in the group include introducing irrelevant topics, giving personal opinions, and presenting unvalidated assumptions as facts. Usually the highly verbal individual is displaying an habitual behavior pattern which has developed over a long period of time.

Some highly verbal individuals seem to "use words" either to avoid involvement with others or to avoid thinking. It is almost characteristic that such persons tend to have difficulty relating theory to practice. They are masters of the art of "waffling"—a British term which means to talk a great deal while saying nothing. It is recommended that the supervisor assist all group members to remain on the point under discussion. However, the highly verbal person usually requires guided practice in remaining on the subject without adding irrelevant data or relating interesting personal experiences which have nothing to do with the point under discussion. The highly verbal practitioner should be challenged by the supervisor (and group members) whenever she makes unsubstantiated assumptions, relates inconsequential data, or in any way contributes irrelevant material in group session. The aim of the supervisor is not to stop the highly verbal person from talking too much; rather, it is to assist the individual to keep to the point and to apply theory to practice.

Difficulties in Applying Theory to Practice

Assisting learners to apply content to process, i.e., theory to practice, is one of the most difficult tasks of the educator-supervisor. There are many reasons for this. For example, the learner may not have understood the pertinent theoretical concepts, and hence cannot apply that which has not been learned. More commonly, the learner does not comprehend the relationship between theory and practice. Some learners, because of their prior educational experiences, seem to believe that theory is "classwork" and has little or no application to "what you do in practice." Emphasis is therefore placed on assisting learners consciously to apply theory to practice and to give evidence of ability to do so. Knowledge must be translated into action, i.e. into behavior which can be observed. The learner who can apply theory to practice is able to state the theoretical basis for judgments made and interventive measures taken. The supervisor is a role model for the learner—an individual who demonstrates her ability consciously to apply theory in practice. Through repetitive emphasis on the *why*, i.e., the rationale underlying nursing action, the supervisor can assist learners to bridge the gap between theory and practice.

Difficulties in Assuming Reponsibility for Learning

A basic assumption underlying this work is that practitioners are responsible for their own learning. It is the task of the supervisor-educator to provide learning experiences; it is the task of the practitioner to learn. This assumption in no way excuses the supervisor-educator from providing a milieu conducive to learning. Teaching, guiding and evaluating are activities which lie within the province of the supervisor; however, learning is the task of the student or practitioner. It is one matter to believe practitioners and students are responsible for their own learning and quite another to implement this belief. Most supervisors have encountered learners whose general attitude seems to be that of passivity, a lack of initiative. Some practitioners verbalize or exemplify in their behavior the "you tell me what to do and I will do it" attitude. There are various reasons for this. Past "educational" experiences may have generally been of such a nature that the learner discovered the best way to pass a course is to find out "what the teacher (or supervisor) wants" and then to meet the expectations of these authority figures; learners who have been penalized because they used initiative may well adopt this attitude.

Some learners are seemingly unable (or unwilling) to ask clarifying questions for fear of appearing "stupid." Past experiences with authority figures may predispose the learner to this level of behavior. It is recommended that supervisors unequivocally state, and demonstrate by their behavior, that it is the practitioner's task to learn. It is the practitioner's responsibility to raise questions and clarify ambiguities.

Difficulties in Assessing Self

Most learners experience some difficulty in assessing self in terms of abilities and limitations. This behavior is normal, very human, and to be expected. However, in psychiatric nursing it is necessary that the practitioner develop the difficult art of assessing self and noting the effect of one's behavior on others. A hoped-for outcome of self-assessment is an increased knowledge of one's capacities, abilities as well as limitations.

Many learners quite glibly recount their limitations and "bad points" but have difficulty in assessing capabilities and areas of strength. Surely knowledge of what one is "good at" is as important as knowledge of one's "bad points." Perhaps cultural prohibitions regarding bragging about one's abilities are, in part, responsible for this proclivity. Whatever the cause, it is important for individuals to possess knowledge of their areas of strength in order to develop their talents and capabilities to the fullest extent. As much emphasis should be placed, by educators and others, on assisting learners to harness and productively use their talents as is placed on helping them to recognize their shortcomings. It is not a sign of humility to deny one's talents or make light of one's assets; rather, it is a sign of pride. Humility is truth. An individual who is six feet tall yet insists he is only five feet is not only untruthful but is also denying reality. This is not to say that the learner's limitations are to be ignored. However, it is recommended that supervisors and all who evaluate the competencies of others place an equal emphasis on the learner's strengths as on her weaknesses.

Learners may have difficulty in assessing self because they have never been expected to audit their own behavior. A practitioner may be able to assess self and have some degree of self-knowledge yet be reluctant to reveal her strengths and weaknesses to others. As the learner develops trust in the supervisor, this disinclination tends to weaken.

Some practitioners may apparently be able to assess self, but in conference with them it soon becomes clear that they are only repeating what others have told them. In such individuals, motivation to audit their behavior is lacking. Educators have never expected them to assess self. Instead they have been told, by supervisors and others, of their faults and shortcomings. These individuals need to be taught to assess self and not to rely exclusively on the opinions of others.

If the ability to assess self is expected of learners, then it follows that it is also expected of supervisors. The ability to assess self is never easy, and there is a natural reluctance to audit one's behavior. However, self-assessment is a major prerequisite to the practice of psychiatric nursing.

Inability to Make Use of Supervision

Some practitioners have difficulty in using supervision to enhance learning. There may be many reasons for this. The learner's concept of supervision may be such that she is unable to view supervision as a helping process. The supervisor may be perceived as an authority figure whose sole purpose is to discover the learner's mistakes. Because of past experiences, some practitioners may be reluctant to use the supervisor as a resource person for fear of being accused of a "lack of initiative."

It is one of the tasks of the supervisor to present herself as an individual whose primary interest is the development of the human potential of the learner. The practitioner must unlearn old ways of relating with supervisors before she will be able to make use of supervision. It is therefore necessary for the supervisor to assist the practitioner consciously to identify the way in which she perceives supervision, to discover the genesis of this attitude, and to revise her preconceptions through interaction with the supervisor.

SELECTED BIBLIOGRAPHY: SUGGESTED READING REFERENCES FOR EACH CHAPTER

CHAPTER I: THE NATURE OF PSYCHIATRIC NURSING

Articles

ATKINSON, C. ALBERT, AND VANKAMPEN, J. FRANK: Community psychiatric nursing. Canad. Nurse 63:31, 1967.

BLACK, SISTER KATHLEEN: An existential model for psychiatric nursing. Perspect. Psychiat. Care 6:178, 1968.

BUEKER, KATHLEEN: The treatment role of the psychiatric nurse—one point of view. Perspect. Psychiat. Care 4:15, 1966.

CROLEY, M. JAY: What does a psychiatric nursing specialist do? Amer. J. Nurs. 62:72, 1962.

FAGIN, CLAIRE M.: Psychotherapeutic nursing. Amer. J. Nurs. 67:298, 1967.

FIELD, WILLIAM E. JR., AND PIERCE-JONES, JOHN: Role perception and acquisition in psychiatric nursing. Nurs. Res. 16:61, 1967.

GREGG, DOROTHY E.: The therapeutic roles of the nurse. Perspect. Psychiat. Care 1:18, 1963.

HAYS, JOYCE SAMHAMMER: The psychiatric nurse as sociotherapist. Amer. J. Nurs. 62:62, 1962.

HUBER, HELEN: Defining the role of the psychiatric nurse. J. Psychiat. Nurs. 2:595, 1964.

MALONEY, ELIZABETH: Does the psychiatric nurse have independent functions? Amer. J. Nurs. 62:61, 1962.

MCBRIEN, MICHAEL: What is wrong with psychiatric nursing? Nurs. Mirror Midwives J. 126:31, 10 May, 1968.

MERENESS, DOROTHY: The potential significant role of the nurse in community mental health services. Perspect. Psychiat. Care 1:34, 1963.

MERENESS, DOROTHY: Problems and issues in contemporary psychiatric nursing. Perspect. Psychiat. Care 2:14, 1964.

NORRIS, CATHERINE M.: Psychiatric crises. Perspect. Psychiat. Care 5:20, 1967.

PEPLAU, HILDEGARD E.: Interpersonal techniques: the crux of psychiatric nursing. Amer. J. Nurs. 62:50, 1962.

WOLFF, ILSE S.: The psychiatric nurse in community health—a rebuttal. Perspect. Psychiat. Care 2:11, 1964.

Books and Reports of Organizations

ACKNER, BRIAN (Ed.): Handbook for Psychiatric Nurses, 9th ed. Royal Medico-Psychological Association. Balliere, Tindall & Cox, London, 1964. (See: The role of the psychiatric nurse, pp. 5-11)

BRAY, R. E., AND BIRD, T. E.: The Practice of Psychiatric Nursing. The Williams & Wilkins Co., Baltimore, 1964. (See: The role of the nurse, pp. 2-7)

EVANS, FRANCES MONET CARTER: The Role of the Nurse in Community Mental Health. The Macmillan Co., New York, 1968. (See: The nurse as a helping person. Supportive role of the nurse, pp. 43-62, and The nurse as consultant, pp. 173-186)

FUJIKI, SUMIKO, et al.: Defining Clinical Content. Graduate Programs. Psychiatric Nursing. Western Interstate Commission for Higher Education, Boulder, 1967. (See p. 4 for a definition of the nursing process)

HOLMES, MARGUERITE J., AND WERNER, JEAN A.: Psychiatric Nursing in a Therapeutic Community. The Macmillan Co., New York, 1966. (See: Clinical psychiatric nursing, pp. 75-95)

HOULISTON, MAY: The Practice of Mental Nursing, 4th ed. E. & S. Livingstone Ltd., Edinburgh and London, 1965. (See: The general duties of a mental nurse, pp. 12-20, and Special duties of the nurse, pp. 86-105)

KALKMAN, MARION E. (WITH MARTIN, EUGENE V., et al.): Psychiatric Nursing, 3rd ed. McGraw-Hill Book Co., Blakiston Div., New York, 1967. (See: The psychiatric nurse—historical development of the role, pp. 3-11)

MADDISON, DAVID, DAY, PATRICIA, AND LEABEATER, BRUCE: Psychiatric Nursing, 2nd ed. The Williams & Wilkins Co., Baltimore, 1965. (See: The role of the nurse in the psychiatric hospital, pp. 15-30)

MATHENEY, RUTH V., AND TOPALIS, MARY: Psychiatric Nursing, 4th ed. The C. V. Mosby Co., St. Louis, 1965. (See: The nurse in the mental health program, pp. 9-15, and Psychiatric nursing: what is it? pp. 10-13)

MERENESS, DOROTHY, AND KARNOSH, LOUIS J.: Essentials of Psychiatric Nursing, 7th ed. The C. V. Mosby Co., St. Louis, 1966. (See: Introduction—the nature of psychiatric nursing, pp. 3-8, and Therapeutic roles of the psychiatric nurse, pp. 9-19)

PATERSON, JOSEPHINE G.: Concepts used to promote mental health in nursing visits to families. In Zderad, Loretta T., and Belcher, Helen C.: Developing Behavioral Concepts in Nursing. Report of the Regional Project in Teaching Psychiatric Nursing in Baccalaureate Programs. Southern Regional Education Board, Atlanta, 1968.

PEPLAU, HILDEGARD E.: Principles of psychiatric nursing. In Arieti, Silvano (Ed.): American Handbook of Psychiatry, vol. 2. Basic Books, Inc., New York, 1959.

RENDER, HELENA WILLIS, AND WEISS, M. OLGA: Nurse-Patient Relationships in Psychiatry, 2nd ed. McGraw-Hill Book Co., Blakiston Div., New York, 1959. (See: Psychiatric nursing: meaning and objectives, pp. 1-39)

Statement on Psychiatric Nursing Practice. Division on Psychiatric-Mental Health Nursing. American Nurses Association, New York, 1967.

STRAUSS, ANSELM, et al.: Psychiatric Ideologies and Institutions. The Macmillan Co., Free Press of Glencoe, New York, 1964. (See: Psychiatric nurses as an ideologically uncommitted group, pp. 71-73, and The nurses at P.P., pp. 206-227)

TRAVELBEE, JOYCE: Interpersonal Aspects of Nursing. F. A. Davis Co., Philadelphia, 1966. (See: The nature of nursing, pp. 5-21)

Social Problems

Articles

ALLEN, JAMES R., AND WEST, LOUIS JOLYON: Flight from violence: hippies and the green rebellion. Amer. J. Psychiat. 125:364, 1968.

BERKOWITZ, LEONARD: Impulse, aggression and the gun. Psychol. Today 2:18, 1968.

BERNS, ROBERT S.: The Berkeley uprisings: a study of the conditions of riotous behavior. Amer. J. Psychiat. 123:1165, 1967.

BERWICK, KEITH: The senior citizen in America: a study in unplanned obsolescence. Gerontologist 7:257, 1967.

BLUHM, HILDE O.: How did they survive? Mechanisms of defense in Nazi concentration camps. Amer. J. Psychother. 2:3, 1948.

BROWN, WILLIAMS NEAL: Alienated youth. Ment. Hyg. 52:330, 1968.

BROWNE, IVOR W., AND KIERNAN, T. J.: The dilemma of the human family—a cycle of growth and decline. J. Irish Med. Assoc. 60:1, 1967.

BÜHLER, CHARLOTTE: The course of human life as a psychological problem. Hum. Develop. 11:184, 1968.

CAPLAN, NATHAN S., AND PAIGE, JEFFERY M.. A study of ghetto rioters. Sci. Amer. 219:15, 1968.

COHEN, NATHAN E.: The Los Angeles riot study. Soc. Work 12:14, 1967.

COLES, ROBERT: Psychiatric observations on students demonstrating for peace. Amer. J. Orthopsychiat. 37:107, 1967.

DARLEY, JOHN M., AND LATANE, BIBB: Bystander intervention in emergencies: diffusion of responsibility. J. Personality Soc. Psychol. 8:377, 1968.

DUHL, LEONARD J.: The shame of the cities. Amer. J. Psychiat. 124:1184, 1968.

DUNLAP, RALPH L., BEIGEL, ASTRID, AND ARMON, VIRGINIA: Young children and the Watts revolt. Comm. Ment. Health J. 4:201, 1968.

ELKIND, DAVID: Middle-class delinquency. Ment. Hyg. 51:80, 1967.

FREEDMAN, DANIEL X.: On the use and abuse of LSD. Arch. Gen. Psychiat. 18:330, 1968.

GIOVACCHINI, PETER L.: Compulsory happiness. Adolescent despair. Arch. Gen. Psychiat. 18:650, 1968.

GUNN, ALEXANDER D. G.: Vulnerable Groups 2. Life at the top. The health of the business executive. Nurs. Times 64:433, 29 March, 1968; Vulnerable Groups 3. High life in the sky. The medical-social problems of multi-storey living. Ibid 64:468, 5 April, 1968; Vulnerable Groups 4. A life with bars. The medical-social problems of imprisonment. Ibid 64:499, 12 April, 1968; Vulnerable Groups 5. The bedsitter life. The medical-social problems of the young single girl. Ibid 64:522, 19 April, 1968; Vulnerable Groups 6. The underprivileged and underpaid. The medical-social problems of the working wife. Ibid 64:563, 26 April, 1968.

HARTOG, JOSEPH: The mental health problems of poverty's youth. Ment. Hyg. 51:85, 1967.

NOWLIS, HELEN H.: Why students use drugs. Amer. J. Nurs. 68:1680, 1968.

OSTWALD, PETER, AND BITTNER, EGON: Life adjustment after severe persecution. Amer. J. Psychiat. 124:1393, 1968.

POUSSAINT, ALVIN F., AND LADNER, JOYCE: Black power. A failure for racial integration. Within the civil rights movement. Arch. Gen. Psychiat. 18:385, 1968.

SANKOT, MARGARET, AND SMITH, DAVID E.: Drug problems in the Haight-Ashbury. Amer. J. Nurs. 68:1686, 1968.

SHAINESS, NATALIE: The problem of sex today. Amer. J. Psychiat. 124:1076, 1968. Discussion by Harold I. Lief, pp. 1081-1084.

Special Section: Alcoholism and emergency psychiatric services. Amer. J. Psychiat. 124:1659, 1968. (Seven papers)

Special Section: On the culturally deprived child. J. Learning Disabil. 1:561, 1968. (Seven papers)

Special Section: Geriatrics. Amer. J. Psychiat. 123:1226, 1967, (Five papers)

Special Section: LSD, STP, and marihuana. Amer. J. Psychiat. 125:341, 1968. (Eight papers)

Special Section: Eight papers on drug dependence and alcohol problems. Amer. J. Psychiat. 122:727, 1966.

Special Section: Family processes. Amer. J. Psychiat. 124:340, 1967. (Five papers)

SPIEGEL, JOHN P.: Psychosocial factors in riots—old and new. Amer. J. Psychiat. 125:281, 1968.

SYMONDS, MARTIN: Disadvantaged children growing in a climate of hopelessness and despair. Amer. J. Psychoanal. 28:15, 1968. Discussion by Andrew K. Ruotolo, pp. 22-24.

Symposium: Alienation and the search for identity. Amer. J. Psychoanal. 21:117, 1961. (Sixteen papers)

Symposium: Forces affecting the family today. Robert T. Porter, moderator. New York J. Med. 68:2509, 1968. (Six papers)

Symposium: Our youth: apathy, rebellion and growth. Amer. J. Psychoanal. 28:13, 1968. (Six papers)

TANENBAUM, DAVID E.: Loneliness in the aged. Ment. Hyg. 51:91, 1967.

TOUSSIENG, POVL W.: Hangloose identity, or living death. The agonizing choice of growing up today. Adolescence 3:307, 1968.

Books and Reports of Organizations

CHILMAN, CATHERINE S.: Growing Up Poor. U.S. Department of Health, Education and Welfare, Welfare Administration, Division of Research. Welfare Administration Publication No. 13, U.S. Government Printing Office, Washington, 1966.

CHODOFF, PAUL: Effects of extreme coercive and oppressive forces: brainwashing and concentration camps. *In* Arieti, Silvano (Ed.): American Handbook of Psychiatry, vol. 3. Basic Books, Inc. New York, 1966.

COOK, FRED J.: The Corrupted Land: The Social Morality of Modern America. The Macmillan Co., New York, 1967.

DEUTSCHER, IRWIN, AND THOMPSON, ELIZABETH J. (Eds.): Among the People: Encounters with the Poor. Basic Books, Inc., New York, 1968.

FEUER, LEWIS S.: The Conflict of Generations. Basic Books, Inc., New York, 1968.

FORTAS, ABE: Concerning Dissent and Civil Disobedience. We Have an Alternative to Violence. The New American Library, New York, 1968.

GRIER, WILLIAM H., AND COBBS, PRICE M.: Black Rage. Basic Books, Inc., New York, 1968.

HERZOG, ELIZABETH: About the Poor. Some Facts and Some Fictions. U.S. Department of Health, Education and Welfare, Social and Rehabilitation Service, Children's Bureau. Children's Bureau Publication Number 451-1967, U.S. Government Printing Office, Washington, 1967.

IRELAN, LOLA M. (Ed.): Low-Income Life Styles. U.S. Department of Health, Education and Welfare, Welfare Administration, Division of Research. Welfare Administration Publication No. 14, U.S. Government Printing Office, Washington, 1966.

KNIGHT, JAMES A.: For the Love of Money. Human Behavior and Money. J. B. Lippincott Co., Philadelphia, 1968.

LOWENTHAL, MARJORIE FISKE: Lives in Distress: The Paths of the Elderly to the Psychiatric Ward. Basic Books, Inc., New York, 1964.

MINUCHIN, SALVADOR, et al.: Families of the Slums. An Exploration of Their Structure and Treatment. Basic Books, Inc., New York, 1967.

PARKER, SEYMOUR, AND KLEINER, ROBERT J.: Mental Illness in the Urban Negro Community. The Macmillan Co., Free Press, New York, 1966.

Report of the National Advisory Commission on Civil Disorders. Otto Kerner, chairman. U.S. Government Printing Office, Washington, 1968.

STRATTON, JOHN R., AND TERRY, ROBERT M. (Eds.): Prevention of Delinquency. Problems and Programs. The Macmillan Co., New York, 1968.

TAYLOR, GORDON RATTRAY: The Biological Time Bomb. An N.A.L. Book. World Publishing Co., New York, 1968. (See: Is death necessary? pp. 91-124, and New minds for old, pp. 125-158)

Mental Health

Articles

ARBUCKLE, DUGALD S.: Psychology, medicine and the human condition known as mental health. Comm. Ment. Health J. 2:129, 1966.

BARRETT-LENNARD, G. T.: The mature person. Ment. Hyg. 46:98, 1962.

BERES, DAVID: The humanness of human beings. Psychoanalytic considerations. Psychoanal. Quart. 37:487, 1968.

BLATT, SIDNEY J.: An attempt to define mental health. J. Consult. Psychol. 28:146, 1964.

BOLMAN, WILLIAM H.: Theoretical and empirical bases of community mental health. Amer. J. Psychiat. 124: Suppl. 8, 1967.

BONNEY, MERL E.: A descriptive study of the normal personality. J. Clin. Psychol. 18:256, 1962.

Conference on Normal Behavior. Arch. Gen. Psychiat. 17:258, 1967. (Ten papers)

FOOTE, NELSON: Love. Psychiatry 16: 245, 1953.

FRANKL, VIKTOR E.: Beyond self-actualization and self-expression. J. Exist. Psychiat. 1:5, 1960. Comment on Dr. Frankl's paper by R. H. Turner, pp. 21-23.

GOMBERG, WALTER: The paradox of mental health. J. Occup. Med. 9:239, 1967.

GRAY, ROBERT MACK, et al.: Stress and health in later maturity. J. Geront. 20:65, 1965.

GRINKER, ROY R. SR., with the collaboration of GRINKER, ROY R. JR., AND TIMBERLAKE, JOHN: Mentally healthy young males (homoclites). A study. Arch. Gen. Psychiat. 6:405, 1962.

HEISLER, VERDA: Toward a process model of psychological health. J. Couns. Psychol. 11:59, 1964.

HERZBERG, FREDERICK, AND HAMLIN, ROY M.: A motivation-hygiene concept of mental health. Ment. Hyg. 45:394, 1961.

KASL, STANISLAV V., AND COBB, SIDNEY: Effects of parental status incongruence and discrepancy on physical and mental health of adult offspring. J. Personality Soc. Psychol. 7:1, 1967.

KAUFMANN, MARGARET A.: High-level wellness, a pertinent concept for the health professions. Ment. Hyg. 47:57, 1963.

LIVSON, NORMAN, AND PESKIN, HARVEY: Prediction of adult psychological health in a longitudinal study. J. Abnorm. Psychol. 72:509, 1967.

LUNDSTEDT, SVEN: Mental health and illness: the search for a general theory. Ment. Hyg. 51:343, 1967.

MEHLMAN, BENJAMIN: Love as the measure of man. Ment. Hyg. 45:84, 1961.

MOSAK, HAROLD H.: Subjective criteria of normality. Psychother. Theory Res. Pract. 4:159, 1967.

OFFER, DANIEL, AND OFFER, JUDITH LYNN: Profiles of normal adolescent girls. Arch. Gen. Psychiat. 19:513, 1968.

PHILLIPS, DEREK L.: Mental health status, social participation and happiness. J. Health Soc. Behav. 8:285, 1967.

REDLICH, F. C.: The concept of normality. Amer. J. Psychother. 6:551, 1955.

REIDER, NORMAN: The concept of normality. Psychoanal. Quart. 19:43, 1950.

RINDER, IRWIN D.: New directions and an old problem: the definition of normality. Psychiatry 27:107, 1964.

ROGERS, CARL R.: The concept of the fully functioning person. Psychother. Theory Res. Prac. 1:17, 1963.

ROGERS, CARL R.: Toward a modern approach to values: the valuing process in the mature person. J. Abnorm. Soc. Psychol. 68:160, 1964.

SCHNEIDERS, ALEXANDER A.: Religion and psychological health—a new approach. J. Exist. Psychiat. 2:93, 1961.

SMITH, M. BREWSTER: Optima of mental health. Psychiatry 13:503, 1950.

Special Section: College students and mental health. Amer. J. Psychiat. 124:642, 1967. (Seven papers)

Symposium: The mental health of aging people. J. Amer. Geriat. Soc. 8: 327, 1960. (Seven papers)

THORNE, FREDERICK C., AND PISHKIN, VLADIMIR: A factorial study of ideological composition in vocationally successful adults. J. Clin. Psychol. 24:269, 1968.

TIFFANY, DONALD W.: Mental health: a function of experienced control. J. Clin. Psychol. 23:311, 1967.

TUCKER, D. K., AND LE RICHE, W. HARDING: Mental health: the search for a definition. Canad. Med. Assoc. J. 90: 1160, 1964.

VANDERVELDT, REVEREND JAMES: Religion and mental health. Ment. Hyg. 35:177, 1951.

VICKERS, SIR GEOFFREY: Mental health and spiritual values. Lancet 1:521, 1955.

WHITEHORN, JOHN C.: A working concept of maturity of personality. Amer. J. Psychiat. 119:197, 1962.

WILSON, WARNER: Correlates of avowed happiness. Psychol. Bull. 67:294, 1967.

Books and Reports of Organizations

BRADBURN, NORMAN M., AND CAPLOVITZ, DAVID: Reports on Happiness: A Pilot Study on Behavior Related to

Mental Health. National Opinion Research Center Monograph in Social Research, No. 3. Aldine Publishing Co., Chicago, 1965.

Conceptual Problems in Developing an Index of Health. Vital and Health Statistics. Data Evaluation and Methods Research. National Center for Health Statistics. Series 2, Number 17. U.S. Department of Health, Education and Welfare. Publication 1000, Office of Health Statistics Analysis, Washington, 1966.

DAVID, HENRY P. (Ed.): International Trends in Mental Health, vol. 1, Community and School. McGraw-Hill Book Co., New York, 1965.

DAVIS, JAMES A.: Education For Positive Mental Health. National Opinion Research Center. Aldine Publishing Co., Chicago, 1966.

DUNN, HALBERT L.: High-Level Wellness. R. W. Beatty Co., Arlington, 1961.

HARPER, RALPH: Human Love—Existential and Mystical. The Johns Hopkins Press, Baltimore, 1966.

FRANKL, VIKTOR E.: Man's Search For Meaning. An Introduction to Logotherapy. Washington Square Press, Inc., New York, 1963.

JAHODA, MARIE: Current Concepts of Positive Mental Health. Basic Books, Inc., New York, 1958.

KESSLER, JANE W.: Psychopathology of Childhood. Prentice-Hall, Inc., Englewood Cliffs, 1966. (See: Concept of normality, pp. 68-70)

LANGNER, THOMAS S., AND MICHAEL, STANLEY T.: Life Stress and Mental Health, vol. II, The Midtown Manhattan Study. Free Press, The Macmillan Co., New York, 1963.

MARTIN, JAMES G.: The Tolerant Personality. Wayne State Univ. Press, Detroit, 1964.

MASLOW, A. H.: Motivation and Personality. Harper & Brothers, New York, 1954. (See: Self-actualizing people: a study of psychological health, pp. 199-234; Love in self-actualizing people, pp. 235-260; and Normality, health and values, pp. 335-352)

MAY, ROLLO: Man's Search For Himself. New American Library Inc., New York, 1953. (See: Courage, the virtue of maturity, pp. 191-216, and Man, the transcender of time, pp. 217-236)

MEERLOO, JOOST A. M.: Illness and Cure—Studies on the Philosophy of Medicine and Mental Health. Grune & Stratton Inc., New York, 1964.

OFFER, DANIEL, AND SABSHIN, MELVIN: Normality: Theoretical and Clinical Concepts of Mental Health. Basic Books, Inc., New York, 1966.

Mental Illness

Articles

ADAMS, HENRY B.: Mental illness or interpersonal behavior? Amer. Psychol. 19:191, 1964. (See: What is mental illness? p. 194)

ALVAREZ, WALTER: Some psychoanalysts who blame the family (editorial). J. Schizo. 2:1, 1968.

AYLLON, T., HAUGHTON, E., AND HUGHES, H. B.: Interpretation of symptoms: fact or fiction? Behav. Res. Ther. 3:1, 1965.

BARTON, RUSSELL: Institutional neurosis. Nurs. Mirror Midwives J. 122:x, 29 April, 1966.

BATES, JOSEPHINE A.: Attitudes toward mental illness. Ment. Hyg. 52:250, 1968.

CORNWELL, GEORGIA: Scapegoating: a study in family dynamics. Amer. J. Nurs. 67:1862, 1967.

CRUMPTON, EVELYN, et al.: How patients and normals see the mental patient. J. Clin. Psychol. 23:46, 1967.

CUMMING, JOHN, AND CUMMING, ELAINE: On the stigma on mental illness. Comm. Ment. Health J. 1:135, 1965.

ELLIS, ALBERT: Should some people be labeled mentally ill? J. Consult. Psychol. 31:435, 1967.

FERREIRA, ANTHONY: Psychosis and family myth. Amer. J. Psychother. 21:186, 1967.

FLETCHER, C. RICHARD: Attributing responsibility to the deviant: a factor in psychiatric referrals by the general public. J. Health Soc. Behav. 8:185, 1967.

FONTANA, ALAN F., GESSNER, THEODORE, AND LORR, MAURICE: How sick and what treatment: patient presentations and staff judgments. Amer. J. Psychother. 22:26, 1968.

HILKER, ROBERT R. J.: Is mental illness a necessary evil? Amer. Assoc. Industr. Nurses J. 16:9, 1968.

KANNER, LEO: Do behavioural symptoms always indicate psychopathology? J. Child. Psychol. Psychiat. 1:17, 1960.

MANIS, JEROME G., et al.: Public and psychiatric conceptions of mental illness. J. Health Hum. Behav. 6:48, 1965.

MARGOLIN, REUBEN J.: The concept of mental illness, a new look at some old assumptions. Comm. Ment. Health J. 4:417, 1968.

PHILLIPS, DEREK L.: Rejection of the mentally ill: the influence of behavior and sex. Amer. Sociol. Rev. 29:679, 1964.

PHILLIPS, DEREK L.: Identification of mental illness: its consequences for rejection. Comm. Ment. Health J. 3:262, 1967.

RUESCH, JURGEN: Hospitalization and social disability. J. Nerv. Ment. Dis. 142:203, 1966.

RUESCH, JURGEN, AND BRODSKY, CARROLL M.: The concept of social disability. Arch. Gen. Psychiat. 19:394, 1968.

SARBIN, THEODORE R.: On the futility of the proposition that some people be labeled mentally ill. J. Consult. Psychol. 31:447, 1967.

SCHOFIELD, WILLIAM: In sickness and in health. Comm. Ment. Health J. 2:244, 1966. (See: Mental illness, unhappiness, and philosophical neurosis, pp. 244-246)

SIEGLER, MIRIAM, CHEEK, FRANCES E., AND OSMOND, HUMPHRY: Attitudes towards naming the illness. Ment. Hyg. 52:226, 1968.

SZASZ, THOMAS: The myth of mental illness. Amer. Psychol. 15:113, 1960.

SZASZ, THOMAS: The uses of naming and the origin of the myth of mental illness. Amer. Psychol. 16:59, 1961.

SZASZ, THOMAS, AND ALEXANDER, GEORGE J.: Mental illness as an excuse for civil wrongs. J. Nerv. Ment. Dis. 147:113, 1968. (See: The concept of mental illness, pp. 113-116)

Books and Reports of Organizations

Diagnostic and Statistical Manual of Mental Disorders (DSM-II), 2nd ed. Prepared by The Committee on Nomenclature and Statistics of The American Psychiatric Association. American Psychiatric Assoc., Washington, 1968.

HOLLINGSHEAD, AUGUST B., AND REDLICH, FREDERICK C.: Social Class and Mental Illness. John Wiley & Sons, Inc., New York, 1958.

KANNER, LEO: In Defense of Mothers: How to Bring Up Children in Spite of the More Zealous Psychologists. Charles C Thomas, Publisher, Springfield, 1962.

MYERS, JEROME K., AND ROBERTS, BERTRAM H.: Family and Class Dynamics in Mental Illness. John Wiley & Sons, Inc., New York, 1964.

RUFF, GEORGE E., Isolation and deprivation. In Arieti, Silvano (Ed.): American Handbook of Psychiatry, vol. 3. Basic Books, Inc., New York, 1966.

SCHEFF, THOMAS J.: Being Mentally Ill: A Sociological Theory. Aldine Publishing Co., Chicago, 1966.

SCHWARTZ, MORRIS S., SHOCKLEY, EMMY LANNING (with the assistance of CHARLOTTE GREEN SCHWARTZ): The Nurse and the Mental Patient. A Study in Interpersonal Relations. Russell Sage Foundation, New York, 1956. (See: A conception of mental illness, pp. 218-221)

SZASZ, THOMAS S.: The Myth of Mental Illness: Foundations of a Theory of Personal Conduct. Harper & Row, Hoeber Med. Div., New York, 1961.

Perceptions of Mental Illness

Articles and Books

ANON (MISS G.): The other side of depression. Canad. Med. Assoc. J. 81:678, 1959.

ANON: Alcoholism addiction, depression: a nurse's story. Nurs. Outlook 13:48, 1965.

ANON: Case report. An autobiography of a schizophrenic experience. J. Abnorm. Soc. Psychol. 51:677, 1955.

ANONYMOUS MOTHER: Inside schizophrenia: Cindy. J. Schizo. 1:260, 1967.

BLASS, BETTY V.: One step at a time. Ment. Hyg. 45:504, 1961.

BOWERS, MALCOLM: The onset of psychosis—a diary account. Psychiatry 28: 346, 1965.

BY A PRACTICING PSYCHIATRIST: The experience of electro-convulsive therapy. Brit. J. Psychiat. 111:365, 1965.

CHRISTIENN, FELICITY: Who will heal the ills? Nurs. Times 62:221, 18 February, 1966. (Account of a nurse suffering from depression)

COX, JAMES: A patient's view of psychotherapy. Lancet 1:103, 1965.

JONES, ANN: My birthday is not the day I was born. Amer. J. Nurs. 67: 1434, 1967.

KERSCHBAUMER, L.: A schizophrenic's knowledge of himself. J. Nerv. Ment. Dis. 101:65, 1945.

LANDIS, CARNEY: Varieties of Psychopathological Experience (Fred A. Mettler, Ed.). Holt, Rinehart and Winston Inc., New York, 1964. (A collection of subjective accounts of mental illness)

LANG, JONATHAN: The other side of hallucinations. Part I. Phenomena. Amer. J. Psychiat. 94:1089, 1938; Part II. Interpretations. Ibid 96:423, 1939.

MACDONALD, NORMA: The other side. Living with schizophrenia. Canad. Med. Assoc. J. 82:218, 1960.

MEYER, EUGENE, AND CORRI, LINO: The experience of depersonalization: a written report by a patient. Psychiatry 23:215, 1960.

PALOMBO, STANLEY R., AND BRUCH, HILDE: Falling apart: the verbalization of ego failure. Psychiatry 27: 248, 1964.

PSYCHE: Suicide: the patient's viewpoint. Nurs. Times 61:1700, 10 December, 1965.

PSYCHE: The other side of the counter. Nurs. Times 60:402, 27 March, 1964.

SONMER, ROBERT, AND OSMOND, HUMPHRY: Autobiographies of former mental patients. J. Ment. Sci. 106: 648, 1960.

SONMER, ROBERT, AND OSMOND, HUMPHRY: Autobiographies of former mental patients. Addendum. J. Ment. Sci. 107:1030, 1961.

TAYLOR, ROSEMARY: Stigma attached. Nurs. Times 61:279, 26 February, 1965.

WALLACE, CLARE MARC: Suicide. Nurs. Mirror Midwives J. 127:16, 30 August, 1968.

WALLACE, CLARE MARC: Nursing the schizophrenic patient. Nurs. Times 127:36, 26 July, 1968.

WALLACE, CLARE MARC: Friendliness should be the keynote. Nurs. Mirror Midwives J. 127:19, 23 August, 1968.

WALLACE, CLARE MARC: Schizophrenia —from both sides. Nurs. Mirror Midwives J. 121:iv, 12 November, 1965.

WALLACE, CLARE MARC: Portrait of a Schizophrenic Nurse. Hammond, Hammond & Co., Ltd., London, 1965.

Prevention of Mental Illness

Articles, Books and Reports of Organizations

ALLINSMITH, WESLEY, AND GOETHALS, GEORGE W.: The Role of Schools in Mental Health. Joint Commission on Mental Illness and Health. Basic Books, Inc., New York, 1962.

ARSENIAN, JOHN: Life cycle factors in mental illness. A biosocial theory with implications for prevention. Ment. Hyg. 52:19, 1968.

ARSENIAN, JOHN: Toward prevention of mental illness in the United States. Comm. Ment. Health J. 1:320, 1965.

BELLAK, LEOPOLD (Ed.): Handbook of Community Psychiatry and Community Mental Health. Grune & Stratton Inc., New York, 1964.

BOLMAN, WILLIAM M.: An outline of preventive psychiatric programs for children. Arch. Gen. Psychiat. 17:5, 1967.

BOLMAN, WILLIAM M.: Theoretical and empirical bases of community mental health. Amer. J. Psychiat. 124: Suppl. 8, 1967.

BOLMAN, WILLIAM M., AND WESTMAN, JACK C.: Prevention of mental disorder: an overview of current programs. Amer. J. Psychiat. 123:1058, 1967.

CAPLAN, GERALD: Principles of Preventive Psychiatry. Basic Books, Inc., New York, 1964.

CAPLAN, GERALD, AND GRUNEBAUM, HENRY: Perspectives on primary prevention. A review. Arch. Gen. Psychiat. 17:331, 1967.

CARLTON, M. GANT: The pre-admission period and precare programs for the mentally ill: a review of the literature. Comm. Ment. Health J. 1:43, 1965.

CUMMING, ELAINE: Unsolved problems of prevention. Canad. Ment. Health J. 16: Suppl. 56:3, 1968.

DARBONNE, ALLEN R.: Crisis: a review of theory, practice and research. Psychother. Theory Res. Prac. 4:49, 1967.

EVANS, FRANCES MONET CARTER: The Role of the Nurse in Community Mental Health. The Macmillan Co., New York, 1968. (See: Elements of community mental health, pp. 6-42; Concepts of prevention, pp. 82-145)

HANKOFF, L. D.: Emergency Psychiatric Treatment: A Handbook of Secondary Prevention. Charles C Thomas, Publisher, Springfield, 1968.

HAUGHTON, ANSON B.: Suicide prevention programs—the current scene. Amer. J. Psychiat. 124:1692, 1968.

HORSLEY, STEPHEN: Key people in community mental welfare. 1. Introduction. Nurs. Mirror Midwives J. 125: 325, 5 January, 1968. 2. Janus and the health visitor. Ibid 125:359, 12 January, 1968. 3. Communication through psychodrama. Ibid 125:xi, 19 January, 1968. 4. Emotional factors in midwifery. Ibid 126:20, 26 January, 1968. 5. A glimpse into the future. Ibid 126:37, 2 February, 1968.

HUME, PORTIA BELL: General principles of community psychiatry. In Arieti, Silvano (Ed.): American Handbook of Psychiatry, vol. 3. Basic Books, Inc., New York, 1966.

KYSAR, JOHN E.: Preventive psychiatry on the college campus. Comm. Ment. Health J. 2:27, 1966.

LEON, ROBERT L.: Some implications for a preventive program for American Indians. Amer. J. Psychiat. 125:232, 1968.

LEMKAU, PAUL V.: Prospects for the prevention of mental illness. Ment. Hyg. 50:172, 1966.

McGEE, THOMAS F.: Some basic considerations in crisis intervention. Comm. Ment. Health J. 4:319, 1968.

MacLEOD, A. W., SILVERMAN, B., AND POLAND, PHYLLIS: The well-being clinic: a study of the effectiveness of an attempt to provide routine mental health check-ups for community groups. Amer. J. Psychiat. 113:795, 1957.

PARAD, HOWARD J. (Ed.): Crisis Intervention: Selected Readings. Family Service Assoc., New York, 1965.

RAINER, JOHN D.: Genetic counseling and preventive psychiatry. Ment. Hyg. 50:593, 1966.

RICHMOND, JULIUS B., AND COVERT, CATHY: Mental health and education conference. A report. Arch. Gen. Psychiat. 17:513, 1967.

RIESSMAN, FRANK, AND HALLOWITZ, EMMANUEL: The neighborhood service center: an innovation in preventive psychiatry. Amer. J. Psychiat. 123: 1408, 1967.

SALK, LEE: On the prevention of schizophrenia. Dis. Nerv. Syst. 29: Suppl. 11, 1968.

SCHULBERG, HERBERT C., AND SHELDON, ALAN: The probability of crisis and strategies for preventive intervention. Arch. Gen. Psychiat. 18:553, 1968.

SILVERMAN, PHYLLIS ROLFE: Services to the widowed: first steps in a program of preventive intervention. Comm. Ment. Health J. 3:37, 1967.

STICKNEY, STONEWALL B.: Schools are our community mental health centers. Amer. J. Psychiat. 124:1407, 1968.

Supplement: Community psychiatry. Amer. J. Psychiat. 124:1, 1967. (Ten papers)

Symposium: Mental health services. Canad. Psychiat. Assoc. J. 13:3, 1968. (Four papers)

TUCKMAN, JACOB, AND REGAN, RICHARD: A note on secondary prevention. Ment. Hyg. 49:334, 1965.

CHAPTER II: THE PROCESS OF PSYCHIATRIC NURSING

Articles

ATTA, RALPH E. VAN: Concepts employed by accurate and inaccurate clinicians. J. Couns. Psychol. 15:338, 1968.

BAILEY, DANIEL E.: Clinical inference in nursing: analysis of nursing action patterns. Nurs. Res. 16:154, 1967.

BAZIAK, ANNA T.: Concept-attainment in a practice setting. Perspect. Psychiat. Care 4:32, 1966.

EDWARDS, WARD: The theory of decision making. Psychol. Bull. 51:380, 1954.

FORGUS, RONALD H.: The hierarchial organization of perception. Int. J. Neurol. 6:138, 1967.

GARNER, W. R.: To perceive is to know. Amer. Psychol. 21:11, 1966.

GAURON, EUGENE F., AND DICKINSON, JOHN K.: Diagnostic decision making in psychiatry. I. Information usage. Arch. Gen. Psychiat. 14:225, 1966. II. Diagnostic styles. Ibid 14:233, 1966.

GENDLIN, EUGENE T.: Experiencing: a variable in the process of therapeutic change. Amer. J. Psychother. 15:233, 1961.

GERARD, HAROLD B.: Choice difficulty, dissonance and the decision sequence. J. Personality 35:91, 1967.

HAMMOND, KENNETH R., et al.: Clinical inference in nursing: analyzing cognitive tasks representative of nursing problems. Nurs. Res. 15:134, 1966. Use of information-seeking strategies by nurses. Ibid 15:330, 1966. Revising judgments. Ibid 16:38, 1967.

HOLT, ROBERT: Clinical judgment as a disciplined inquiry. J. Nerv. Ment. Dis. 133:369, 1961.

JOHNSON, DOROTHY E.: Theory in nursing: borrowed and unique. Nurs. Res. 17:206, 1968.

KAHN, EUGENE: On experiencing. Amer. J. Psychiat. 120:131, 1963.

LYONS, JOSEPH: Whose experience? J. Project. Techn. 31:11, 1967.

NATSOULAS, THOMAS: What are perceptual reports about? Psychol. Bull. 67:249, 1967.

OLSON, MARIAN: Social influence on decision-making. J. Nurs. Ed. 7:11, 1968.

PEPITONE, ALBERT: Motivations in decision making. Trans. N. Y. Acad. Sci. Series II, No. 7, 920, 1967.

SCHLESSINGER, NATHAN, MUSLIN, HYMAN L., AND BAITTLE, MARGERY: Teaching and learning psychiatric observational skills. Arch. Gen. Psychiat. 18:549, 1968.

SINGER, ESTELLE, AND ROBY, THORNTON B.: Dimensions of decision-making behavior. Percept. Motor Skills 24: 571, 1967. (Monograph Suppl. 3-V20)

STARK, STANLEY: Toward a psychology of knowledge: II. Two kinds of foresight and foresight theorizing. Percept. Motor Skills 23:547, 1966. (Monograph Suppl. 4-V23)

Symposium: Theory development in nursing. Nurs. Res. 17:196, 1968. (Seven papers and a panel discussion)

TRIPODI, TONY, AND MILLER, HENRY: The clinical judgment process: a review of the literature. Soc. Work 11:63, 1966.

WILDE, WILLIAM A.: Decision-making in a psychiatric screening agency. J. Health Soc. Behav. 9:215, 1968.

WITKIN, HERMAN A., GOODENOUGH, DONALD R., AND KARP, STEPHEN A.: Stability of cognitive style from childhood to young adulthood. J. Personality Soc. Psychol. 7:291, 1967.

WITKIN, HERMAN A., AND OLTMAN, PHILIP: Cognitive style. Int. J. Neurol. 6:119, 1967.

Books and Reports of Organizations

BERELSON, BERNARD, AND STEINER, GARY A.: Human Behavior. An Inventory of Scientific Findings. Harcourt, Brace & World Inc., New York, 1964. (See: Perceiving, pp. 87-131)

BRUNER, JEROME S., GOODNOW, JACQUELINE J., AND AUSTIN, GEORGE A.: A Study of Thinking. John Wiley & Sons, Inc., New York, 1956.

COHEN, JOHN: Behaviour in Uncertainty. Basic Books, Inc., New York, 1965.

DEMBER, WILLIAM N.: Psychology of Perception. Holt, Rinehart and Winston, Inc., New York, 1960.

DUNCAN, CARL P. (Ed.): Thinking: Current Experimental Studies. J. B. Lippincott Co., Philadelphia, 1967.

EPSTEIN, WILLIAM: Varieties of Perceptual Learning. An Examination of the Role of Learning in Visual Perception. McGraw-Hill Book Co., New York, 1966.

GORE, WILLIAM J. AND DYSON, J. W. (Eds.): The Making of Decisions. A Reader in Administrative Behavior. The Macmillan Co. New York, 1964.

HABER, RALPH NORMAN (Ed.): Contemporary Theory and Research in Visual Perception. Holt, Rinehart and Winston, Inc., New York, 1968.

HOCH, P. H. AND ZUBIN, J. (Eds.): Psychopathology of Perception, vol. XX. Fifty-third Meeting of the American Psychopathological Association. Grune & Stratton, Inc., New York, 1965.

KLAUSMEIER, H. G. AND HARRIS, C. W. (Eds.): Analyses of Concept Learning. Academic Press, New York, 1966.

KLEINMUNTZ, BENJAMIN (Ed.): Problem Solving: Research, Method and Theory. John Wiley & Sons, Inc., New York, 1966.

LAING, R. D.: The Politics of Experience. Random House Inc., Pantheon Books, New York, 1967. (See: Persons and experience, pp. 3-25)

MANASER, JANICE C.: Clinical judgment in psychotherapeutic nurse-patient situations. In Zderad, Loretta T., and Belcher, Helen C.: Developing Behavioral Concepts in Nursing. Report of the Regional Project in Teaching Psychiatric Nursing in Baccalaureate Programs. Southern Regional Education Board, Atlanta, 1968.

PARKER, J. CECIL, AND RUBIN, LOUIS J.: Process as Content: Curriculum Design and the Application of Knowledge. Rand McNally & Co., Chicago, 1966. (See: Process and content defined, pp. 1-3)

PASCAL, G. R., AND JENKINS, W. O.: Systematic Observation of Gross Human Behavior. Grune & Stratton, Inc., New York, 1961.

PEPLAU, HILDEGARD E.: Operational definitions and nursing practice. In Zderad, Loretta T., and Belcher, Helen C.: Developing Behavioral Concepts in Nursing. Report of the Regional Project in Teaching Psychiatric Nursing in Baccalaureate Programs. Southern Regional Education Board, Atlanta, 1968.

Perceiving Behaving Becoming. A New Focus for Education. Yearbook, 1962. Prepared by the ASCD 1962 Yearbook Committee, Arthur W. Combs, chairman. Association for Supervision and Curriculum Development. National Education Assoc., Washington, 1962. (See: Perceiving and behaving, pp. 65-82)

PIKAS, ANATOL: Abstraction and Concept Formation. An Interpretative Investigation into a Group of Psychological Frames of Reference. (Translated by Neil Tomkinson) Harvard Univ. Press, Cambridge, 1965.

SHELLY, MAYNARD W. II, AND BRYAN, GLENN L. (Eds.): Human Judgments and Optimality. John Wiley & Sons, Inc., New York, 1964.

SOLLY, CHARLES M., AND MURPHY, GARDNER: Development of the Perceptual World. Basic Books, Inc., New York, 1960.

TRAVELBEE, JOYCE: The concept of observation. In Communication in the Helping Process in Nursing. Proceedings of a nursing conference sponsored by Louisiana State Board of Health, Louisiana State Department of Hospitals, and the National Institute of Mental Health. New Orleans, February 15-18, 1965.

TRAVELBEE, JOYCE: Interpersonal Aspects of Nursing. F. A. Davis Co., Philadelphia, 1966. (See: Observation, pp. 100-101, and Steps in meeting nursing needs, pp. 127-132)

WEINLAND, JAMES D.: How to Think Straight. Littlefield, Adams & Co., Totowa, 1966. (See: Thinking comes from experience, pp. 1-8)

CHAPTER III: ASPECTS OF THE ONE-TO-ONE RELATIONSHIP

Articles, Books and Reports of Organizations

BURTON, ARTHUR: The clinician as moralist. J. Exist. Psychiat. 1:207, 1960.

CARTER, ELIZABETH W.: Support: a lay concept in nursing. *In* Burd, Shirley F., and Marshall, Margaret A. (Eds.): Some Clinical Approaches to Psychiatric Nursing. The Macmillan Co., New York, 1963.

CHESSICK, RICHARD: Greed and vanity in the life of the psychotherapist. Psychiat. Dig. 28:40, 1967.

CHODOFF, PAUL: Reassurance. Med. Ann. D.C. 21:671, 1952.

CONNOLLY, MARY GRACE: What acceptance means to patients. Amer. J. Nurs. 60:1754, 1960.

GREGG, DOROTHY: Reassurance. Amer. J. Nurs. 55:171, 1955.

HAGERMAN, ZERITA: The concept of love as it relates to nursing intervention. Conference on Teaching Psychiatric Nursing in Baccalaureate Programs. Southern Regional Education Board, Atlanta, 1967.

HALMOS, PAUL: The Faith of the Counsellors. A Study in the Theory and Practice of Social Case Work and Psychotherapy. Schocken Books, New York, 1966. (See: The counsellor's love as therapeutic skill, pp. 49-74)

HOLMES, MARGUERITE: What's wrong with getting involved? Nurs. Outlook 8:250, 1960.

OHNMACHT, FRED W., AND MURO, JAMES J.: Self-acceptance: some anxiety and cognitive style relationships. J. Psychol. 67:235, 1967.

RENTZ, R. ROBERT, AND WHITE, WILLIAM F.: Congruence of the dimensions of self-as-object and self-as-process. J. Psychol. 67:277, 1967.

SIMMONS, CAROLYN H., AND LERNER, MELVIN J.: Altruism as a search for justice. J. Personality Soc. Psychol. 9:216, 1968.

SMITH, HENRY CLAY: Sensitivity to People. McGraw-Hill Book Co., New York, 1966.

TRAVELBEE, JOYCE: What do we mean by rapport? Amer. J. Nurs. 63:70, 1963.

TRAVELBEE, JOYCE: What's wrong with sympathy? Amer. J. Nurs. 64:68, 1964.

TRAVELBEE, JOYCE: Interpersonal Aspects of Nursing. F. A. Davis Co., Philadelphia, 1966. (See: Acceptance, p. 145, and Sympathy in nursing situations, pp. 144-155)

UJHELY, GERTRUDE E.: What is realistic emotional support? Amer. J. Nurs. 68:758, 1968.

WALLACE, CAROLINE OGILVIE: Acceptance. Conference on Teaching Psychiatric Nursing in Baccalaureate Programs. Southern Regional Education Board, Atlanta, 1967. (Includes an operational definition of the concept of acceptance)

WASLI, EVELYN: Hope—a basic nursing concept. Conference on Teaching Psychiatric Nursing in Baccalaureate Programs. Southern Regional Education Board, Atlanta, 1967. (Includes an operational definition of the concept of hope)

WYATT, FREDERICK: How objective is objectivity? Reflections on scope and limitations of a basic tenet in the study of personality. J. Project. Techn. 31:3, 1967.

CHAPTER IV: INTRODUCTION TO THE ONE-TO-ONE RELATIONSHIP

Articles, Books and Reports of Organizations

BERGENTAL, J. F. T.: The Search for Authenticity. An Existential Analytic Approach to Psychotherapy. Holt, Rinehart and Winston, Inc., New York, 1965.

BURTON, ARTHUR: The meaning of psycotherapy. J. Exist. 8:49, 1967.

CHURCHILL, JULIA: An issue: nurses and psychotherapy. Perspect. Psychiat. Care 5:160, 1967.

COLLITON, MARGARET A.: The history of nursing therapy. A reactionnaire to the work of June Mellow. Perspect. Psychiat. Care 3:10, 1965.

FAGIN, CLAIRE M.: Psychotherapeutic nursing. Amer. J. Nurs. 67:298, 1967.

GREGG, DOROTHY E.: The therapeutic roles of the nurse. Perspect. Psychiat. Care 1:18, 1963.

GRENE, MARJORIE: The Knower and the Known. Basic Books, Inc., New York, 1966.

KESSEL, PAUL, AND MCBREARTY, JOHN F.: Values and psychotherapy: a review of the literature. Percept. Motor Skills 25:669, 1967. (Monograph Suppl. 2-V25)

LAING, R. D.: The Politics of Experience. Random House, Inc., Pantheon Books, New York, 1967. (See: The psychotherapeutic experience, pp. 26-34)

MAY, ROLLO: Psychology and the Human Dilemma. D. Van Nostrand Co.,

Inc., Princeton, 1967. (See: The context of psychotherapy, pp. 87-110, and A phenomenological approach to psychotherapy, pp. 111-127)

MULLAN, HUGH, AND SANGIULIANO, IRIS: The Therapist's Contribution to the Treatment Process. His Person, Transactions and Treatment Methods. Charles C Thomas, Publisher, Springfield, 1964. (See: The psychotherapist becomes process, pp. 56-88; The Interpretation: the therapeutic experience leads to authentic communication, pp. 135-163; and Being is becoming: the process of termination, pp. 230-271)

NALLS, SANDRA: Developing a therapeutic relationship. Amer. J. Nurs. 65:114, 1965.

CHAPTER V: COMMUNICATING WITH PATIENTS

Articles

ARLOW, JACOB A.: Silence and the theory of technique. J. Amer. Psychoanal. Assoc. 9:44, 1961.

ARTEBERRY, JOAN: The disturbed communication of a schizophrenic patient: an approach to a clinical nursing problem. Perspect. Psychiat. Care 3:24, 1965.

BUCK, LUCIEN A., AND CUDDY, JOSEPH M.: A theory of communication in psychotherapy. Psychother. Theory Res. Prac. 3:7, 1966.

DAVIDSON, HENRY A.: Non-verbal communication in a hospital setting. Perspect. Psychiat. Care 1:12, 1963.

DRIEMANN, G. H. J.: Differences between written and spoken language. Acta Psychol. 20:78, 1962.

FOULDS, G. A., et al.: Cognitive disorder among the schizophrenias. I. The validity of some tests of thought-process disorder. Brit. J. Psychiat. 113:1361, 1967. II. Differences between the sub-categories. Ibid 113:1369, 1967.

HAYS, JOYCE SAMHAMMER: Analysis of nurse-patient communications. Nurs. Outlook 14:32, 1966.

JONES, ELIZABETH A.: The use of speech as a security operation. Perspect. Psychiat. Care 3:18, 1965.

KEW, JOHN K.: A comparison of thought processes in various nosological groups. J. Clin. Psychol. 19:162, 1963.

LEVY, WILLIAM H.: The communication of affect in psychotherapy. Arch. Gen. Psychiat. 16:102, 1967.

LIVINGSTON, PETER B., AND SHADER, RICHARD I.: Thought disorder in schizophrenia. Soc. Casework 49:489, 1968.

LORENZ, MARIA: Problems posed by schizophrenic language. Arch. Gen. Psychiat. 4:603, 1961.

MAHL, GEORGE F.: Some clinical observations on nonverbal behavior in interviews. J. Nerv. Ment. Dis. 144:492, 1967.

MATRAZZO, JOSEPH D., HOLMAN, DAVID C., and WIENS, ARTHUR N.: A simple measure of interviewer and interviewee speech durations. J. Psychol. 66:7, 1967.

MATRAZZO, JOSEPH D., et al.: Interviewer "mm-hmm" and interviewee speech durations. Psychother. Theory Res. Prac. 1:109, 1964.

MAZZANTI, VINCENT E., AND BESSELL, HAROLD: Communication through the latent language. Amer. J. Psychother. 10:250, 1956.

MCGUIRE, MICHAEL T., AND LORCH, STEPHEN: Natural language conversation modes. J. Nerv. Ment. Dis. 146:239, 1968.

MEHRABIAN, ALBERT, AND WIENER, MARLON: Decoding of inconsistent communications. J. Personality Soc. Psychol. 6:109, 1967.

MEHRABIAN, ALBERT: Attitudes inferred from neutral verbal communication. J. Consult. Psychol. 31:414, 1967.

MEHRABIAN, ALBERT: Communication without words. Psychol. Today 2:52, 1968.

ORLINSKY, DAVID E., AND HOWARD, KENNETH I.: Communication rapport and patient progress. Psychother. Theory, Res. Prac. 5:131, 1968.

PEPLAU, HILDEGARD E.: Talking with patients. Amer. J. Nurs. 60:964, 1960.

PHILLIPS, LORRAINE W.: Language in disguise: non-verbal communication with patients. Perspect. Psychiat. Care 4:18, 1966.

PETRIE, C. R. JR.: What we don't know about listening. J. Commun. 14:248, 1964.

RUESCH, JURGEN: Synopsis of the theory of human communication. Psychiatry 16:215, 1963.

SCHEFLEN, ALBERT E.: The significance of posture in communication systems. Psychiatry 27:316, 1964.

SLUZKI, CARLOS, et al.: Transactional disqualification research on the double bind. Arch. Gen. Psychiat. 16:494, 1967.

SPIEGEL, JOHN P.: Classification of body messages. Arch. Gen. Psychiat. 17:298, 1967.

SYMONDS, MARTIN: Faulty verbal communication between parents and children. Amer. J. Psychoanal. 22:98, 1962.

WENDER, PAUL H.: Communicative unclarity: some comments on the rhetoric of confusion. Psychiatry 30:332, 1967.

WILMER, HARRY A.: "You know" observations on interjectory, seemingly meaningless phrases in group psychotherapy. Psychiat. Quart. 41:296, 1967.

Books and Reports of Organizations

ARMSTRONG, SHIRLEY W.: Thought disorders of psychiatric patients. *In* Burd, Shirley F., and Marshall, Margaret A. (Eds.): Some Clinical Approaches to Psychiatric Nursing. The Macmillan Co., New York, 1963.

BARBARA, DOMINICK: The Art of Listening. Charles C Thomas, Publisher, Springfield, 1966.

BUBER, MARTIN: Between Man and Man. (Translated by Ronald Gregor Smith) Beacon Press, Boston, 1955.

CHERRY, COLIN: On Human Communication: A Review, a Survey, and a Criticism, 2nd ed. Mass. Inst. Tech. Press, Cambridge, 1966.

DAVITZ, JOEL R. (Ed.): The Communication of Emotional Meaning. McGraw-Hill Book Co., New York, 1964.

DIXON, THEODORE R., AND HORTON, DAVID L. (Eds.): Verbal Behavior and General Behavior Theory. Prentice-Hall Inc., Englewood Cliffs, 1968.

FELDMAN, SANDOR: Mannerisms of Speech and Gesture in Everyday Life. International Univ. Press, New York, 1959.

GOULD, GRACE: Helping process in nursing—problems in communication. *In* Communication in the Helping Process in Nursing. Proceedings of a nursing conference sponsored by Louisiana State Board of Health, Louisiana State Department of Hospitals and the National Institute of Mental Health. New Orleans, February 15-18, 1965.

HAYS, JOYCE SAMHAMMER, AND LARSON, KENNETH H.: Interacting with Patients. The Macmillan Co., New York, 1963.

HOCH, P. H., AND ZUBIN, J. (Eds.): Psychopathology of Communication. Forty-sixth meeting of The American Psychopathological Association. Grune & Stratton Inc., New York, 1958.

KAPLAN, BERNARD: The study of language in psychiatry. The comparative developmental aproach and its application to symbolization and language in psychopathology. *In* Arieti, Silvano (Ed.): American Handbook of Psychiatry, vol. 3. Basic Books, Inc., New York, 1966.

KESSLER, JANE W.: Psychopathology of Childhood. Prentice-Hall Inc., Englewood Cliffs, 1966. (See: Developmental problems in speech and language, pp. 129-165)

LAFFAL, JULIUS: Pathological and Normal Language. Atherton Press, New York, 1965.

ODEN, GLORIA: An outline of the normal thought process. *In* Burd, Shirley F., and Marshall, Margaret A. (Eds.): Some Clinical Approaches to Psychiatric Nursing. The Macmillan Co., New York, 1963.

PARRY, JOHN: The Psychology of Human Communication. American Elsevier Publishing Co., Inc., New York, 1968.

PIAGET, JEAN: The Construction of Reality In the Child. (Translated by Margaret Cook) Basic Books, Inc., New York, 1954.

RUESCH, JURGEN: Therapeutic Communication. W. W. Norton & Co., Inc., New York, 1961.

RUESCH, JURGEN, AND BATESON, GREGORY: Communication: The Social Matrix of Psychiatry. W. W. Norton & Co., Inc., New York, 1951.

RUESCH, JURGEN, AND KEES, WELDON: Non-Verbal Communication. Univ. of Cal. Press, Berkeley and Los Angeles, 1956.

SMOYAK, SHIRLEY A.: Nonverbal communication. *In* Burd, Shirley F., and Marshall, Margaret A. (Eds.): Some Clinical Approaches to Psychiatric Nursing. The Macmillan Co., New York, 1963.

SPIEGEL, ROSE: Specific problems of communication in psychiatric conditions. *In* Arieti, Silvano (Ed.): American Handbook of Psychiatry, vol. 1. Basic Books, Inc., New York, 1959.

TRAVELBEE, JOYCE: Interpersonal Aspects of Nursing. F. A. Davis Co., Philadelphia, 1966. (See: Concept: communication, pp. 93-117)

CHAPTER VI: THE SELECTION OF PATIENTS

Articles

BROWN, FRANCES GOLD: Ritualism and patient reactions. Amer. J. Nurs. 61: 63, 1961.

GRANN, VICTOR: The interesting patient syndrome. Arch. Intern. Med. 116: 442, 1965.

HAWKINS, ELSIE, CLAGHORN, JAMES L., AND ZENTAY, WANDA: Nursing dress, an experimental evaluation of its effect on psychiatric patients. J. Psychiat. Nurs. 4:148, 1966.

HURTEAU, PHYLLIS: Street clothes or uniform for psychiatric nursing personnel. Nurs. Outlook 11:359, 1963.

LARSON, RUTH B., AND ELLSWORTH, ROBERT B.: The nurse's uniform and its meaning in a psychiatric hospital. Nurs. Res. 2:100, 1962.

MEYER, GEORGE G., et al.: Staff perceptions of the white coat on a psychiatric ward. Dis. Nerv. Syst. 27: 586, 1966.

SEGAL, BERNARD E.: Nurses and patients: a case study in stratification. J. Health Hum. Behav. 5:54, 1964.

SIEGEL, HILDEGARDE: The nurse's uniform. Symbolic or sacrosanct? Nurs. Forum 7:314, 1968.

CHAPTER VII: PROCESS RECORDING

Articles, Books and Reports of Organizations

ABELES, NORMAN: Liking for clients—its relationship to therapists' personality: unexpected results. Psychother. Theory, Res. Pract. 4:19, 1967.

ADAMS, JACK A.: Human Memory. McGraw-Hill Book Co., New York, 1967.

BLOOM, BENJAMIN S. (Ed.): Taxonomy of Educational Objectives. The Classification of Educational Goals. Handbook 1. Cognitive Domain. David McKay Co., Inc., New York, 1956. (See discussion of abilities and skills, pp. 38-43)

EKSTEIN, RUDOLF, AND WALLERSTEIN, ROBERT S.: The Teaching and Learning of Psychotherapy. Basic Books, Inc., New York, 1958 (See: The utilization of recordings, pp. 267-281)

HAGGARD, ERNEST A., HIKEN, JULIA R., AND ISAACS, KENNETH S.: Some effects of recording and filming on the psychotherapeutic process. Psychiatry 28:169, 1965.

HUDSON, BERNICE E.: The nursing process record. Nurs. Outlook 3:224, 1955.

KING, JOAN M.: The initial interview: assessment of the patient and his difficulties. Perspect. Psychiat. Care 5:256, 1967.

MAGER, ROBERT F.: Preparing Instructional Objectives. Fearon Publishers, Palo Alto, 1962.

MARSDEN, GERALD: Content-analysis studies of therapeutic interviews 1954-1964. Psychol. Bull. 63:298, 1965.

NEHREN, JEANNETTE G., AND BATEY, MARJORIE E.: The process recording —a method of teaching interpersonal relationship skills. Nurs. Forum 2:65, 1963.

O'NEILL, AUDREY MYERSON: The bases of clinical inference. J. Clin. Psychol. 24:366, 1968.

PEPLAU, HILDEGARD E.: Process recording as one technique for studying elements of the nursing process. In Communication in the Helping Process in Nursing. Proceedings of a nursing conference sponsored by Louisiana State Board of Health, Louisiana State Department of Hospitals and the National Institute of Mental Health. New Orleans, February 15-18, 1965.

STRAKER, M.: Comprehensive history taking for the non-psychiatrist. Canad. Med. Assoc. J. 96:39, 1967.

Symposium: The role of experiential data in personality assessment. J. Project. Techn. 31:3, 1967. (Five papers)

TYLER, RALPH W.: Basic Principles of Curriculum and Instruction. Syllabus for Education 305. Syllabus Division. Univ. of Chicago Press, Chicago, 1950.

UNDERWOOD, BENTON J.: Forgetting. Sci. Amer. 210:91, 1964.

WALKER, JANET F., AND MCQUILLEN, MARY: Process recording in public health nursing. Public Health Nurs. 44:542, 1952.

WILMER, HARRY A.: Television as participant recorder. Amer. J. Psychiat. 124:1157, 1968.

CHAPTER VIII. THE NURSE-PATIENT RELATIONSHIP

Articles, Books and Reports of Organizations

BABRICK, MARIE: Re-learning through a one-to-one relationship. Perspect. Psychiat. Care 2:23, 1964.

BANDURA, ALBERT: Psychotherapy as a learning process. Psychol. Bull. 58:143, 1961.

BRISCOE, MAY E., WOODYARD, HOWARD D., AND SHAW, MARVIN E.: Personality impression change as a function of the favorableness of first impressions. J. Personality 35:343, 1967.

CARL, MARY KATHRYN: Establishing a relationship with a schizophrenic patient. Perspect. Psychiat. Care 1:20, 1963.

CHARNEY, E. JOSEPH: Psychosomatic manifestations of rapport in psychotherapy. Psychosom. Med. 28:305, 1966.

CHARNLEY, JEAN: What's in a client's name? Soc. Work 9:109, 1964.

CHRISTOFFERS, CAROL A.: Identification of phases in the nurse-patient relationship. An existential encounter. Perspect. Psychiat. Care 5:174, 1967.

COLM, HANNA: Healing as participation: comments based on Paul Tillich's existential philosophy. Psychiatry 16:99, 1953.

GENDLIN, EUGENE T.: Initiating psychotherapy with unmotivated patients. Psychiat. Quart. 35:134, 1961.

GOFFMAN, ERVING: Interaction Ritual: Essays on Face-to-Face Behavior. Aldine Publishing Co., Chicago, 1967.

HALE, SHIRLEY L., AND RICHARDSON, JULIA H.: Terminating the nurse-patient relationship. Amer. J. Nurs. 63:116, 1963.

HAYS, JOYCE SAMHAMMER, AND MYERS, JANESY B.: Learning in the nurse-patient relationship. Perspect. Psychiat. Care 2:20, 1964.

HAYES, SISTER IMMACULATA: When professionals are psychiatric patients. Amer. J. Nurs. 67:760, 1967.

KEMPLER, WALTER: The experiential therapeutic encounter. Psychother. Theory Res. Prac. 4:166, 1967.

KEPECS, JOSEPH G.: Theories of transference neurosis. Psychoanal. Quart. 35:497, 1966.

KLOES, KAREN B., AND WEINBERG, ANN: Countertransference: a bilateral phenomenon in the learning model. Perspect. Psychiat. Care 6:152, 1968.

KOVACS, LIBERTY W.: A therapeutic relationship with a patient and family. Perspect. Psychiat. Care 4:11, 1966.

LEE, JANE M.: Working through—a conceptual framework for nursing. Conference on Teaching Psychiatric Nursing in Baccalaureate Programs. Southern Regional Education Board, Atlanta, 1967.

MARMOR, JUDD: Theories of learning and the psychotherapeutic process. Psychiatry 112:363, 1966.

MCGUIRE, MICHAEL T., AND LORCH, STEPHEN: A model for the study of dyadic communication. I. Orientation and model. J. Nerv. Ment. Dis. 146:221, 1968.

MCGUIRE, MICHAEL T., AND COLEMAN, ROGER: A model for the study of dyadic communication. II. Research approach, research and discussion. J. Nerv. Ment. Dis. 146:230, 1968.

MCMAHON, ARTHUR W., AND SHORE, MILES F.: Some psychological reactions to working with the poor. Arch. Gen. Psychiat. 18:562, 1968.

MELLOW, JUNE: Nursing therapy. Amer. J. Nurs. 68:2365, 1968.

MOLDE, DONALD A., AND WIENS, ARTHUR N.: Interview interaction behavior of nurses with task versus person orientation. Nurs. Res. 17:45, 1968.

PARKS, SUZANNE LOWRY: Allowing physical distance as a nursing approach. Perspect. Psychiat. Care 4:31, 1966.

PEABODY, DEAN: Trait inferences: evaluative and descriptive aspects. J. Personality Soc. Psychol. 7:1, 1967.

PEPLAU, HILDEGARD E.: Interpersonal techniques: the crux of psychiatric nursing. Amer. J. Nurs. 62:50, 1962.

PEPLAU, HILDEGARD E.: Process of developing a relationship: some general considerations. In Communication in The Helping Process in Nursing. Proceedings of a nursing conference sponsored by Louisiana State Board of Health, Louisiana State Department of Hospitals and the National Institute of Mental Health. New Orleans, February 15-18, 1965.

RECTOR, CYNTHIA: Content in the initial therapist-patient interview. Perspect. Psychiat. Care 3:33, 1965.

RHODES, MARTHA: Nursing the acutely ill psychiatric patient. Nurs. Outlook 14:25, 1966.

SCHLICHT, WILLIAM J. JR.: The anxieties of the psychotherapist. Ment. Hyg. 52:439, 1968.

SCHMIDEBERG, MELITTA: A major task of therapy: developing volition and purpose. Amer. J. Psychother. 15:251, 1961.

SCHNEIDER, IRVING: The use of patients to act out professional conflicts. Psychiatry 26:88, 1963.

SCHULTZ, FRANCES K.: The mourning phase of relationships. J. Psychiat. Nurs. 2:37, 1964.

SELZER, MELVIN L.: The use of first names in psychotherapy. Arch. Gen. Psychiat. 3:215, 1960.

SHEAR, HOWARD J.: Choice and determinancy in psychological illness. Int. J. Neuropsychiat. 2:572, 1966.

SHULMAN, LAWRENCE: A game-model theory of interpersonal strategies. Soc. Work 13:16, 1968.

Special Section: Hospitalization: patterns and alternatives. Amer. J. Psychiat. 124:934, 1968. (Five papers)

TYLER, FORREST B., AND SIMMONS, WILLIAM L.: Patients' conceptions of therapists. J. Clin. Psychol. 20:122, 1964.

WATTS, WILLIAM A.: Commitment under conditions of risk. J. Personality Soc. Psychol. 3:507, 1966.

WICK, JOHN H., CAMERON, DOROTHY I. H., AND HARVOIS, GASTON P.: A nurse-patient interview as a learning experience for the nurse and the patient. Perspect. Psychiat. Care 1:12, 1963.

CHAPTER IX. PROBLEMATIC AREAS OF THE NURSE-PATIENT RELATIONSHIP

BOURNE, HAROLD: Main's syndrome and a nurse's reaction to it. Arch. Gen. Psychiat. 2:576, 1960.

BRONNER, ALFRED: Psychotherapy with religious patients. A review of the literature. Amer. J. Psychother. 18: 475, 1964.

BURNHAM, DONALD L.: Special-problem patient: victim or agent of splitting? Psychiatry 29:105, 1966.

CLANCY, KATHLYN: Concerning gifts. Perspect. Psychiat. Care 6:169, 1968.

DANIELS, MARVIN: Further observations on the development of the vindictive character. Amer. J. Psychother. 21:822, 1967.

EIDUSON, BERNICE T.: Retreat from help. Amer. J. Orthopsychiat. 38:910, 1968.

EKDAWI, M. Y.: The difficult patient. Brit. J. Psychiat. 113:547, 1967.

KING, JOAN M.: Denial. Amer. J. Nurs. 66:1010, 1966.

LENNY, MARY RUTH: Acting-out behavior of the psychiatric nurse. Perspect. Psychiat. Care 4:10, 1966.

LUDWIG, ARNOLD M., AND FARRELLY, FRANK: The code of chronicity. Arch. Gen. Psychiat. 15:562, 1966.

MAIN, T. F.: The ailment. Brit. J. Med. Psychol. 30:129, 1957.

MARTIN, PETER A.: Psychoanalytic aspects of that type of communication termed "small talk." J. Amer. Psychoanal. Assoc. 12:392, 1964.

POKORNY, ALEX D.: The multiple readmission psychiatric patient. Psychiat. Quart. 39:70, 1965.

POLANSKY, NORMAN A.: On duplicity in the interview. Amer. J. Orthopsychiat. 37:568, 1967.

POLLACK, IRWIN W., AND BATTLE, WILLIAM C.: Studies of the special patient. The sentence. Arch. Gen. Psychiat. 9:344, 1963. (A discussion of Main's syndrome)

ROSEKRANS, FRANK M.: Choosing to suffer as a consequence of expecting to suffer. A replication. J. Personality Soc. Psychol. 7:419, 1967.

SCHRODER, DAVID, AND EHRLICH, DANUTA: Rejection by mental health professionals: a possible consequence of not seeking appropriate help for emotional disorders. J. Health Soc. Behav. 9:222, 1968.

SCHWARTZ, BARRY: The social psychology of the gift. Amer. J. Sociol. 73:1, 1967.

Special Section: Some aspects of psychotherapy. Amer. J. Psychiat. 124: 1202, 1968. (Six papers)

STEIN, MARTIN H.: The cliché: a phenomenon of resistance. J. Amer. Psychoanal. Assoc. 6:263, 1958.

WAAGE, J.: On symbiosis and symbiotic relations in the mental hospital. Psychiat. Neurol. Neurochir. 71:141, 1968.

WEINTRAUB, WALTER: The VIP syndrome: a clinical study in hospital psychiatry. J. Nerv. Ment. Dis. 138: 181, 1964.

Detachment

Articles

ARIETI, SILVANO: New views on the psychodynamics of schizophrenia. Amer. J. Psychiat. 124:453, 1967.

ARIETI, SILVANO: The psychodynamics of schizophrenia. Amer. J. Psychother. 22:366, 1968.

BALDESSARINI, ROSS J., AND SNYDER, SOLOMON H.: Schizophrenia: critique of recent genetic-biochemical formulations. Nature 206:1111, 1965.

BETZ, BARBARA J.: Studies of the therapist's role in the treatment of the schizophrenic patient. Amer. J. Psychiat. 123:963, 1967.

BOWERS, MALCOLM B. JR.: Pathogenesis of acute schizophrenic psychosis. An experiential approach. Arch. Gen. Psychiat. 19:348, 1968.

BRAGINSKY, BENJAMIN M., AND BRAGINSKY, DOROTHEA D.: Schizophrenic patients in the psychiatric interview: an experimental study of their effectiveness at manipulation. J. Consult. Psychol. 31:543, 1967.

BROWN, GEORGE W., AND BIRLEY, J. L. T.: Crises and life changes and the onset of schizophrenia. J. Health Soc. Behav. 9:203, 1968.

BRUCH, HILDE: Psychotherapy with schizophrenics. Arch. Gen. Psychiat. 14:346, 1966.

D'ELIA, FRANK, AND GRALNICK, ALEX-
ANDER: Recent considerations in the
broad spectrum treatment of inpa-
tient schizophrenia. Amer. J. Psychother. 22:405, 1968.

DRAPER, FRANKLIN M.: The doctor's
personality and social recovery of
schizophrenics. Arch. Gen. Psychiat.
16:633, 1967.

ECKHARDT, MARIANNE H.: The detached
person. Amer. J. Psychoanal. 20:139,
1960.

FISH, FRANK: The concept of schizophrenia. Brit. J. Med. Psychol. 39:269,
1966.

GIBSON, ROBERT W.: On the therapeutic
handling of aggression in schizophrenia. Amer. J. Orthopsychiat. 37:
926, 1967.

GLICK, IRA D.: The "sick" family and
schizophrenia—cause and effect. Dis.
Nerv. Syst. 29:Suppl. 129, 1968.

GOSHEN, CHARLES E.: The importance
of patient-laid traps in the psychotherapeutic study of schizophrenia.
Amer. J. Psychother. 19:75, 1965.

HARMON, ROBERTA: Helping a schizophrenic patient learn to trust. Amer.
J. Nurs. 63:111, 1963.

HAYWOOD, MALCOLM L.: Schizophrenia
and the double bind. Psychiat. Quart.
34:89, 1960.

HIGGINS, JERRY: The concept of process-
reactive schizophrenia: criteria and
related research. J. Nerv. Ment. Dis.
138:9, 1964.

HOFFER, A., AND OSMOND, H.: Some
psychological consequences of perceptual disorder and schizophrenia.
Int. J. Neuropsychiat. 2:1, 1966.

HURTEAU, PHYLLIS: The psychiatric
nurse and the mute patient. Amer.
J. Nurs. 62:55, 1962.

JANSSON, BENGT, AND ALSTROM, JAN:
The relation between prognosis, symptoms and background factors in suspected schizophrenic insufficiencies in
young people. Acta Psychiat. Scand.
Suppl. 198: 43:5, 1967.

KALLMAN, FRANZ J.: The genetic theory
of schizophrenia. An analysis of 691
schizophrenic twin index families
Amer. J. Psychiat. 103:309, 1946.

KELLAM, SHEPPARD G., et al.: Ward
atmosphere and outcome of treatment
of acute schizophrenia. J. Psychiat.
Res. 5:145, 1967.

LUDWIG, ARNOLD M.: The influence of
nonspecific healing techniques with
chronic schizophrenics. Amer. J. Psychother. 22:382, 1968.

LUDWIG, ARNOLD M., AND MARX, ARN-
OLD J.: Influencing techniques of
chronic schizophrenics. Arch. Gen.
Psychiat. 18:681, 1968.

LUDWIG, ARNOLD M., AND FARRELLY,
FRANK: The weapons of insanity.
Amer. J. Psychother. 21:737, 1967.

MELAT, SHIRLEY A.: The development
of trust. Perspect. Psychiat. Care 3:
28, 40, 1965.

MOORE, JUDITH ANNE: The dynamics of
schizophrenia. Perspect. Psychiat.
Care 4:10, 1966.

OSMOND, H., AND HOFFER, A.: A comprehensive theory of schizophrenia.
Int. J. Neuropsychiat. 2:302, 1966.

PAVY, DAVID: Verbal behavior in schizophrenia: a review of recent studies.
Psychol. Bull. 70:164, 1968.

PROBST, MARJORIE E.: Helping the schizophrenic patient enlarge his perceptual field (the bundle lady). Perspect.
Psychiat. Care 5:236, 1967.

RODNICK, ELIOT H.: The psychopathology of development: investigating
the etiology of schizophrenia. Amer.
J. Orthopsychiat. 38:784, 1968.

ROSENBAUM, C. PETER: Metabolic, physiological, anatomic and genetic studies
in the schizophrenias: a review and
analysis. J. Nerv. Ment. Dis. 146:103,
1968.

Schizophrenia — recent   approaches.
Amer. J. Psychother. 22:366, 1968.
(Five papers)

SCHUHAM, ANTHONY I.: The double-
bind hypothesis a decade later. Psychol. Bull. 68:409, 1967.

SCHORER, C. E.: Mistakes in the diagnosis of schizophrenia. Amer. J. Psychiat. 124:1057, 1968.

SEARLES, HAROLD F.: The schizophrenic
individual's experience of his world.
Psychiatry 30:119, 1967.

SHEINER, SARA: Intensity of casual relationships in schizophrenia: living
in imagination. Amer. J. Psychoanal.
28:156, 1968.

SHERRILL, LATTICE: Nursing the patient
who expresses concern for self-iden-
tity. Perspect. Psychiat. Care 2:24,
1964.

SHIELDS, JAMES, GOTTESMAN, IRVING I., AND SLATER, ELIOT: Kallman's 1946 schizophrenic twin study in the light of new information. Acta Psychiat. Scand. 43:385, 1967.

SMITH, ARNOLD L.: Schizophrenia: a synthesis. Int. J. Neuropsychiat. 1: 199, 1965.

STASTNY, JOY P.: Helping a patient learn to trust. Perspect. Psychiat. Care 3:16, 1965.

Symposium: Follow-up studies. Canad. Psychiat. Assoc. J. 13:201, 1968. (Four papers)

Symposium: Aspects of schizophrenia. Brit. J. Med. Psychol. 39:269, 1966. (Four papers)

Toward a definition of schizophrenia. Tenth Annual Meeting of the Group Without a Name (Psychiatric Research Society). Dis. Nerv. Syst. 29: Suppl. 5, 1968. (Twenty-four papers)

TRUNNELL, THOMAS L.: Thought disturbance in schizophrenia. Pilot study utilizing Piaget's theories. Arch. Gen. Psychiat. 11:126, 1964.

TURNER, R. JAY: Social mobility and schizophrenia. J. Health Soc. Behav. 9:194, 1968.

WILDMAN, LAURA LINTHICUM: Reducing the schizophrenic patient's resistance to involvement. Perspect. Psychiat. Care 3:26, 1965.

Books and Reports of Organizations

ARIETI, SILVANO: Interpretation of Schizophrenia. Basic Books, Inc., New York, 1955.

ARIETI, SILVANO: Schizophrenia: other aspects; psychotherapy. *In* American Handbook of Psychiatry, vol. 1, Basic Books, Inc., New York, 1959. (See also: Schizophrenia: the manifest symptomatology, the psychodynamic and formal mechanisms. Ibid pp. 455-484.

ARTISS, K. L.: Milieu Therapy in Schizophrenia. Grune & Stratton, Inc., New York, 1962.

BELLAK, LEOPOLD, AND LOEB, LAURENCE (Eds.): Schizophrenia. Grune & Stratton, Inc., New York, 1968. (An updating of the earlier volumes Dementia Praecox, 1948, and Schizophrenia: A Review of the Syndrome, 1958)

FARIS, ROBERT E. L., AND DUNHAM, H. WARREN: Mental Disorders in Urban Areas. An Ecological Study of Schizophrenia and Other Psychoses. Univ. of Chicago Press, Chicago, 1965.

HALEY, JAY: Strategies of Psychotherapy. Grune & Stratton, Inc., New York, 1963. (See: The schizophrenic: his methods and his therapy, pp. 86-116)

HOCH, P. H., AND ZUBIN, J. (Eds.): Vol. XXI, Psychopathology of Schizophrenia. Fifty-fourth Meeting of the American Psychopathological Association. Grune & Stratton, Inc., New York, 1966.

HOFFER, ABRAM, AND OSMOND, HUMPHRY: How To Live With Schizophrenia. University Books, New York, 1966.

KANTOR, ROBERT E., AND HERRON, WILLIAM G.: Reactive and Process Schizophrenia. Science and Behavior Books, Palo Alto, 1966.

JACKSON, DON D. (Ed.): The Etiology of Schizophrenia. Basic Books, Inc., New York, 1960.

ROGERS, CARL R. with the collaboration of EUGENE T. GENDLIN, DONALD J. KIESLER, AND CHARLES B. TRUAX: The Therapeutic Relationship and Its Impact. A Study of Psychotherapy With Schizophrenics. Univ. of Wisconsin Press, Madison, 1967. (See: Therapeutic procedures in dealing with schizophrenics by Eugene T. Gendlin, pp. 369-400, and Appendix B.2 A tentative scale for the rating of unconditional positive regard by Charles B. Truax, pp. 569-579)

SMOYAK, SHIRLEY A.: Self-concept and the schizophrenic patient. *In* Burd, Shirley F., and Marshall, Margaret A. (Eds.): Some Clinical Approaches To Psychiatric Nursing. The Macmillan Co., New York, 1963.

Special Section: Schizophrenia. Amer. J. Psychiat. 123:947, 1967. (Eight papers)

Hallucinations

Articles and Books

CHARLTON, M. H.: Visual hallucinations. Psychiat. Quart. 37:389, 1963.

ERICKSON, GERALD D., AND GUSTAFSON, GARY J.: Controlling auditory hallucinations. Hosp. Community Psychiat. 19:327, 1968.

FIELD, WILLIAM E. JR.: When a patient hallucinates. Amer. J. Nurs. 63: 80, 1963.

GRAVENKAMPER, KATHERINE H.: Hallucinations. *In* Burd, Shirley F., and Marshall, Margaret A. (Eds.): Some Clinical Approaches to Psychiatric Nursing. The Macmillan Co., New York, 1963.

HOROWITZ, MARDI J.: The imagery of visual hallucinations. J. Nerv. Ment. Dis. 138:513, 1964.

MODELL, ARNOLD H.: The theoretical implications of hallucinatory experiences in schizophrenia. J. Amer. Psychoanal. Assoc. 6:442, 1958.

MODELL, ARNOLD H.: An approach to the nature of auditory hallucinations in schizophrenia. Arch. Gen. Psychiat. 3:259, 1960.

MOTT, RICHARD H., AND SMALL, IVER F.: Comparative study of hallucinations. Arch. Gen. Psychiat. 12:595, 1965.

SARBIN, THEODORE R.: The concept of hallucination. J. Personality 35:359, 1967.

SARBIN, THEODORE R., AND JUHASZ, JOSEPH B.: The historical background of the concept of hallucinations. J. Hist. Behav. Sci. 3:399, 1967.

SCHAECHTER, FRIEDA: The language of the voices. Med. J. Aust. 2:870, 1964.

SEDMAN, G.: A phenomenological study of pseudohallucinations and related experiences. Acta Psychiat. Scand. 42:35, 1966.

SEDMAN, G.: "Inner voices." Phenomenological and clinical aspects. Brit. J. Psychiat. 112:485, 1966.

SMALL, IVER F., SMALL, JOYCE G., AND ANDERSEN, JOHN M.: Clinical characteristics of hallucinations of schizophrenia. Dis. Nerv. Syst. 27:349, 1966.

WEST, LOUIS JOLYON (Ed.): Hallucinations. Grune & Stratton, Inc., New York, 1962.

Dejection

Articles, Books and Reports of Organizations

AYD, FRANK J. JR.: Recognizing the Depressed Patient. With Essentials of Management and Treatment. Grune & Stratton, Inc., New York, 1961.

BECK, AARON T.: Depression: Clinical, Experimental and Theoretical Aspects. Harper & Row, Hoeber Med. Div., New York, 1967.

BONIME, WALTER: The psychodynamics of neurotic depression. *In* Arieti, Silvano (Ed.): American Handbook of Psychiatry, vol. 3. Basic Books, Inc., New York, 1966.

BOWLBY, JOHN: Childhood mourning and its implications for psychiatry. Amer. J. Psychiat. 118:481, 1961.

BRIGGS, PETER F, LAPERRIERE, ROBERT, AND GREDEN, JOHN: Working outside the home and the occurrence of depression in middle-aged women. Ment. Hyg. 49:438, 1965.

BURKE, LEE, et al.: The depressed woman returns. A study of post hospital adjustment. Arch. Gen. Psychiat. 16:548, 1967.

CRUMB, FREDERICK W.: A resonance of agony. A subjective account of nursing in a depressed culture. Perspect. Psychiat. Care 1:16, 1963.

DAVIS, HARRY K., AND FARLEY, ARTHUR J.: Psychodynamics of depressive illness. Fantasy love-object loss as an etiologic factor. Dis. Nerv. Syst. 28: 105, 1967.

DORFMAN, WILFRED: Hypochondriasis as a defense against depression. Psychosomatics 9:248, 1968.

FAST, IRENE, AND BROEDEL, JOHN W.: Intimacy and distance in the interpersonal relationships of persons prone to depression. J. Project. Techn. 31:7, 1967.

FLYNN, GERTRUDE E.: The development of the psychoanalytic concept of depression. J. Psychiat. Nurs. Ment. Health Serv. 6:138, 1968.

GERSHON, ELLIOT S., CROMER, MARJORIE, AND KLERMAN, GERALD L.: Hostility and depression. Psychiatry 31:224, 1968.

GLASER, KURT: Masked depression in children and adolescents. Amer. J. Psychother. 21:565, 1967.

GREENSON, RALPH R.: The psychology of apathy. Psychoanal. Quart. 18:290, 1949.

GREENSON, RALPH R.: On boredom. J. Amer. Psychoanal. Assoc. 1:7, 1953.

GUTHEIL, EMIL A.: Reactive depressions. In Arieti, Silvano (Ed.): American Handbook of Psychiatry, vol. 1. Basic Books, Inc., New York, 1959.

HARGREAVES, WILLIAM A., AND STARKWEATHER, J. A.: Vocal and verbal indicators of depression. Calif. Ment. Health Res. Dig. 3:59, 1965.

KESSELMAN, SAMUEL R.: The hostility index. An objective measure of psycho-aggressiveness. J. Med. Soc. New Jersey 64:131, 1967.

KRAINES, S. H.: Therapy of the chronic depressions. Dis. Nerv. Syst. 28:577, 1967.

LORR, MAURICE, SONN, THOMAS M., AND KATZ, MARTIN M.: Toward a definition of depression. Arch. Gen. Psychiat. 17:183, 1967.

MALERSTEIN, A. J.: Depression as a pivotal affect. Amer. J. Psychother. 22:202, 1968.

MCKINLEY, CAMERON K., AND DREISBACH, LINDA KAY: Variations in depressive symptomatology as a function of age. Texas Rep. Biol. Med. 25:179, 1967.

NEYLAN, MARGARET PROWSE: The depressed patient. Amer. J. Nurs. 61:77, 1961.

OSTOW, MORTIMER: The consequences of ambivalence. Psychosomatics 9:255, 1968.

Proceedings of the Scandinavian Symposium on Depression. (Erik Sarauw Kristiansen, Ed.): Acta Psychiat. Scand. 37: Suppl. 162:13, 1961. (Thirty-two papers)

Programmed Instruction: Understanding hostility. Prepared by the staff of Education Design, Inc., New York, under the direction of Caleb E. Crowell. Amer. J. Nurs. 67:2131, 1967.

RISLEY, JOAN: Nursing intervention in depression. Perspect. Psychiat. Care. 5:65, 1967.

ROSENTHAL, SAUL H., AND GUDEMAN, JON E.: The self-pitying constellation in depression. Brit. J. Psychiat. 113:485, 1967.

RUBINS, JACK L.: A holistic approach to the psychoses: Part I—The affective psychoses. Amer. J. Psychoanal. 28:139, 1968.

SELLERS, LOIS BELLE: Hostility: nursing implications. Conference on Teaching Psychiatric Nursing in Baccalaureate Programs. Southern Regional Education Board, Atlanta, 1967.

SILVERMAN, CHARLOTTE: The epidemiology of depression—a review. Amer. J. Psychiat. 124:883, 1968.

Special Section: Affective disorders. Amer. J. Psychiat. 123:671, 1966. (Seven papers)

SPIEGEL, ROSE: Anger and acting out: masks of depression. Amer. J. Psychother. 21:597, 1967.

STUART, RICHARD B.: Casework treatment of depression viewed as an interpersonal disturbance. Soc. Work 12:27, 1967.

STOCKWELL, MARTHA L.: Depression: an operational definition with themes related to the nurse's role. Conference on Teaching Psychiatric Nursing in Baccalaureate Programs. Southern Regional Education Board, Atlanta, 1967.

SYMONDS, MARTIN: The depressions in childhood and adolescence. Amer. J. Psychoanal. 28:189, 1968.

WEINTRAUB, WALTER, AND ARONSON, H.: The application of verbal behavior analysis to the study of psychological defense mechanisms. IV. Speech pattern associated with depressive behavior. J. Nerv. Ment. Dis. 144:22, 1967.

WOLMAN, BENJAMIN B.: Dr. Jekyll and Mr. Hyde: a new theory of the manic-depressive disorder. Trans. N. Y. Acad. Sci. 28:1020, 1966.

Suicide

Articles, Books and Reports of Organizations

ACKERLY, WILLIAM C.: Latency-age children who threaten or attempt to kill themselves. J. Amer. Acad. Child Psychiat. 6:242, 1967.

ADAM, KENNETH STUART: Suicide: a critical review of the literature.

Canad. Psychiat. Assoc. J. 12:413, 1967.

BARTER, JAMES T., SWABACK, DWIGHT O., AND TODD, DOROTHY: Adolescent suicide attempts. A follow-up study of hospitalized patients. Arch. Gen. Psychiat. 19:523, 1968.

BODIE, MARILYNN K.: When a patient threatens suicide. Perspect. Psychiat. Care 6:76, 1968.

CAIN, ALBERT C., AND FAST, IRENE: Children's disturbed reactions to parent suicide. Amer. J. Orthopsychiat. 36:873, 1966.

CAIN, ALBERT C., AND FAST, IRENE: The legacy of suicide. Observations on the pathogenic impact of suicide upon marital partners. Psychiatry 29:406, 1966.

DEAN, R. A., et al.: Prediction of suicide in a psychiatric hospital. J. Clin. Psychol. 23:296, 1967.

DUBLIN, LOUIS I.: Suicide—A Sociological and Statistical Study. The Ronald Press Co., New York, 1963.

DUBLIN, LOUIS I.: Suicide: an overview of a health and social problem. Bull. Suicidology (National Clearinghouse for Mental Health Information), December, 1967.

DURKHEIM, EMILE: Suicide. A Study in Sociology. (Translated by John A. Spaulding and George Simpson) The Macmillan Co., Free Press Paperback, New York, 1966.

FARBEROW, NORMAN L., AND SHNEIDMAN, EDWIN S. (Eds.): The Cry For Help. McGraw-Hill Book Co., Blakiston Div., New York, 1961.

FARBEROW, NORMAN L., SHNEIDMAN, EDWIN S., AND NEURINGER, CHARLES: Case history and hospitalization factors in suicides of neuropsychiatric hospital patients. J. Nerv. Ment. Dis. 142:32, 1966.

FREEMAN, WALTER: Psychiatrists who kill themselves: a study in suicide. Amer. J. Psychiat. 124:846, 1967.

GRAFF, HAROLD, AND MALLIN, RICHARD: The syndrome of the wrist cutter. Amer. J. Psychiat. 124:36, 1967.

GREER, S., AND LEE, H. A.: Subsequent progress of potentially lethal attempted suicides. Acta Psychiat. Scand. 43:361, 1967.

GREER, S., AND GUNN, J. C.: Attempted suicides from intact and broken parental homes. Brit. Med. J. 2:1355, 1966.

GRUNEBAUM, HENRY, AND KLERMAN, GERALD L.: Wrist slashing. Amer. J. Psychiat. 124:527, 1967.

HARTELIUS, HANS: A study of suicides in Sweden 1951-1963, including a comparison with 1925-1950. Acta Psychiat. Scand. 43:121, 1967.

HENDIN, HERBERT: Suicide and Scandinavia. Grune & Stratton, Inc., New York, 1964.

KAHNE, MERTON J.: Suicides in mental hospitals: a study of the effects of personnel and patient turnover. J. Health Soc. Behav. 9:255, 1968.

LEONARD, CALISTA V.: Understanding and Preventing Suicide. Charles C Thomas, Publisher, Springfield, 1967.

LESLIE, MARGARET D.: Nursing care of the suicidal patient. Canad. Nurse 62:39, 1966.

MARGOLIN, N. LIONEL, AND TEICHER, JOSEPH D.: 13 adolescent male suicide attempts: dynamic considerations. J. Amer. Acad. Child Psychiat. 7:296, 1968.

McCANDLESS, FREDERICK D.: Suicide and the communication of rage: a cross-cultural case study. Amer. J. Psychiat. 125:197, 1968.

McGEE, RICHARD K.: The suicide prevention center as a model for community mental health programs. Comm. Ment. Health J. 1:162, 1965.

MEERLOO, JOOST A. M.: Suicide and Mass Suicide. Grune & Stratton, Inc., New York, 1962.

SHNEIDMAN, EDWIN S.: Some current developments in suicide prevention. Bull. Suicidology, December, 1967.

SHEA, FRANK, AND HURLEY, ELIZABETH: Hopelessness and helplessness. Perspect. Psychiat. Care 2:32, 1964.

STONE, ALAN A., AND SHEIN, HARVEY M.: Psychotherapy of the hospitalized suicidal patient. Amer. J. Psychother. 22:15, 1968.

UMSCHEID, SISTER THEOPHANE: With suicidal patients: caring for is caring about. Amer. J. Nurs. 67:1230, 1967.

Manipulation

Articles, Books and Reports of Organizations

ABROMS, GENE M.: Setting limits. Arch. Gen. Psychiat. 19:113, 1968.

ABT, L. E., AND WEISMAN, S. L. (Eds.): Acting Out: Theoretical and Clinical Aspects. Grune & Stratton, Inc., New York, 1965.

AKUTAGAWA, DONALD, SISKO, FRANK J., AND KEITEL, NORMA B.: Beartrapping: a study in interpersonal behavior. Amer. J. Psychother. 19:54, 1965.

BERGER, MILTON M., AND ROSENBAUM, MAX: Notes on help-rejecting complainers. Int. J. Group Psychother. 17:357, 1967.

BRAGINSKY, B. M., GROSSE, M., AND RING, K.: Controlling outcomes through impression management: an experimental study of the manipulative tactics of mental patients. J. Consult. Psychol. 30:295, 1966.

CLECKLEY, HERVEY M.: Psychopathic states. *In* Arieti, Silvano (Ed.): American Handbook of Psychiatry, vol. 1. Basic Books, Inc., New York, 1959.

EKDAWI, M. Y.: The difficult patient. Brit. J. Psychiat. 113:547, 1967.

GREENBERG, HARVEY R.: The manipulator and the mental hygiene consultation service. Amer. J. Psychiat. 122:313, 1965.

KUMLER, FERN R.: An interpersonal interpretation of manipulation. *In* Burd, Shirley F., and Marshall, Margaret A. (Eds.): Some Clinical Approaches to Psychiatric Nursing. The Macmillan Co., New York, 1963.

LOMAS, PETER: The origin of the need to be special. Brit. J. Med. Psychol. 35:339, 1962.

MEERLOO, JOOST A. M.: The meaning of crying. Amer. J. Psychother. 18:298, 1964.

MURPHY, GEORGE E., AND GUZE, SAMUEL B.: Setting limits: the management of the manipulative patient. Amer. J. Psychother. 14:30, 1960.

OKKENHAUG, LEE: Nurse-patient manipulation in a relationship. Canad. Nurse 63:46, 1967.

RATTRAY, R. G.: The psychopath and the psychiatric nurse. Nurs. Times 60:709, 10 May, 1964.

SCHORER, C. E.: What do I do when the patient cries? Amer. J. Psychother. 18:500, 1964.

STRICKLER, LAWRENCE J.: The true deceiver. Psychol. Bull. 68:13, 1967.

WEINTRAUB, WALTER, AND ARONSON, H.: The application of verbal behavior analysis to the study of psychological defense mechanisms. II. Speech pattern associated with impulsive behavior. J. Nerv. Ment. Dis. 139:75, 1964.

WILEY, PATRICIA L.: Manipulation. Conference on Teaching Psychiatric Nursing in Baccalaureate Programs. Southern Regional Education Board, Atlanta, 1967.

WOLFE, NANCY ANDERSON: Setting reasonable limits on behavior. Amer. J. Nurs. 62:104, 1962.

Suspiciousness

Articles, Books and Reports of Organizations

ACHTE, K. A.: On prognosis and rehabilitation in schizophrenic and paranoid psychoses. A comparative follow-up study of two series of patients first admitted to hospital in 1950 and 1960 respectively. Acta Psychiat. Scand. 43: Suppl. 196:5, 1967.

ARONSON, ELLIOT, AND COPE, VERNON: My enemy's enemy is my friend. J. Personality Soc. Psychol. 8:8, 1968.

ARTISS, KENNETH, AND BULLARD, DEXTER M.: Paranoid thinking in everyday life. The function of secrets and disillusionment. Arch. Gen. Psychiat. 14:89, 1966.

ARTHUR, A. Z.: Theories and explanations of delusions: a review. Amer. J. Psychiat. 121:105, 1964.

BRAMEL, DANA, TAUB, BARRY, AND BLUM, BARBARA: An observer's reaction to the suffering of his enemy. J. Personality Soc. Psychol. 8:384, 1968.

CAMERON, NORMAN: Paranoid conditions and paranoia. *In* Arieti, Silvano (Ed.): American Handbook of Psychiatry, vol. 1. Basic Books, Inc., New York, 1959.

CHRZANOWSKI, GERARD: Cultural and pathological manifestations of paranoia. Perspect. Psychiat. Care 1:34, 1963.

DUPONT, ROBERT L. JR., AND GRUNE-
BAUM, HENRY: Willing victims: the
husbands of paranoid women. Amer.
J. Psychiat. 125:151, 1968.

KOVAR, LEO: A reconsideration of paranoia. Psychiatry 29:289, 1966.

LERNER, MELVIN J., AND SIMMONS, CAR-
OLYN H.: Observer's reaction to the
"innocent victim": compassion or rejection? J. Personality Soc. Psychol.
4:203, 1966.

MELAT, SHIRLEY A.: The development
of trust. Perspect. Psychiat. Care 3:
28, 40, 1965.

ROKEACH, MILTON: The Three Christs
of Ypsilanti. A Psychological Study.
Alfred A. Knopf, New York, 1964.

SCOTT, MARVIN B., AND LYMAN, STAM-
FORD: Paranoia, homosexuality and
game theory. J. Health Soc. Behav.
9:179, 1968.

SLETTEN, IVAN W., AND BALLOU, SUSAN
R.: The selection of delusional persecutors. Canad. Psychiat. Assoc. J.
12:327, 1967.

STANKIEWICZ, BARBARA: Guides to nursing intervention in the projective patterns of suspicious patients. Perspect.
Psychiat. Care 2:39, 1964.

STASTNY, JOY P.: Helping a patient
learn to trust. Perspect. Psychiat.
Care 3:16, 1965.

TRAVELBEE, JOYCE: The concept of envy.
Conference on Teaching Psychiatric
Nursing in Baccalaureate Programs.
Southern Regional Education Board,
Atlanta, 1967.

Anxiety

*Articles, Books and Reports of
Organizations*

BENJAMIN, JOHN D.: Some developmental observations relating to the
theory of anxiety. J. Amer. Psychoanal. Assoc. 9:652, 1961.

BREGGIN, PETER ROGER: The psycho-
physiology of anxiety. J. Nerv. Ment.
Dis. 139:558, 1964.

BURD, SHIRLEY F.: Effects of nursing
intervention in anxiety of patients.
In Some Clinical Approaches to Psychiatric Nursing. The Macmillan Co.,
New York, 1963.

CALLIERI, BRUNO, AND FRIGHI, LUIGI:
An approach to the problem of exis-
tential vs. psychoanalytic anxiety. J.
Exist. Psychiat. 2:323, 1962.

DARBONNE, ALLEN R.: Crisis: a review
of theory, practice and research.
Psychother. Theory Res. Prac. 4:49,
1967.

DAY, MERLE E.: An eye-movement in-
dicator of type and level of anxiety:
some clinical observations. J. Clin.
Psychol. 23:438, 1967.

DRAGE, ELAINE MURRAY: Helping patients recall panic episodes. Amer. J.
Nurs. 68:1254, 1968.

EPSTEIN, SEYMOUR: Toward a unified
theory of anxiety. *In* Progress in Experimental Personality Research, vol.
4. Academic Press, New York, 1968.

GOTTSCHALK, LOUIS A., AND FRANK,
EDWARD C.: Estimating the magni-
tude of anxiety from speech. Behav.
Sci. 12:289, 1967.

GREGG, DOROTHY E.: Anxiety—a factor
in nursing care. Amer. J. Nurs. 52:
1363, 1952.

HENDRIX, HARVILLE: The ontological
character of anxiety. J. Rel. Health
6:46, 1967.

HOCH, PAUL H., AND ZUBIN, JOSEPH
(Eds.): Anxiety. Proceedings of the
Thirty-ninth Annual Meeting of the
American Psychopathological Associ-
ation. Hafner Publishing Co., New
York, 1950.

IBOR, J. J. LOPEZ: Basic anxiety as the
core of neuroses. Acta Psychiat.
Scand. 41:329, 1965.

KAPLAN, FRANCES: Effects of anxiety
and defense in a therapy-like situation. J. Abnorm. Psychol. 71:449,
1966.

KELMAN, HAROLD: A unitary theory of
anxiety. Amer. J. Psychoanal. 17:
127, 1957.

LAUGHLIN, HENRY P.: The Neuroses.
Butterworths, Washington, 1967.
(See: The nature and origins of anxiety . . . Fear in the absence of a
known cause, pp. 1-54)

LAING, R. D.: An examination of Tillich's theory of anxiety and neurosis.
Brit. J. Med. Psychol. 30:88, 1957.

MAY, ROLLO: The Meaning of Anxiety.
The Ronald Press Co., New York,
1950.

NEYLAN, MARGARET PROWSE: Anxiety.
Amer. J. Nurs. 62:110, 1962.

PEPLAU, HILDEGARD E.: A working definition of anxiety. In Burd, Shirley F., and Marshall, Margaret A. (Eds.): Some Clinical Approaches to Psychiatric Nursing. The Macmillan Co., New York, 1963.

PORTNOY, ISIDORE: The anxiety states. In Arieti, Silvano (Ed.): American Handbook of Psychiatry, vol. 1. Basic Books, Inc., New York, 1959.

POST, SEYMOUR C.: The re-evocation of anxiety by its absence. Psychoanal. Quart. 33:526, 1964.

PRICK, J. J. G.: Sketch of anxiety and fear in its normal and pathological appearance. Psychiat. Neurol. Neurochir. 71:155, 1968.

Programmed Instruction: Anxiety. Recognition and intervention. Prepared by Basic Systems, Inc. under the supervision of Journal editors. Amer. J. Nurs. 65:130, 1965.

RANGELL, LEO: A further attempt to resolve the "problem of anxiety." J.

Amer. Psychoanal. Assoc. 16:371, 1968.

ROSENBERG, MORRIS: The association between self-esteem and anxiety. J. Psychiat. Res. 1:135, 1962.

RUDOLPHSON, S.: A critique of Horney's theory of anxiety. Amer. J. Psychoanal. 21:27, 1961.

SPIELBERGER, CHARLES D. (Ed.): Anxiety and Behavior. Academic Press, New York, 1966.

STEIN, MAURICE, VIDICH, A. J., AND WHITE, D. M. (Eds.): Identity and Anxiety. The Macmillan Co., Free Press, New York, 1960.

SULLIVAN, HARRY STACK: The theory of anxiety and the nature of psychotherapy. Psychiatry 12:3, 1949.

Supplement: Proceedings of the Canadian Conference on Coexistent Anxiety and Depression: Recognition and Treatment. Canad. Psychiat. Assoc. J. 7:S1, 1962. (Fifteen papers)

CHAPTER X: SUPERVISION OF THE PRACTITIONER: THE SUPERVISORY PROCESS

Articles

AARSON, DORIS: Temporal factors in perception and short-term memory. Psychol. Bull. 67:130, 1967.

ALLEN, VERNON L., AND BRAGG, BARRY W.: Effect of social pressure on concept identification. J. Educ. Psychol. 59:302, 1968.

ALTUCHER, NATHAN: Constructive use of the supervisory relationship. J. Couns. Psychol. 14:165, 1967.

ARBUCKLE, DUGALD S.: The learning of counseling: process not product. J. Couns. Psychol. 10:163, 1963.

ARONSON, ELLIOT, AND METTEE, DAVID R.: Dishonest behavior as a function of differential levels of induced self esteem. J. Personality Soc. Psychol. 9:121, 1968.

BERNS, ROBERT S.: Regressive emotional behavior in college students. Amer. J. Psychiat. 122:1378, 1966.

BLATT, SIDNEY J., AND QUINLAN, PAUL: Punctual and procrastinating students: a study of temporal parameters. J. Consult. Psychol. 31:169, 1967.

BORDIN, EDWARD S.: The ambivalent quest for independence. J. Couns. Psychol. 12:339, 1965.

BURKETT, BARBARA J.: The relationship of thought processes to methods of teaching. J. Nurs. Educ. 3:5, 30, 1964.

CLELAND, VIRGINIA: Effects of stress on thinking. Amer. J. Nurs. 67:108, 1967.

DAVIS, FRED, AND OLESEN, VIRGINIA L.: The career outlook of professionally educated women: the case of collegiate student nurses. Psychiatry 28:334, 1965.

DICKOFF, JAMES, AND JAMES, PATRICIA: A theory of theories: a position paper. Symposium on theory development in nursing. Nurs. Res. 17:197, 1968.

FAGIN, CLAIRE M.: The clinical specialist as supervisor. Nurs. Outlook 15:34, 1967.

FLEMING, JOAN, AND BENEDEK, THERESE: Supervision. A method of teaching psychoanalysis. Psychoanal. Quart. 33:71, 1964.

HART, HENRY HARPER: A review of the literature on passivity. Psychiat. Quart. 35:331, 1961.

HEINEMANN, M. EDITH: The conflicting life of a student. Nurs. Outlook 12:35, 1964.

HOLLANDER, EDWIN P., AND WILLIS, RICHARD H.: Some current issues in the psychology of conformity and nonconformity. Psychol. Bull. 68:62, 1967.

HOLMES, MARGUERITE J.: Teaching interpersonal skills through the supervisory process. In Zderad, Loretta T., and Belcher, Helen C.: Developing Behavioral Concepts in Nursing. Report of the Regional Project in Teaching Psychiatric Nursing in Baccalaureate Programs. Southern Regional Education Board, Atlanta, 1968.

JONES, E. E.: Conformity as a tactic of ingratiation. Science 149:144, 1965.

JONES, ROBERT G., AND JONES, EDWARD E.: Optimum conformity as an ingratiation tactic. J. Personality 32:436, 1964.

KADUSHIN, ALFRED: Games people play in supervision. Soc. Work 13:23, 1968.

KOCH, HARRIET B.: Television in nursing education. J. Nurs. Educ. 7:37, 1968.

KOGAN, NATHAN, AND WALLACH, MICHAEL A.: Group risk taking as a function of members' anxiety and defensiveness level. J. Personality 35:50, 1967.

KYSAR, JOHN E.: Social class and adaptation of college students. A review and prospectus. Ment. Hyg. 50:398, 1966.

LILLIBRIDGE, JOHN, AND LUNDSTEDT, SVEN: Some initial evidence for an interpersonal risk theory. J. Psychol. 66:119, 1967.

LUCHINS, ABRAHAM S., AND LUCHINS, EDITH H.: On conformity with judgments of a majority or an authority. J. Soc. Psychol. 53:303, 1961.

MAIER, NORMAN R. F., AND JANZEN, JUNIE C.: Reliability of reasons used in making judgments of honesty and dishonesty. Percept. Motor Skills 25:141, 1967.

MERENESS, DOROTHY: Freedom and responsibility for nursing students. Amer. J. Nurs. 67:69, 1967.

MUSLIN, HYMAN L., et al.: Research on the supervisory process. I. Supervisor's appraisal of the interview data. Arch. Gen. Psychiat. 16:427, 1967.

NEHREN, JEANETTE G., AND LARSON, MARGARET L.: Supervised supervision. Perspect. Psychiat. Care 6:25, 42, 1968.

PATERSON, JOSEPHINE G.: Group supervision: a process and philosophy. Comm. Ment. Health J. 2:315, 1966.

PATTERSON, C. H.: Supervising students in the counseling practicum. J. Couns. Psychol. 11:47, 1964.

PEPLAU, HILDEGARD E.: What is experiential teaching? Amer. J. Nurs. 57:884, 1957.

PESZNECKER, BETTY, BAKER, JOAN M., AND KOGAN, KATE L.: Testing students' ability to grasp principles. Nurs. Outlook 13:57, 1965.

QUINT, JEANNE C.: Hidden hazards for nurse teachers. Nurs. Outlook 15:34, 1967.

REID, CLYDE H.: Toward a definition of authority. J. Rel. Health 6:7, 1967.

RITVO, MIRIAM, AND FISK, CLAIRE: Role conflict. Amer. J. Nurs. 66:2248, 1966.

ROBITAILLE, NORMAND D.: The organization of nursing service for the establishment of nurse-patient relationships. Perspect. Psychiat. Care 2:30, 1964.

ROSENBERG, LOUIS M., RUBIN, SAM S., AND FINZI, HILDA: Participant-supervision in the teaching of psychotherapy. Amer. J. Psychother. 22:280, 1968.

SARBIN, THEODORE R., AND ALLEN, VERNON L.: Increasing participation in a natural group setting: a preliminary report. Psychol. Rec. 18:1, 1968.

SHAW, DALE J.: Personality patterns associated with level of adjustment to psychiatric affiliation. J. Clin. Psychol. 23:222, 1967.

SHOPPER, MOISY, AND LEVY, NORMAN B.: Emotional difficulties in nursing students. Childhood factors: a preliminary report. Arch. Gen. Psychiat. 16:180, 1967.

STOTLAND, EZRA, AND BLUMENTHAL, ARTHUR L.: The reduction of anxiety as a result of the expectation of making a choice. Canad. J. Psychol. 18:139, 1964.

VAN HUBEN, BETTY L.: Exploration of reciprocal feelings. Perspect. Psychiat. Care 2:43, 1964.

WALSTEDT, JOYCE J.: Teaching empathy. Ment. Hyg. 52:600, 1968.

WILMER, HARRY A.: The undisguised camera in videotape psychiatric teaching. Calif. Ment. Health Res. Dig. 4:147, 1966.

WINTER, SARA K., GRIFFITH, JEFFERY C., and KOLB, DAVID A.: Capacity for self direction. J. Consult. Clin. Psychol. 32:35, 1968.

WOLFORD, HELEN G.: Dialogue as a method of teaching. J. Nurs. Educ. 4:21, 1965.

Books and Reports of Organizations

AMIDON, EDMUND, AND HUNTER, ELIZABETH: Improving Teaching: The Analysis of Classroom Verbal Interaction. Holt, Rinehart and Winston Inc., New York, 1966.

BERNE, ERIC: Games People Play. The Psychology of Human Relationships. Grove Press, Inc., New York, 1964. (See: Why don't you—yes but, pp. 116-122)

CARTWRIGHT, DORWIN, AND ZANDER, ALVIN (Eds.): Group Dynamics: Research and Theory, 3rd ed. Harper & Row, New York, 1968.

DE BONO, EDWARD: New Think: The Use of Lateral Thinking in the Generation of New Ideas. Basic Books, Inc., New York, 1968.

EKSTEIN, RUDOLF, AND WALLERSTEIN, ROBERT S.: The Teaching and Learning of Psychotherapy. Basic Books, Inc., New York, 1958.

FINGARETTE, HERBERT: On Responsibility. Basic Books, Inc., New York, 1967.

JOHN, E. R.: Mechanisms of Memory. Academic Press, New York, 1967.

MCGRATH, JOSEPH, AND ALTMAN, IRWIN: Small Group Research: A Synthesis and Critique of the Field. Holt, Rinehart and Winston Inc., New York, 1966.

NEWCOMB, THEODORE M.: The Acquaintance Process. Holt, Rinehart and Winston Inc., New York, 1961.

ROKEACH, MILTON: The Open and Closed Mind. Basic Books, Inc., New York, 1960.

ROSENTHAL, ROBERT, AND JACOBSON, LEONORE: Pygmalion in the Classroom. Teacher Expectation and Pupil's Intellectual Development. Holt, Rinehart and Winston Inc., New York, 1968.

TRABASSO, TOM, AND BOWER, GORDON H.: Attention in Learning. Theory and Research. John Wiley & Sons, Inc., New York, 1968.

A SELECTED LIST OF GENERAL REFERENCE SOURCES IN PSYCHIATRIC NURSING AND RELATED FIELDS

Knowledge of source materials and ability to utilize research findings are essential if the practitioner is to intervene effectively and to act as a change agent in improving the quality of care given the mentally ill. Practitioners must know how to find, and use, source materials in the library with a minimum of time and effort. Because of the proliferation of literature in the behavioral sciences and the "knowledge explosion," emphasis is placed on assisting practitioners to use abstracts, indexes and bibliographies.

The reference sources in this Appendix are categorized as: book indexes, reference books, indexes and guides to the literature, abstract, digest and review journals, bibliographies, and references regarding bibliographic tools and methods.

BOOK INDEXES

A book index lists the name(s) of author(s), title of book, place of publication and/or publisher.

American Book Publishing Record Annual Cumulatives. R. R. Bowker Co., New York, (see latest publication). (Cumulates all books listed in the monthly issues of American Book Publishing Record. Arrangement is by subject)

British Books in Print. The Reference Catalog of Current Literature. R. R. Bowker Co., New York, (see latest publication). (Lists titles of ap-proximately 1,900 publishers in the United Kingdom. Arrangement is by author and title)

BUTTERFIELD, RITA, AND RICHER, JULIA (Eds.): Canadian Books in Print 1967. Published by Canadian Books in Print Committee. Univ. of Toronto Press, Toronto, 1968.

Cumulative Book Index. A World List of Books in the English Language. H. W. Wilson Co. Inc., Bronx, monthly. (Author, title and subject index to current books in the English language. Does not include government publications)

LYONS, NATALIE (Ed.): Forthcoming Books. R. R. Bowker Co., New York, bimonthly. (Indexes books to be published in the coming five-month season)

PRAKKEN, SARAH L. (Ed.): Books in Print 1968. An Author-Title Index to the Publishers' Trade List Annual. R. R. Bowker Co., New York, 1968. (In two volumes: Authors Index and Title Index. Published annually in October. Includes hardbacks, paperbacks, trade books, text-

books, adult books and juveniles)

WALFORD, A. J. (Ed.): Guide to Reference Material, 2nd ed. R. R. Bowker Co., New York, 1966-1970. (In three volumes: Vol. 1, Science and Technology, 1966; Vol. 2, Social and Historical Sciences, Philosophy, Religion, 1968; Vol. 3, General Works, Language, Literature, Fine Arts, 1970)

WEBER, OLGA S. (Ed.): Paperbound Books in Print. R. R. Bowker Co., New York, monthly.

BASIC REFERENCE BOOKS

Dictionaries

ENGLISH, HORACE B., AND ENGLISH, AVA CHAMPNEY.: A Comprehensive Dictionary of Psychological and Psychoanalytical Terms. A Guide to Usage. David McKay Co., Inc., New York, 1958.

HINSIE, LELAND E., AND CAMPBELL, ROBERT JEAN: Psychiatric Dictionary, 3rd ed. Oxford Univ. Press, New York, 1960.

MITCHELL, G. DUNCAN (Ed.): A Dictionary of Sociology. Aldine Publishing Co., Chicago, 1967.

RYCROFT, CHARLES: A Critical Dictionary of Psychoanalysis. Basic Books, Inc., New York, 1968.

Directories

American Medical Directory, 24th ed. American Medical Assoc., Chicago, 1967. (In three volumes)

American Men of Science, Social and Behavioral Sciences, 11th ed. Edited by the Jaques Cattell Press, R. R. Bowker Co., New York, 1968. (In two volumes)

Biographical Directory of the American Psychiatric Association, 4th ed. R. R. Bowker Co., New York, 1968.

Canadian Medical Directory, 14th annual. Seccombe House, Toronto, 1968.

Directory For Exceptional Children, 6th ed. Porter Sargent Publisher, Boston, 1968. (Lists facilities for the care and development of the exceptional child)

Directory of American Scholars, 5th ed. Published with the cooperation of the American Council of Learned Societies, R. R. Bowker Co., New York. (In four volumes: Vol. I, History, 1968; Vol. II, English, Speech and Drama, 1968; Vol. III, Foreign Languages, Linguistics and Philology, 1969; Vol. IV, Philosophy, Religion and Law, 1969)

Directory of Professional Social Workers, 2nd ed. National Assoc. of Social Workers, New York, 1966.

Directory Sociological Association. American Sociological Assoc., Washington, 1963.

Handbook of Scientific & Learned Societies of Great Britain. Hillary House Publishers, New York, 1964.

Mental Health Directory (Reference Guide to Mental Health Programs and Services Throughout the United States). National Clearinghouse for Mental Health Information, National Institute of Mental Health, U.S. Department of Health, Education and Welfare, Public Health Service. U.S. Government Printing Office, Washington, (see latest publication). (Contains a federal, state and community listing of mental health facilities)

Scientific and Technical Societies of the United States, 8th ed. National Academy of Sciences—National Research Council Publication 1499, Washington, 1968.

The Medical Directory, 119th annual issue. J. & A. Churchill Ltd., London,

WASSERMAN, CLARA SEDACCA, AND WASSERMAN, PAUL: Health Organizations of the United States, Canada and Internationally: A Directory of Voluntary Associations, Professional Societies and Other Groups Concerned With Health and Related Fields, 2nd ed. Cornell Univ. Graduate School of Business and Public Administration, Ithaca, 1965.

WILSON, B. J. (Ed) · Aslib Directory, vol. 1, Information Sources in Science Technology and Commerce. Aslib Services, London, 1968.

Encyclopedias

ADAMS, ROGERS, et al. (Eds.) : The McGraw-Hill Encyclopedia of Science and Technology. An International Reference Work in Fifteen Volumes Including An Index. McGraw-Hill Book Co., New York, 1966.

DEUTSCH, ALBERT, et al. (Eds.) : The Encyclopedia of Mental Health. Franklin Watts, Inc., New York, 1963. (In six volumes)

EDWARDS, PAUL (Ed.) : The Encyclopedia of Philosophy. Collier-Macmillan Library Service, New York, 1966. (In eight volumes)

EIDELBERG, LUDWIG (Ed.) : Encyclopedia of Psychoanalysis. The Macmillan Co., Free Press, New York, 1967.

LURIE, HARRY L. (Ed.) : Encyclopedia of Social Work. National Assoc. Social Workers, New York, 1965.

RUFFNER, FREDERICK G. JR. (Ed.) : Encyclopedia of Associations, 5th ed. Gale Research Co., Detroit, 1968. (In three volumes)

SILLS, DAVID L., et al. (Eds.) : International Encyclopedia of the Social Sciences. Crowell-Collier, The Macmillan Co., New York, 1967. (In seventeen volumes)

Review Series and Yearbooks

Advances in Child Development and Behavior. 1, 1963—. Academic Press, New York.

Advances in Computers. 1, 1960—. Academic Press, New York.

Advances in Drug Research. 1, 1964—. Academic Press, New York.

Advances in Experimental Social Psychology. 1, 1964—. Academic Press, New York.

Advances in Genetics. 1, 1947—. Academic Press, New York.

Advances in Gerontological Research. 1, 1964—. Academic Press, New York.

Advances in Pharmacology. 1, 1962—. Academic Press, New York.

Advances in the Study of Behavior. 1, 1965—. Academic Press, New York.

Annual Review of Genetics. 1, 1967—. Annual Reviews Inc., Palo Alto.

Annual Review of Information Science and Technology. 1, 1966—. John Wiley & Sons, Inc., Interscience Publishers, New York.

Annual Review of Pharmacology. 1, 1961—. Annual Reviews Inc., Palo Alto.

Annual Review of Psychology. 1, 1950—. Annual Reviews Inc., Palo Alto.

Contributions to Sensory Physiology. 1, 1965—. Academic Press, New York.

Current Psychiatric Therapies. 1, 1961—. Grune & Stratton, Inc., New York.

International Review of Neurobiology. 1, 1959—. Academic Press, New York.

Legal Medicine Annual. 1, 1967—. Appleton-Century-Crofts, New York.

National Society for the Study of Education Yearbooks (Henry, Nelson B., Ed.) Univ. of Chicago Press, Chicago.

Neuroendocrinology. 1, 1966—. Academic Press, New York.

Progress in Brain Research. 1, 1963—. American Elsevier Publishing Co., Inc., New York.

Progress in Clinical Psychology. 1, 1952—. Grune & Stratton, Inc., New York.

Progress in Experimental Personality Research. 1, 1964—. Academic Press, New York.

Progress in Learning Disabilities. 1, 1968—. Grune & Stratton, Inc., New York.

Progress in Neurology and Psychiatry. An Annual Review. 1, 1944-45—. Grune & Stratton, Inc., New York.

Recent Advances in Biological Psychiatry. 1, 1959—. Plenum Press, New York.

Science and Psychoanalysis. 1, 1958—. Grune & Stratton, Inc., New York.

The Psychoanalytic Study of the Child. 1, 1945—. International Univ. Press, New York.

The Yearbook of Drug Therapy. Annual. 1900—. Year Book Medical Publishers Inc., Chicago.

The Yearbook of Neurology, Psychiatry and Neurosurgery. Annual. 1900

—. Year Book Medical Publishers Inc., Chicago.

Yearbook of International Congress Proceedings. Union of International Assoc., Brussels, 1968.

INDEXES

Periodical Indexes

A periodical index lists the name of the periodical, editor's name, frequency of issue, name and address of publisher, year first published and other information.

Catalogue of Scientific and Technical Research Journals in All Languages. Scientific International Inc., Long Island City.

CHICOREL, MARIETTA, (Ed.): Ulrich's International Periodicals Directory, 12th ed. R. R. Bowker Co., New York. (In two volumes: Vol. 1, Scientific, Technical, Medical Periodicals, 1967; Vol. II, Arts, Humanities, Social Sciences, Business Periodicals, 1968)

Directory of Periodicals Published by International Organizations, 3rd ed. Union of International Assoc., Brussels, 1968.

International Periodical Index. Oxbridge Publishing Co., New York. (In press)

KOLTAY, EMERY (Ed.): Irregular Serials and Annuals. An International Directory. R. R. Bowker Co., New York, 1967.

Medical and Nursing Indexes

Medical and nursing indexes list name(s) of author(s), title of article, name of periodical and date of publication.

Cumulated Index Medicus. National Library of Medicine. Public Health Service, U.S. Department of Health, Education and Welfare. (Formerly published by the American Medical Assoc. Since 1965 published by the National Library of Medicine)

Index Medicus. National Library of Medicine. Public Health Service, U.S. Department of Health Education and

Welfare, monthly. (First series 1879-1899 published by the Library of the Surgeon-General's Office. Discontinued in 1927. Superseded by the Quarterly Cumulative Index Medicus. Since 1960 published by the National Library of Medicine)

N.B. For references prior to 1960 consult the following:

Index-Catalogue of The Library of The Surgeon-General's Office. U.S. Army, U.S. Government Printing Office, Washington. (First series 1880-1895. Discontinued with publication of fifth series, vol. 3, 1961)

Quarterly Cumulative Index to Current Medical Literature. American Medical Assoc. Chicago, 1916-1926. (In 1927 merged with Index Medicus to form The Quarterly Cumulative Index Medicus, Q.C.I.M.)

Current List of Medical Literature. National Library of Medicine, Washington, 1941-1959. (Superseded in 1960 by the monthly Index Medicus published by the National Library of Medicine and the Cumulative Index Medicus published by the American Medical Assoc. until 1965)

Quarterly Cumulative Index Medicus, 1927-1956. (Resulted from merger in 1927 of the Index Medicus and The Quarterly Cumulative Index to Current Medical Literature. Sponsored by the American Medical Assoc. and the Army Medical Library. Superseded by the Cumulated Index Medicus and by the Index Medicus)

N.B. The Army Medical Library was renamed the Armed Forces Medical Library in 1952 and in 1956 was named the National Library of Medicine.

Cumulative Index to Nursing Literature. 1, 1956—. Glendale Adventist Hospital Publication Services, Glendale, bimonthly.

International Nursing Index. 1, 1966—.
Amer. J. Nurs., New York. (Published as a cooperative effort between
the National Library of Medicine
and American Journal of Nursing)
Nursing Studies Index. J. B. Lippincott
Co., Philadelphia. (An annotated
guide to reported studies, research in
progress, research methods and historical materials in periodicals, books
and pamphlets published in English.
Prepared by Yale University School
of Nursing Index Staff under the
direction of Virginia Henderson)
Physicians' Basic Index. 1, February
1966—. Charles F. Kettering Hospital, Kettering, monthly.

*Special Indexes and Guides to the
Literature*

ANDREWS, THOMAS G., AND KERR,
FRANCES E.: Index of literature reviews and summaries in the Psychological Bulletin, 1940-1966. Psychol.
Bull. 68:178, 1967.
Applied Science & Technology Index.
H. W. Wilson Co., Inc., Bronx,
monthly. (A subject index to approximately 225 periodicals. Permanent bound annual cumulations)
Author Index to Psychological Index
1894 to 1935 and Psychological Abstracts 1927-1958. (Compiled by the
Psychology Library, Columbia University) G. K. Hall & Co., Boston,
1960.
Bibliographic Index. H. W. Wilson Co.,
Inc., Bronx, semi-annually. (Indexes
by subject current bibliographies.
Bound annual and three-year cumulations)
Bioresearch Titles. BioSciences Information Service, Philadelphia, monthly.
Book Review Index. Gale Research Co.,
Detroit, monthly. (Guide to current
book reviews)
Behavior & Physiology Index. Science
Search Associates, Kansas City.
BORING, EDWIN GARRIGUES, AND ANNIN,
EDITH L. (Eds.): The Harvard List
of Books in Psychology, 3rd ed. Harvard Univ. Press, Cambridge, 1964.
British Education Index. Library Assoc., London.
Brain Biochemistry Monthly. Literature
Searchers, Kettering.

Canadian Government Publications
Monthly Catalogue. Queens Printer,
Ottawa.
Cumulated Subject Index to Psychological Abstracts. G. K. Hall & Co.,
Boston, 1966.
Cumulative Author Index to Psychological Abstracts. G. K. Hall & Co.,
Boston, 1965.
Cumulative Index of Hospital Literature. Amer. Hosp. Assoc., Chicago.
Current Contents. Life Sciences. Institute for Scientific Information, Philadelphia. (Reports weekly table of
contents in original format of more
than 800 foreign and domestic research journals)
Education Index. H. W. Wilson Co.,
Inc., Bronx, monthly. (Subject index
to approximately 200 educational periodicals published in the United States,
Canada and Great Britain)
Educational Periodicals. UNESCO
Publications Center, New York, 1963.
(Data on approximately 5,000 educational periodicals published in 100
countries)
GRINSTEIN, ALEXANDER: The Index of
Psychoanalytic Writings. International Univ. Press, New York. (In
nine volumes)
Hospital Literature Index. Library
Amer. Hosp. Assoc., Chicago.
Monthly Catalog of United States Government Publications. Superintendent
of Documents. U.S. Government
Printing Office, Washington.
Public Affairs Information Service Bulletin. Public Affairs Information Service Inc., New York. (Lists books,
pamphlets, government periodicals,
reports of public and private agencies relating to economic and social
conditions)
Readers Guide to Periodical Literature.
H. W. Wilson Co., Inc., Bronx. (Indexes approximately 158 nontechnical
periodicals)
Social Sciences & Humanities Index. H.
W. Wilson Co., Inc., Bronx, quarterly.
(Author and subject index to 206
periodicals. Includes publications in
the fields of anthropology, economics,
history, language and literature, political science, religion, sociology and
others)

ABSTRACT, DIGEST AND REVIEW JOURNALS

Abstracts For Social Workers. National Association of Social Workers, New York, quarterly. (Prepared under contract with the National Clearinghouse for Mental Health Information of the National Institute of Mental Health)

Abstracts of Hospital Management Studies. Univ. of Michigan, Ann Arbor, quarterly.

Abstracts of World Medicine. British Medical Assoc., London. (Includes a section on neurology, neurosurgery and psychiatry)

Biological Abstracts. BioSciences Information Service, Philadelphia, semimonthly. (Includes abstracts re behavioral science, genetics, pharmacology, public health, etc.)

Child Development Abstracts and Bibliography. Society for Research in Child Development, Washington, three times a year.

Communications in Behavioral Biology. Part B: Abstracts and Index. Academic Press, New York, monthly. (Includes abstracts re behavioral pharmacology, neurology and psychiatry)

Communication Disorders. The Johns Hopkins Medical Institutions, Baltimore. (Includes articles and abstracts re hearing and speech impairment, language and language disorders, neurophysiology and other areas)

Contemporary Psychology: A Journal of Reviews. American Psychological Assoc., Inc., Washington, monthly. (Includes book reviews in the behavioral sciences. Reviews some nursing books)

Crime and Delinquency Abstracts and Current Projects—An International Bibliography. U.S. Department of Health, Education and Welfare. Public Health Service, National Institute of Mental Health, Chevy Chase.

Digest of Neurology and Psychiatry. Abstracts and Reviews of Selected Literature in Psychiatry, Neurology and Their Related Fields. Institute of Living, Hartford.

Dissertation Abstracts. The Humanities and Social Sciences. Universal Microfilms, Inc., Ann Arbor. (Includes abstracts of dissertations in nursing)

Epilepsy Abstracts. Prepared for the National Institute of Neurological Diseases and Blindness by the Excerpta Medica Foundation. U.S. Department of Health, Education and Welfare, Public Health Service, National Institutes of Health, Bethesda.

Excerpta Criminologica. Excerpta Criminologica Foundation, Amsterdam. (An international abstracting service covering the etiology of crime and juvenile delinquency, the control and treatment of offenders, criminal procedure and the administration of justice)

Excerpta Medica. Excerpta Medica Foundation, Amsterdam. (Section VIII-B, Psychiatry)

International Pharmaceutical Abstracts. American Society of Hospital Pharmacists, Washington, semimonthly.

Language and Language Behavior Abstracts. Center for Research on Language and Language Behavior, Ann Arbor, and the Bureau pour l'Enseignement de la Langue et de la Civilisation Francaises a l'Etranger, Paris. Appleton-Century-Crofts Inc., New York.

Mental Health Book Review Index: An Annual Bibliography of Books and Book Reviews in the Behavorial Sciences. Council on Research on Bibliography, Research Center for Mental Health, New York Univ., New York.

Mental Health Digest. National Clearinghouse for Mental Health Information. U.S. Department of Health, Education and Welfare, Public Health Service, National Institute of Mental Health, Chevy Chase.

Mental Retardation Abstracts. National Clearinghouse for Mental Health Information. U.S. Department of Health, Education and Welfare, Public Health Service, National Institute of Mental Health, Chevy Chase. U.S. Government Printing Office, Washington.

Poverty and Human Resources Abstracts. Institute of Labor and Industrial Relations, Univ. Michigan, Ann Arbor.

Psychiatry Digest. A Summary of the World's Psychiatric Literature. Psychiatry Digest Inc., Northfield, monthly.

Psychological Abstracts. Amer. Psychological Assoc. Inc., Washington, monthly. (Nonevaluative summaries of the world's literature in psychology and related disciplines)

Rehabilitation Literature. National Society for Crippled Children and Adults, Chicago. (Includes abstracts re rehabilitation of psychiatric patients)

BIBLIOGRAPHIES

ALDOUS JOAN, AND HILL, REUBEN: International Bibliography of Research in Marriage and the Family. 1900-1964. Univ. Minnesota Press, Minneapolis, 1967.

ANDERSON, MARIAN P.: Mental Health Consultation to Schools, A Selected Annotated Bibliography. Office of Planning, California Department of Mental Hygiene, Sacramento, 1965.

Annual Educational Bibliography of the International Bureau of Education UNESCO. UNESCO Publications Center, New York. (See most recent publication)

BALL, JOHN C. (compiler): Topical Bibliography on Drug Addiction. National Institute of Mental Health, Addiction Research Center, Lexington, 1966.

Bibliography and Abstracts on Suicide. See issues of Bulletin of Suicidology. National Clearinghouse For Mental Health Information, U.S. Department of Health, Education and Welfare, Public Health Service. U.S. Government Printing Office, Washington.

Bibliography of the History of Medicine. National Library of Medicine. U.S. Department of Health, Education and Welfare, Public Health Service, Bethesda. U.S. Government Printing Office, Washington.

Bibliography of Military Psychiatry 1947-1952. National Library of Medicine. U.S. Government Printing Office, 1953. (Literature relating to the U.S. armed forces with selected references to British forces)

Bibliography of Military Psychiatry 1952-1958. National Library of Medicine. U.S. Government Printing Office, Washington, 1959.

Bibliography on Drug Dependence and Abuse. 1928-1966. American Social Health Association under contract to the National Clearinghouse for Mental Health Information. U.S. Government Printing Office, Washington, 1967.

Bibliography on Religion and Mental Health 1960-1964. National Clearinghouse for Mental Health Information, U.S. Department of Health, Education and Welfare, Public Health Service, National Institute of Mental Health, Chevy Chase. U.S. Government Printing Office, Washington, 1967. (An annotated bibliography on the theoretical and practical relationships between religion and mental health)

BOOTH, ROBERT E., et al.: Culturally Disadvantaged. A Keyword-Out-of-Context Index. (KWOC). Wayne State Univ., Detroit, 1967.

BRACKBILL, YVONNE, et al.: Research in Infant Behavior: A Cross-Indexed Bibliography. The Williams & Wilkins Co., Baltimore, 1964.

BROWN, MYRTLE IRENE, BASSON, PRISCILLA HOLMES, AND BURCHETT, DOROTHY ELLEN: Nursing Care of the Aged. An Annotated Bibliography for Nurses. U.S. Department of Health, Education and Welfare, Division of Medical Care Administration, Adult Health Protection and Aging Branch, Arlington. U.S. Government Printing Office, Washington, 1967.

Community Care of the Mentally Ill. A Selected Annotated Bibliography. National Clearinghouse for Mental Health Information, U.S. Department of Health, Education and Welfare, Public Health Service, National Institute of Mental Health. U.S. Government Printing Office, Washington, 1966.

DAVIS, E. E.: Attitude Change. UNESCO Publications Center, New York, 1965. (A review and selected bibliography on attitude change)

EDWARDS, MABEL I.: Selected References on Home Care Services for the Chronically Ill and Aged. An Annotated Bibliography. Institute of Gerontology, Univ. of Iowa, Iowa City, 1967.

FORRESTER, GERTRUDE: Occupational Literature. An Annotated Bibliography. H. W. Wilson Co., Inc., Bronx, 1964.

FREEMAN, RUTH ST. JOHN, AND FREEMAN, HARROP A.: Counseling. A Bibliography (with Annotations). Scarecrow Press, Inc., New York, 1964.

GOLDFARB, WILLIAM, AND DORSEN, MARILYN M.: Annotated Bibliography of Childhood Schizophrenia and Related Disorders. Basic Books, Inc., New York, 1956.

HEGGESTED, WAYNE A.: Family Care Treatment of the Mentally Ill. A Selectively Annotated Bibliography. Veterans Administration, Department of Medicine and Surgery, 1966.

International Bibliography of Social and Cultural Anthropology. Prepared by the International Committee for Social Sciences Documentation in cooperation with International Congress of Anthropological and Ethnological Sciences. Aldine Publishing Co., Chicago. (See most recent publication)

International Bibliography of Sociology. Prepared by the International Committee for Social Sciences Documentation in cooperation with the International Sociological Association. Aldine Publishing Co., Chicago. (See most recent publication)

JONES, DOROTHY M.: Children Who Need Protection: An Annotated Bibliography. U.S. Children's Bureau. U.S. Government Printing Office, Washington, 1966.

KANTER, LOUISE, AND ANDERSON, MARIAN P.: Social Class, Ethnicity and Mental Illness, A Selected Annotated Bibliography. Office of Planning, Cal-

ifornia Department of Mental Hygiene, Sacramento, 1964.

KELLER, MARK (Ed.): International Bibliography of Studies on Alcohol. Rutgers Center of Alcohol Studies, New Brunswick.

KENDALL, M. G., AND DOIG, A. L.: Bibliography of Statistical Literature. Hafner Publishing Co., New York.

KNOP, EDWARD, AND APARICIO, KATHRYN: Current Sociocultural Change Literature. An Annotated Classification of Selected Interdisciplinary Sources. Univ. of North Dakota, Grand Forks, 1967.

LEVY, C. MICHAEL, HARTNAGLE, KAREN, AND LEVY, ELEANOR: The psychology of memory—1960-1964: A bibliography. Percept. Motor Skills 25:921, 1967. (Monograph Suppl. 5-V25)

LEVY, C. MICHAEL, AND HARTNAGLE, KAREN: Psychology of memory— 1966: A bibliography. Percept. Motor Skills 25:825, 1967. (Monograph Suppl. 4-V25)

LUBIN, BERNARD, AND LUBIN ALICE: Group Psychotherapy: A Bibliography of the Literature From 1956 Through 1964. Michigan State Univ. Press, East Lansing, 1966.

MacLENNAN, BERYCE W., AND LEVY, NAOMI: The group psychotherapy literature 1967. Int. J. Group Psychother. 18:375, 1968.

MILLER, GENEVIEVE (Ed.): Bibliography of the History of Medicine of the United States and Canada. 1939-1960. The Johns Hopkins Press, Baltimore, 1964.

National Library of Medicine Literature Searches. National Library of Medicine, Office of Public Information, Bethesda. Abortion and mental disorders. Mid-1963-June, 1965, L.S. No. 6-65. Brain RNA and memory. Mid-1963-March, 1966, L.S. No. 13-66. Frontal lobe tumors presenting as anxiety or anxiety-like symptoms. References from the current list of medical literature 1955-59, Index Medicus 1960-66 and cited literature, L.S. No. 16-66. Emergency psychiatric services. January 1964-November, 1967, L.S. 4-68. Epidemiology of suicide. Mid-1963-September, 1967, L.S. No. 21-67.

PALTIEL, FREDA L.: Poverty: An Annotated Bibliography and References. Canadian Welfare Council, Ottawa, 1966.

PEARSALL, MARION: Medical Behavioral Science: A Selected Bibliography of Cultural Anthropology, Social Psychology, and Sociology in Medicine. Univ. of Kentucky Press, Lexington, 1963.

PETRAS, JOHN W., AND CURTIS, JAMES E.: Critique and comment. The current literature on social class and mental illness in America: critique and bibliography. Behav. Sci. 13:382, 1968.

SCHERMERHORN, RICHARD A. (Ed.): Psychiatric Index for Interdisciplinary Research; A Guide to the Literature. 1950-1961. U.S. Government Printing Office, Washington, 1964.

SCHLESINGER, BENJAMIN: The Multi-Problem Family. A Review and Annotated Bibliography. Univ. of Toronto Press, Toronto, 1963.

SCHLESINGER, BENJAMIN: Poverty in Canada and the United States: Overview and Annotated Bibliography. Univ. of Toronto Press, Toronto, 1966.

SHOCK, NATHAN W.: A Classified Bibliography of Gerontology and Geriatrics. Stanford Univ. Press, Stanford, 1951. (Supplement 1 published in 1957. Supplement 2 published in 1963)

TILTON, JAMES R., DeMYER, MARIAN K., AND LOEW, LOIS HENDRICKSON: Annotated Bibliography on Childhood Schizophrenia. 1955-1964. Grune & Stratton Inc., New York, 1966.

BIBLIOGRAPHIC TOOLS AND METHODS

ALDRICH, ELLA V.: Using Books and Libraries, 5th ed. Prentice-Hall Inc., Englewood Cliffs, 1967.

BURKE, ARVID J., AND BURKE, MARY A.: Documentation in Education. Teachers College Press, Columbia Univ., New York, 1967.

CAMPBELL, WILLIAM GILES: Form and Style in Thesis Writing. Houghton Mifflin Co., Boston, 1954.

GATES, JEAN: A Guide to the Use of Books and Libraries. McGraw-Hill Book Co., New York, 1962.

HENDERSON, VIRGINIA: Library resources in nursing: their development and use. Part I. Int. Nurs. Rev. 15: 164, 1968; Part II, Ibid., 15:236, 1968.

THOMPSON, ALICE M. C.: The literature of nursing. Bull. Med. Libr. Assoc. 52:427, 1964.

TRUELSON, STANLEY D. JR.: What the Index Medicus indexes, and why. Bull. Med. Libr. Assoc. 54:329, 1966.

TURABIAN, KATE L.: Student's Guide for Writing College Papers. Univ. of Chicago Press, Chicago, 1963.

TURABIAN, KATE L.: A Manual for the Writers of Term Papers, Theses and Dissertations, 3rd ed. Univ. of Chicago Press, Chicago, 1967.

WEST, K. M.: Using literature indexes in clinical practice. J. Okla. Med. Assoc. 59:393, 1966.

WYATT, H. V.: Paper epidemic: a guide to the use of the biomedical literature. Amer. J. Epidem. 87:509, 1968.

INDEX